Statue in the National Archaeological Museum, Athens, made 3500 BCE in the Cyclades Islands. Photograph taken by author. The statue, arms over chest, is in the position of a dead body in burial, suggesting a body without a soul. There are other remarkable features: the statue is feminine (as souls are in Greek language), with an elongated neck, oversized and mis-shaped head, and absent eyes in a face that by its posture nonetheless seems to be looking at something. All these features make the statue less a representation of a body than of *that which is perceptive when dissociated from the body*, namely, a soul viewing the transcendent. As I interpret Socrates, it was the nature of his soul, most distinctively, to see the transcendent in human life. In this way the image, though predating Socrates by 2000 years, gives us a picture of his very soul.

socrates

George Rudebusch

WILEY-BLACKWELL

A John Wiley & Sons, Ltd., Publication

This edition first published 2009
© 2009 George Rudebusch

Blackwell Publishing was acquired by John Wiley & Sons in February 2007. Blackwell's publishing program has been merged with Wiley's global Scientific, Technical, and Medical business to form Wiley-Blackwell.

Registered Office
John Wiley & Sons Ltd, The Atrium, Southern Gate, Chichester, West Sussex, PO19 8SQ, United Kingdom

Editorial Offices
350 Main Street, Malden, MA 02148-5020, USA
9600 Garsington Road, Oxford, OX4 2DQ, UK
The Atrium, Southern Gate, Chichester, West Sussex, PO19 8SQ, UK

For details of our global editorial offices, for customer services, and for information about how to apply for permission to reuse the copyright material in this book please see our website at www.wiley.com/wiley-blackwell.

Library of Congress Cataloging-in-Publication Data

Rudebusch, George, 1957–
  Socrates / George Rudebusch.
    p. cm. – (Blackwell great minds)
  Includes bibliographical references and index.
  ISBN 978-1-4051-5085-9 (hardcover : alk. paper) – ISBN 978-1-4051-5086-6 (pbk. : alk. paper) 1. Socrates. I. Title.
  B317.R83 2009
  183′.2–dc22
                                                                                    2009007107

A catalogue record for this book is available from the British Library.

Set in 9.5/12pt Trump Mediaeval
by Graphicraft Limited, Hong Kong
Printed in Singapore by Ho Printing Singapore Pte Ltd

4   2013

blackwell great minds

edited by Steven Nadler

The Blackwell Great Minds series gives readers a strong sense of the fundamental views of the great western thinkers and captures the relevance of these figures to the way we think and live today.

1 Kant by Allen W. Wood
2 Augustine by Gareth B. Matthews
3 Descartes by André Gombay
4 Sartre by Katherine J. Morris
5 Charles Darwin by Michael Ruse
6 Schopenhauer by Robert Wicks
7 Shakespeare's Ideas by David Bevington
8 Camus by David Sherman
9 Kierkegaard by M. Jamie Ferreira
10 Mill by Wendy Donner and Richard Fumerton
11 Socrates by George Rudebusch

Forthcoming
Aristotle by Jennifer Whiting
Nietzsche by Richard Schacht
Plato by Paul Woodruff
Spinoza by Don Garrett
Wittgenstein by Hans Sluga
Heidegger by Taylor Carman
Maimonides by Tamar Rudavsky
Berkeley by Margaret Atherton
Leibniz by Christa Mercer
Hume by Stephen Buckle
Hobbes by Edwin Curley
Locke by Samuel Rickless

To
Hope

contents

acknowledgments

Socrates was not entirely successful in saving Athens from its anti-philosophical ways, yet nonetheless Athens owed him thanks. Likewise a number of readers have not entirely succeeded in saving this book from error, yet nonetheless I owe them thanks. Brian Hutler – with his genius for philosophy, his savvy as a manuscript reviewer, his devoted and detailed comments on each chapter as I first drafted it, and his final review of the whole – has played the greatest role in leading me to improve content, structure, and style.

In addition Kofi Ackah, Ashraf Adeel, Mark Budolfson, Mehmet Erginel, Gale Justin, José Lourenço, Fernando Muniz, Debra Nails, Hope Lindsay Rudebusch, and Christopher Turner each gave me a critical review of the entire book and comments that led to substantial changes. For astute help at various points, I thank Michael Baun, Betty Belfiore, Jeffrey Downard, Gail Fine, Steven Funk, Chris Griffin, Stephen Halliwell, Matthew Herbert, Adam Hutler, Rachana Kamtekar, Joe Lauer, Mark McPherran, Sara Rappe, Naomi Reshotko, Nicholas D. Smith, and Mike Stallard. For encouraging me at the outset to undertake the project, I thank Georgios Anagnostopoulos, Julia Annas, Terry Penner, and Gerasimos Santas. Finally, I thank Nick Bellorini, who visited me in Flagstaff and first proposed the project to me in his capacity as editor for Blackwell.

I wrote the bulk of this book while on sabbatical from Northern Arizona University in the academic year 2006–7. Jess Lorona, as an attorney's professional courtesy, provided funding that enabled me to take the whole year for the project. I am grateful for this institutional and personal financial support.

In preparing to write this book, I benefited from the opportunity to make presentations and participate in discussions. For these benefits I am grateful both to the individuals who organized the meetings as well as to the institutions supporting my travel. I thank especially Mark McPherran for organizing each spring in Tucson the Arizona Plato Colloquium, and also Georgios Anagnostopoulos, Julia Annas, Tom Christiano, Chris Maloney, Fernando Muniz, and Terry Penner for bringing me to meetings that were crucial to the development of my ideas. For travel funding, I thank in particular my home institution, Northern Arizona University, and also the University of Arizona. In addition I thank the Olympic Center for Philosophy and Culture in Pyrgos, Greece, the A. G. Leventis Foundation in Nicosia, Cyprus, and the CAPES Foundation of the Brazilian Ministry of Education for their support of my travel to international meetings.

Three chapters are revisions of work published elsewhere. Chapter 7, "Puzzling Pedagogy," is a revision of "Socrates, Wisdom and Pedagogy," *Philosophical Inquiry [Athens]: Festschrift in Honor of Gerasimos Santas*, edited by G. Anagnostopoulos, vol. 30 no. 3–4 (2008) 1–21. Chapter 8, "Love," is a revision of "Socratic Love," in *The Blackwell Companion to Socrates*, edited by R. Kamtekar and S. Ahbel-Rappe, London and New York: Blackwell (2006) 186–99. Chapter 11, "Benevolence," is a revision of "Neutralism in Book I of the *Republic*," in *The Good and the Form of the Good*, edited by D. Cairns, F.-G. Herrmann, and T. Penner, Edinburgh University Press (2007) 76–92. I am grateful to these publishers and their editors for permission to use these works in revision.

translations used

Unattributed translations are mine, except for Bible translations, which are from the New American Standard. The line references I use are standard and should give the reader little trouble.

introduction

Goals of This Book

Plato's dialogues tell a story about Socrates' life, focusing on conversations about human excellence. This book follows that life from age 36 to age 70, from mastery over the "wisest man" Protagoras to death by poison. In those conversations, the conclusions Socrates reaches – sometimes explicitly, sometimes implicitly – are wild:

- No human being knows how to live.
- Bravery, benevolence, righteousness, reverence, the best sort of luck – even the ability to interpret the most divine poetry – are all one and the same thing: expertise at human well-being.
- Such expertise by itself would requite the needy love of any human being, rule the psyche (or soul, as I shall call it) without inner conflict, and ensure happiness and freedom.
- Lacking that expertise, we are guilty of the worst sort of negligence if we do not spend our lives trying to discover it – better not to live at all!

Socrates' arguments eliciting these results are open to obvious objections. Readers who take the objections to be successful have two interpretive options. One is to suppose that Socrates spent his life fascinated by what we easily see to be poor arguments. The second option is to suppose that Socrates did not intend such arguments seriously, but was being playful for some reason or other.

I propose a third option. Finding convincing replies to the obvious objections, I take Socrates' results seriously and endorse the interpretation Alcibiades gives in Plato's *Symposium*. Alcibiades compares Socrates' arguments to "those statues of Silenus that open down the middle" (221d8–e1). This Silenus was a satyr, a mythical creature having a distorted human face and upper body, with the lower body of a goat. Silenus was ridiculous as a lusting drunkard, ever driven by sexual desire and incapable of sober thought – yet these very acts were his worship of the god Dionysus. Hidden inside the grotesque hollow statue was a beautiful *agalma*, that is, a holy image of the god, carved as an act of worship. The *agalma* would delight the lucky person who found it inside. Just so, Alcibiades says,

> Socrates' arguments seem ridiculous the first time you listen . . . but if you see them taken apart and get inside of them, you will find them to be the only arguments that are reasonable, arguments that are the most godlike, arguments holding inside a wealth of *agalmata* of divine excellence, arguments that are largely – no, *completely* – intent on everything proper for becoming a noble and good man.
>
> 221e1–222a4

I follow Alcibiades, seeing in Socrates' arguments the power to bring joy and propriety to human lives.

I emphasize that there are alternatives to my interpretation. While some commentators prefer the first two options I mention above, others prefer a fourth option, which is to take Socrates' arguments seriously, but to give tame interpretations of his conclusions. For example, some have interpreted the wild idea that *expertise ensures happiness* as the tame conventional wisdom that *good people make the best of their circumstances*. The wild idea that any life that does not consist of philosophical examination is *not worth living* becomes the tame advice that an examined life is *the only hope for improving ourselves*. Such taming has advantages: it both judges Socrates' arguments to be good and at the same time leaves conventional moral wisdom unthreatened. Nonetheless, I urge that we recognize the possibility of a deeper and truer moral sensibility than conventional wisdom. Rather than construe Socrates' *view* in the manner most *plausible* by our lights, my goal is to find what in Socratic *argument* will *compel* our assent, even if it turns human life upside down.

Thus 14 chapters that follow aim to show how Socrates gives compelling arguments for wild conclusions. Upon hearing Socrates in the *Gorgias*, Callicles appropriately replied: "If what you say turns out to be true, aren't we human beings living our lives upside down and doing everything quite the opposite of what we ought?" (481c2–5). I agree with Callicles that everything important in human life hangs on the question whether Socrates' views are true.

Socrates speaks to us in ordinary language as human beings, not as academic specialists. It is not rocket science, but it is a philosophical project. Socrates' *method* – beginning from premises accepted by his conversation partner and arguing step by step in ordinary language – to a large degree created the academic discipline of philosophy in European history. Plato and Aristotle took up many of the topics investigated by

Socrates, and those topics have remained essential in the academic tradition of western philosophy. People to this day who have had only one philosophy course are more likely to have read a Socratic dialogue than anything else.

In my opinion the philosophical tradition has not given Socrates' *results* the attention they deserve. His results are as surprising today as they were in his day. Yet it would be difficult to overstate how much my project depends upon a half-century of scholarship that uses the tools of analytic philosophy to interpret and evaluate the premises, inferences, and conclusions of Socratic arguments.

In addition to my goal of providing to readers a conversation with a philosophically astute Socrates, I have another goal. This is to recognize Socrates the Philosopher as one of the great religious inspirations of world history, comparable to such others as Confucius the Master, Krishna the Lord, Siddhartha the Buddha, Jesus the Christ, and Mohammad the Prophet – as they are called by their devotees. These cultural fountainheads make different and sometimes incompatible statements about supernatural beings and the institution of religion in society. But they share the theme that *single-minded devotion to righteousness, done as a holy sacrament, is ideal life.* In chapters 15 and 16 I propose a life of Socratic philosophy not as an alternative to the life of religious devotion but as itself the heavenly way for human beings to live, through the sacrament of cross-examination about human excellence.

To a far greater extent than other religious teachers, we possess in Plato's dialogues step-by-step arguments aimed at demonstrating the truth of their shared theme. It is by considering objections and replies to these arguments that I propose to help readers decide its truth. To put it grandly, my goal is to lead philosophers to religion, to lead the religious to philosophy, and to lead those who are neither to both.

Who Was Socrates?

The Confucius, Siddhartha, and Jesus who have shaped world history are the characters preserved in classic texts. It is a matter of doubt to what degree those texts accurately present historical persons. Likewise the Socrates who has greatly influenced the course of history is the character we find in Plato's dialogues. This Socrates in some ways (but not others) is similar to the Socrates presented in other ancient texts, most extensively in Aristophanes and Xenophon.

Readers want to know to what degree Plato's Socrates is fictional and whether in important ways he *is* the historical figure. I save that question for the epilogue. It is appropriate to put that question last, not first, in this book. The important question for this book – like the important question for us as human beings – is not the *particular flesh and blood* who uttered these words but the *great mind* in the text for us to understand, whether that mind is a literary creation or a historically accurate account.

I sometimes (such as in chapter 5) contrast views of Socrates as he appears in different dialogues written by Plato. It is confusing to speak of Socrates and "another Socrates." Following Aristotle, I refer to the *other Socrates* as Plato, even when the *other Socrates* speaks in the same dialogue with Socrates (as in chapter 16)! In the epilogue I defend the use of Aristotle's distinction as a working hypothesis. But none of the book's goals requires that the distinction between Socrates and the *other Socrates* be more than a convenience for talking about different threads of discussion found in Plato's dialogues.

the *ion*

interpreting socrates

What does it take properly to interpret Socrates? A conversation that Socrates has at age 56 tells us. The conversation is with Ion, a professional *rhapsode*, that is, one who recites and interprets poetic texts. With Ion, Socrates reaches a surprising conclusion: the best interpreter of Homer is not a Homer specialist like Ion, but an expert in human well-being. The same expert, it turns out, will also be the best interpreter of Socrates.

Homer

After getting Ion to recite a passage on chariot racing, Socrates asks a question that is easy for Ion to answer:

> SOCRATES: Tell me what Nestor says to his son Antilochus, when he advises him how to take the turn well in the chariot race honoring Patroclus.
>
> ION: (reciting Homer's *Iliad*, 23.335–40): *Lean*, he says:
>
> Lean in the smooth chariot, just to the left of the pair.
> Then goad the right-hand horse
> As you shout him on and give him free rein.
> Let the left-hand horse skin by the turning post,
> So the hub built into your wheel seems to touch the edge
> – But keep from striking that stone!
>
> SOCRATES: Enough. Now who would know better, Ion, whether or not Homer speaks correctly with these words, a doctor or a charioteer?
>
> ION: A charioteer, of course.
>
> 537a5–c3

Socrates and Ion leave unspecified what it is for Homer to "speak correctly" in these lines. There are many possible standards by which to judge the correctness of these lines. Was Homer speaking correctly in *reporting Nestor's words?* – such a question calls for the expertise of a historian or biographer. Neither a charioteer nor a doctor can answer such a question. Again, if someone wanted to know if Homer was speaking correctly in his *use of poetic form* (for instance, whether the Greek is in proper dactylic hexameter), we would need expertise in poetic grammar to answer. Ion might even have replied to Socrates' question as follows: "A doctor – since it is by expertise in *medical risk* of chariot injuries that we know whether Homer speaks correctly about permitting one's son to participate in chariot racing."

As it happens, Ion evidently takes the words *speaking correctly* to mean speaking correctly about *how to win a chariot race*, not about *whether there is acceptable medical risk in chariot racing*. If we interpret Socrates' words *speaking correctly* the same way as Ion, then we will approve Ion's answer. Ion correctly states that an expert charioteer is a better judge than an expert doctor whether Homer in this passage speaks correctly about how to race a chariot.

Ion goes on to agree to Socrates' generalization from charioteering to any expertise: "Then he who lacks any expertise will not be able to discern well either the words or actions of that expertise?" – "True" (538a5–b1). When it comes to judging good and bad speech about chariot racing, not only is a doctor inferior to a charioteer, so is a rhapsode – even when the speeches are in Homer and the rhapsode is a specialist in Homer. The same is true for judging good and bad speeches about fishing, medicine, and reading omens about the future. The rhapsode will be inferior to the respective experts at assessing the value of the speeches for achieving goals in the spheres of the respective expertises. Ion is right to agree with Socrates.

Now Socrates challenges Ion. As Socrates has pointed out passages in Homer that belong to other expertises, he asks Ion to identify the speeches in Homer that belong to the expertise of the rhapsode, passages which the rhapsode *by his expertise* is able to consider and evaluate better than non-experts. Ion tries to say this is true of *all* the passages in Homer (539e6). After Socrates reminds him that by Ion's own admission "the rhapsode's expertise cannot know everything" (540a5–6), Ion gives a more promising answer. The rhapsode's expertise includes "what's proper for a man to say, or a woman, and a slave or freeman; and a ruler or his subject" (540b3–5).

I judge Ion's answer more promising because it comes close to what Socrates himself stated earlier in the dialogue as the topic of "the most divine of poets," Homer (530b10). According to Socrates, such poetry deals with "*war*, mainly, as well as *social* relationships of human beings with each other, both good and bad, lay and professional, and the relationships of the gods both with each other and with humans, and events in the heavens and in the underworld, and the genesis of gods and heroes" (531c4–d1). Socrates' statement separates poetry from charioteering, fishing, prophecy, and other such arts. Charioteering expertise knows the relations between humans and *chariots* in *racing*. Fishing expertise knows the relations between humans and *fish* in *catching*. Expertise in prophecy knows the relations between humans and *the future* in *reading omens*. By contrast, the main topics of poetry are, first, the relations between humans and *humans* – be they good or bad, lay or professional – in both *war* and *society*; second, the relations between humans and *the gods*; third, the relations between *gods* and *gods*, including supernatural events (that is, events "in the heavens and in the underworld"). Finally, just as the expert at charioteering knows the origin of an expert charioteer – how to make a *hero* or *god* of chariot racing, as it were – so likewise does the expert at the main topic of poetry know how a hero and even a god come to be.

Socrates' statement of the topic of poetry makes it a matter of universal and ultimate human concern. For example, the Bible is ultimately concerned with humanity and divinity as opposed to, say, chariot racing or fishing. We might read the Ten Commandments as giving us a list of religious duties to God ("Remember the Sabbath!") and moral duties to other humans ("Thou shalt not murder!"). Confucius is a second example, from an independent cultural tradition of equal authority. Of ultimate concern to Confucius is *rén* 仁, that is, *the proper way to live among human beings*. In many ways Confucius is as unconcerned with the gods as any atheist. Yet according to Confucius perfect human life will be lived entirely as *lǐ* 禮, that is, as an act of religious devotion in the presence of the divine.[1]

Socrates' account of poetry explains the ultimate benefit and exalted transcendence poetry and great literature in general have. And just as Ion and Socrates understand the chariot speech in Homer not as mere description or history but rather as words advising *how to attain a goal*, likewise we should understand Socrates' statement of the topic of poetry to include words that advise us *how to attain our ultimate goals* as human beings with other human beings and before the gods.

I readily admit that not all poetry aims to help one comprehend and achieve the ultimate aims of human life. Some write poetry simply to communicate an emotion, experience, or point of view. Often we choose literature for entertainment rather than edification. Nonetheless, I say, Socrates' account is correct. For he and Ion agreed upon the scope of their discussion of poetry at the beginning of their conversation: they were concerned with "the best and most divine of poets" (530b10), the most notable of whom in their time was Homer. I cannot conceive a better or more divine topic for any poetry than what Socrates himself stated.

Ion, therefore, is giving a promising answer to Socrates' question – *What parts of Homer are in the scope of the rhapsode's expertise?* – when he says, "what's proper for a man to say, or a woman, and a slave or freeman; and a ruler or his subject." But when Socrates tests Ion's answer, Ion fails to distinguish what a man ought to say as a ruler of *men* from what a man ought to say as a ruler of *soldiers* or *sailors*.

SOCRATES: Are you saying that the rhapsode will know better than the pilot the sort of thing to say when you're ruling a ship at sea and get hit by a storm?

ION: No, the pilot knows better in that case . . .

SOCRATES: Well, will he know what's proper for a man to say, when he is a general advising soldiers?

ION: Yes, that sort of thing the rhapsode will know.

SOCRATES: What? The expertise of the rhapsode is the expertise of the *general*?

540b6–d4

Although Ion fails, there is a successful answer to Socrates' question. I take it that Socrates would agree that a terrorist, for example, might be ever so successful as a ruler of soldiers, or a pirate as a ruler of sailors, yet at the same time they might be failures both as human beings and as rulers of human beings, reckoning that failure in terms of personal depravity or wretchedness. Likewise it is possible to be an excellent doctor, cowherd, or weaver but at the same time be defective as a human being.

Socrates in fact makes this very distinction near the end of the *Charmides*, using nearly the same set of examples of other kinds of expertise in contrast to the expertise at doing well *as a human being*.

SOCRATES: Knowledgeable living does not make us do well and be happy, not even living according to all the other branches of knowledge together, but only according to this single knowledge of good and bad. For, Critias, if you choose to take away this knowledge from all the others, will medicine any the less give us health, or shoemaking give us shoes, or weaving give us clothes, or will the pilot's expertise any the less prevent us dying at sea, or the general's in war?

CRITIAS: None the less.

SOCRATES: But, my dear Critias, if this knowledge is missing, none of these things are well and beneficially given.

174b12–d1

Socrates goes on to describe *this single knowledge of good and bad* as the expertise "whose business is to benefit *us*" (174d3–4), that is, *us ourselves* as opposed to benefiting our health, shoes, clothes, or wars.

With this distinction between expertise at human benefit and the other forms of expertise, we can reinstate Ion's retracted claim (at 539e6) that the rhapsode is the best person to evaluate *every* passage in Homer, from the first page to the last. At the beginning of the *Iliad* (1.10–32), for example, Agamemnon, from desire to keep a young captive as his slave-wife, fails to conform to ritual propriety and disrespects the captive's father, a suppliant priest bearing ransom. The disrespect was evidently a strategic error for Agamemnon *as a general* to make, leading to disastrous dissension in his ranks. But the poet's topic is not military strategy but human strategy, and the passage shows us how Agamemnon fails *as a human being*, regardless of his generalship. It belongs to the expertise of the rhapsode to judge whether Homer speaks correctly not in advising about generalship in war but in advising about humanity in war (and society). At the end of the *Iliad* (24.507–676), to take another example, the poet describes how Achilles, despite blood-lust to defile a corpse, manages to conform to ritual propriety and feel sympathy with the father of the dead victim. Achilles produces financial benefit for himself as a corpse barterer in this passage. But Homer's topic here is not how to make a profit in corpse bartering but how in such a case to produce human well-being through propriety and sympathy.

Likewise we can reclaim the passages Socrates himself mentions. For example, the passage quoted at the beginning of this chapter, where Nestor advises his son Antilochus, certainly is an account of charioteering technique. But Nestor introduces this advice with the following praise of all forms of expertise.

> Dear son, be sure to store in mind all forms of craft,
> So that victory's prizes do not slip out of your hands.
> Craft makes a woodcutter far better than strength.
> It is craft that lets a pilot on the wine-dark sea
> Keep a swift ship on course when a gale strikes.
> And craft makes one charioteer better than another.
> 23.313–318

Nestor's aim in this speech is to advise his son about charioteering, but only because he judges that successful charioteering contributes to his son's successful life as a human being. Given Nestor's subordination of chariot racing to success in human life, the poet's topic likewise is successful chariot racing only insofar as it promotes successful human life. And it belongs to the expertise of the rhapsode to judge whether Nestor advises well to make it one's goal in human life to "store in mind all forms of craft" rather than, as Socrates concluded above with Critias, to aim only at the expertise of knowledge of human well-being, *not* expertise even of "all the other branches of knowledge together." The rhapsode may take the very words that Ion recited from Nestor's speech as a metaphor for expert *human* advice: "Let the left-hand horse skin by the turning post, so the hub built into your wheel seems to touch the edge – but keep from striking that stone!" As the chariot must follow the most direct line best to win the prize, likewise human life must subordinate all else to the most direct line producing well-being, and not be the foolish charioteer, who, "trusting in horses and car, thoughtlessly curves wide to this side and that, and his horses veer up the track uncontrolled" (*Iliad* 23.319–321).

Facing Socrates' challenge, I take myself to have successfully defended Ion's claim that the rhapsode is the best person to evaluate nearly every passage in Homer. The starting point of my defense was Socrates' own premise about poetry's topic: *The best and most divine poets, such as Homer, write mainly on the topic of ultimate concern to human beings, namely, how to live as a human being among human beings and before the gods.* There are objections to this premise. Some will find the reference to *gods* unnecessary. Some will deplore the omission of a reference to *the natural world* apart from humanity. I respond to these objections by interpreting *the gods* as ancient Greeks did: I leave open whether the gods must be supernatural beings or might include those aspects of nature that call for our reverence. Interpreted this way, Socrates' premise is true, as it seems to me and I suppose to most people.

Although nothing I have said so far is wild, there is a wild conclusion to draw. Socrates was no poet, yet his topic in discussion was the poet's topic, namely, ultimate human well-being. Not just Socrates but anyone who discusses ethics discusses that same topic. It follows almost at once that it is one and the same expertise that evaluates both Socrates and Homer, that evaluates both poetry and ethics. I say *almost* because there is one more premise about expertise needed to draw this conclusion: *One expertise differs from another if and only if they are about different topics.* It is no coincidence that Socrates establishes this same premise about expertise in the *Ion:*

> SOCRATES: Then tell me now . . . whether you think this rule holds for all
> expertise – that by the same expertise we must know the same
> things, and by a different expertise things that are not the
> same; but if the expertise is different, the things we know by it
> must be different also.
> ION: I think it is so, Socrates.
>
> 538a1–5

It is wild to say that one and the same expertise evaluates both poetry and ethics. It is bad enough to conclude, as Socrates does with Ion, that anyone who is expert at Homer is also expert at any and every other poet who ever wrote: "We shall not be wrong in saying that Ion is equally skilled in Homer and in the other poets, since Ion agrees that the same man will be a competent judge of all who speak on the same things, and that practically all the poets treat of the same things" (532b3–7). Are literature departments wrong-headed to look for different credentials for expertise at Homer and, say, Emily Dickenson? – and likewise philosophy departments to think there are different branches of expertise for say, Socrates and Confucius? And are universities wrong-headed to house literature and ethics in different departments as if they were two different fields of expertise with different methods?

One might object that, even if they have the same goal, poetry and ethics use different means (say, emotionally charged imagery as opposed to prose argumentation). Dealing with different means, they require different skills and cannot be identified. We can easily broaden this objection from expertise at human well-being to other kinds of expertise. Surgery requires different skills from drug treatments, though both aim at the patient's health. Hiking a desert requires different skills than climbing a mountain, even if the two routes are alternatives to the same destination. In general, it is obvious that one can know one method or means to an end without knowing every other method and means.

But this objections fails. We expect an expert doctor to know the best treatment for our disease. I do not qualify as an expert if I know how to treat your illness with amputation but cannot tell you if amputation is better or worse than drug therapy. Likewise I am not an expert backcountry guide if I can only tell you one route to take but cannot tell you if that route is safer or quicker than other routes. Just as we expect an expert pilot to know the *best* route to the goal and an expert doctor to know the *best* treatment plan, so also we expect the expert at human well-being to know the *best* life plan and therefore to know when emotionally charged images are better than prose argument at guiding a human being.

The Subjectivity Objection

Before agreeing to restructure the academy, we ought to consider a second objection. The *subjectivity objection* is that Socrates' argument ignores the subjectivity of poetry and perhaps ethics. Socrates might be right about the *topic* of ethics and even poetry. But the interpreter's expertise needs to know not *the truth* about that topic but *the subject's thoughts* about the topic. To take again the example of Nestor's advice to his son, the interpreter needs to know Nestor's thought as expressed in his words: "Dear son, be sure to store in mind all forms of craft, so that victory's prizes do not slip out of your hands." This advice is at odds with the advice Socrates gave to Critias: a human being ought to lay up in mind expertise at the "single knowledge of human good and bad," *not* expertise even at "all the other branches of knowledge together."

Since Nestor's advice differs from Socrates', it is possible to know one without knowing the other. Thus it is possible for an interpreter to know Nestor's (or Homer's) thought without knowing Socrates' thought. Our conventional academic distinctions are thereby preserved. If we are looking for a professor of Homer, we want someone who knows Homer's thought. An expert at Socrates' thought, or anyone else's subjective thought, need not apply. And suppose for the sake of argument that we found a scientist of objective human well-being with expert advice about the truth at issue between Nestor and Socrates, an expert who in fact knew whether human beings ought to aim only to learn the single knowledge of human well-being, or whether they ought to aim to learn expertise of every sort related to prize winning. The academy would not be interested in hiring such an expert for professorships either in Homeric or Socratic thought, on the grounds that such objective expertise would not establish one's expertise at knowing either Homer's or Socrates' subjective thoughts.

I recognize that many people are uneasy with the very idea that expertise about human well-being is *objective*. Such people find it incredible that some expert could objectively discover that someone else's subjective moral and religious values are *false*. On the other hand, there are undeniable analogies between the expertise of healing a defective body and that of healing a defective soul, and between navigating a sea voyage and navigating one's way through life. It is surely because of their analogous features that Socrates in his dialogues so often refers to healing and navigation.

But the subjectivity objection remains, even if Socrates is right and there is something objective about human well-being. Let me show how the subjectivity objection holds true even in the case of an objective expertise, like medicine. In that case, the objection would be that it is possible to be a specialist in Homeric medicine without knowing other traditions of healing. We would not expect an expert at healing – that is, the objective truth about healing – to know Homeric thoughts about healing. The academy marks this distinction in its division between the sciences and the humanities: medicine belongs to the sciences while the history of medicine, like the interpretation of poetry, belongs to the humanities. The subjectivity objection holds true for objective branches of expertise like medicine, and so, even if there is an objective science of human well-being – as opposed to it being mere subjective opinions – the objection still holds true.

There is, however, a price to pay to use the subjectivity objection. The objection distinguishes objective truth from subjective opinions about a topic, so that the expert on a subject's thought knows not the truth but mere opinions. The price is that this distinction makes it impossible for such expertise to evaluate how well the subject thinks or speaks about their topic. Such expertise does not have the power to make comparisons of better and worse between poets. But Ion, like other interpreters and professors of poetry, wants to make such comparisons:

SOCRATES: You do say that Homer and the other poets, among whom are Hesiod and Archilochus, all speak about the same things but in different ways, since one does it well, and the rest worse?

ION: Yes, and what I say is true.

532a4–8

Indeed, if Homer or Socrates in truth had anything to teach us about what concerns us most, the expert on subjective thought would not know it.

The subjectivity objection saves for us an identifiable expertise at nothing but Homer's thought, but it does so at the price of making expertise at Homeric thought a thing of no *existential* value, that is, of no practical value for us as human beings. Expertise at Homeric thought would hold our interest only for, as they are called, *academic* reasons that are detached from human concerns.

The subjectivity objection lies behind many readers' reactions to the *Ion*. Most scholarship on the *Ion* falls into two camps. The first takes Socrates at face value and is appalled at his expectation that a truth-seeking expertise governs the topic of poetry. This camp faults Socrates for not recognizing what I have called the subjective nature of poetry. The second camp finds it wildly implausible that Socrates would honestly believe that a truth-seeking expertise governs poetry. This camp gives one or another ironic reading of the dialogue in order to construe the character Socrates as recognizing that absurdity.

Yet the subjectivity objection fails as soon as we interpret Socrates and Ion as themselves existential human beings. At the beginning of the dialogue Socrates says, "I judge rhapsodes worthy of emulation for their expertise . . . To apprehend the thought and not merely learn off the words is worthy of emulation," and Ion agrees (530b5–c1). Socrates and Ion esteem the expertise of the rhapsode not for academic reasons but precisely because it is *practical expertise at achieving the ultimate goals of human well-being*. Given their overriding concern for poetic interpretation as a guide to life, we can be sure that neither would buy the subjectivity objection at the price of making literary interpretation a thing of mere academic interest.

Socrates

Let me turn now to my project of interpreting not Homer but Socrates. It is possible that some study Socrates merely for academic reasons. It is possible to earn money and enjoy a certain prestige, living as I do – a paid professor specializing in the study of Socrates. It is also possible to enjoy puzzling over Socratic texts for the same sort of pleasure one gets from crossword puzzles: an amusement, nothing more. In contrast to those who study Socrates merely to gain money and prestige or who find Socratic texts merely amusing are those readers who come to the texts with existential concerns, whose motive for reading Socrates is that they may gain some expertise how to live as human beings. My interpretation of Socrates is aimed at this *existential* reader, whose overriding concern with Socrates is as a guide to life and who wonders whether Socrates might be a wise guide. Like that reader, my interpretation aims not merely to know the words of the text, but to apprehend Socrates' thought so as to be able to evaluate it as better or worse than the alternatives. My evaluation of Socrates will thus require the very same expertise as needed to evaluate Homer or Confucius or anyone else who writes poetry or ethics, and my evaluation will be as severely limited as my own understanding of human well-being.

If we were able to challenge Socrates with the same question he put to Ion – *Where are the passages that use the rhapsode's expertise?* – what would his answer be? The bare text before us does not give an answer to that question. But the interpretive method I follow does determine an answer. In seeking some expertise for ourselves about human well-being, we do better, facing an interpretive choice about the text, always to make the most charitable assumption consistent with the text. Perhaps this charity is a duty we owe to the dead author, Plato, and his main character. But I have a more practical reason in mind. By seeking the wisest answer we can, consistent with the text, we maximize our own chances of learning something wise from the text.

When Ion agrees with Socrates that to have the expertise of the rhapsode is a condition worthy of emulation, he makes a further claim that distinguishes himself from Socrates: "I consider I speak about Homer better than anybody" (530c8–9). Although Ion appears to be in this happy condition, especially to himself, the course of the dialogue shows that, despite the appearance of this expertise, in reality Ion is unable even to say what this expertise *is*. Socrates' effort to show Ion his ignorance is an example of his divine mission, as the next chapter will show.

note

1 The character *rén* 仁 is composed of the character for *human being* (人) and the character for *two* (二), hence *the proper relationship between two people*. The character *lǐ* (禮) is a combination of two characters, the left depicting *revelation from heaven* and the right depicting *a bowl filled with offering*. Combined, the characters refer to *acts done in and for divine presence*.

further reading

George Rudebusch, "Plato on Knowing a Tradition," *Philosophy East & West* 38 (1988) 324–33. The article gives a further reply to the subjectivity objection.

the *apology*

mission from god

Life

Socrates lived in dangerous times. He survived three tours of duty as an infantry soldier, including one deployment that lasted three years. All three tours ended in battles that were military defeats for Athens, two of them disastrous, with hundreds killed, including the generals in command. Those in the field alongside Socrates recognized him for lifesaving bravery. Although perilous, the three-year deployment may have saved Socrates' life because, while he was away, Athens suffered a plague that killed between a fourth and a third of the population. But Socrates was in the city for the second and third outbreaks of plague, epidemics killing so many people that military rolls were unfilled for the next two decades. He lived to see his city defeated by Sparta and escape a call for annihilation by vindictive Corinthians. He barely survived the murderous tyranny that followed, disobeying an order to make an arrest, and lived through an insurgency that eventually restored democratic self-rule.

It was Socrates' public image that finally killed him. While Ion endured Socrates' cross-examination with good humor, the hostile and threatening reaction of Anytus was probably more typical:

> Socrates, to *say* bad things about people seems easy for you. If you are willing to take my advice, I would advise you to be careful. For to *do* bad things to people is probably easier than to do good in most cities, and especially in this one – and I think you know it.[1]
>
> *Meno* 94e3–95a1

People with a grudge against Socrates found it easy to spread bad stories about him. Socrates had a reputation for dishonoring the religious and social traditions of his fellow citizens with his conversations. For example, in the *Euthyphro*, Socrates said he was defending himself in court because, whenever others tell traditional stories of the gods

hating and fighting each other, "I find it hard to accept. This is why anyone will say I am guilty" (6a8–9).

Socrates disagreed when others told traditional religious stories, trying to reform religious belief to conform to reasonable principles. In this respect he was like the anti-traditional scientists such as Anaxagoras, scientists who were notorious for disagreeing with supernatural poetic fancy on the basis of natural scientific reasoning. Socrates' disagreeable reasoning might have led, via the inevitable distortions of gossip, to a public image confusing him with reductive natural scientists. Thus Athenians would have recognized the Socrates Aristophanes ridicules in his comedy, *The Clouds*. Aristophanes' Socrates states, "There is no Zeus," declaring that the true gods are natural phenomena, "clouds" (lines 316–391).

On trial for his life at age 70, Socrates' reputation made him vulnerable before a jury. In his defense speech, the *Apology*, Socrates calls attention to the fact that many jurors had heard "since they were children" (18b5) that Socrates "did not believe in the city's gods" (18c3) and "taught others these things" (19c1). With the support of the prominent Anytus, a young zealot named Meletus successfully prosecuted him on a rarely used charge of "corrupting the young and believing in new gods, not the gods that the city believes in" (24b9–c1). The jury, composed of hundreds of fellow citizens, convicted him of this wrongdoing and sentenced him to death.

Defense Strategy

In a legal system where jurors take the job more for the entertainment and pay it provides than from a sense of civic duty, Socrates does not follow the conventions of flattering the jury and appealing to their sympathy. As always, he speaks and acts freely, not slavishly.

> You are used to hearing others weep and wail in their defense speech, doing and saying many things that I say are unworthy of me. When I gave my defense speech, I did not think that the danger of losing my case was reason to do anything slavish, and I don't regret it now. I much prefer to die after my sort of defense than to live after a defense of the other sort.
>
> 38d9–e5

Socrates speaks freely, though he is aware that some members of the jury will mistake an earnest but free man's legal defense for foolish jesting at the judicial process: "to some of you it will seem as if I am jesting" (20d4–5).

For example, his choice of witness for his defense causes an uproar. "As a witness to my wisdom, such as it is, I shall produce the god, the one at Delphi" (20e6–8). This god, who spoke through an entranced priestess called the Pythia, is Apollo (as Socrates says at *Protagoras* 341b1–2), though he never calls him by name in the *Apology*.[2] The Athenians relied on this oracle as the most authoritative source of divine word.

Socrates tells a story in introducing the divine testimony about himself. "I suppose you all know Chaerephon" (25e8). Chaerephon was a man so famously eccentric that for 20 years comedians could count on the mention of his name in a play to bring a laugh. "He was my friend since we were young . . . You know the sort of man he was, how impetuous when he got going. Well, once he went to Delphi and dared to request a divine answer to the following question – Gentlemen, please! Do not make an uproar at what I say!" (20e8–21a5). Evidently there are many people in the audience who already know the story and object to Socrates' use of this testimony. "He asked, you know, whether anyone was wiser than I. Then the Pythia answered from on high that no one is wiser. Now Chaerephon is dead, but his brother here will bear witness to this" (21a5–21a8).

The oracle's answer puzzled Socrates:

> When I heard this, I wondered about it: "What in the world is the god saying, and what is he hinting at within the riddle? For I am well aware of being wise in nothing big or small. What is he saying when he states I am as wise as possible? He's not lying, of course – that's not his way."
>
> 21b2–7

Had Socrates lacked reverence to the god at Delphi, he would have had an easy solution to the riddle. The statement about his wisdom might simply be false: either no god was speaking there, or the god was lying. But Socrates was reverent, hence puzzled, and so his life would change, much as Moses' life was changed by the experience of a divine voice in a burning bush.

Unable to solve the riddle, Socrates eventually decided to find a counter-example among those with a reputation for wisdom, thinking that "there, if anywhere, I should test the utterance and show the oracle: 'This man is wiser than I, but you said I was wisest'" (21c1–2). Socrates was in the position of soldiers who are unable to understand their orders and must prepare to return to the commander to say, "Sir, you stated X, but X conflicts with Y!" Respectful soldiers are not thereby presuming that the commanding officer is wrong, or even that the orders are at fault for being unintelligible. They are explaining why they do not understand while they seek explanation. Socrates says that he turned to the task of

finding a counter-example with "great reluctance" (21b8: another parallel with Moses, who shares Socrates' humility and reluctance, Exod. 3:11). Socrates does not say why he was reluctant. In chapter 3 I propose that he wished to avoid the impropriety of going to people to cross-examine them.

But Socrates failed to find a counter-example, confirming the truth of the oracle. Of course Socrates was not able to examine every human being. But he made a sample of different types of people: in the first case political leaders, who take it upon themselves to advise the city about its best interests, in the second case the poets who write about matters of ultimate human concern, and in the last case the craftworkers, who alone of the three classes knew some fine things, but not that on which all else depends (21c–22e).

At some point, Socrates took himself to understand the god's message – if only provisionally, since he introduces his solution saying, "Chances are that . . ." (23a5). His solution interprets the words of the oracle – *no one is wiser* – "as if the god were saying: 'Among you human beings, he is wisest who, like Socrates, recognizes that truly he has no wisdom of value'" (23b1–4). The meaning of these words, that is, what the god is saying at Delphi "*with* the oracle," is that "human wisdom is worth little or nothing" (23a6–7).

Socrates solves the divine riddle by distinguishing three levels of wisdom. The highest level is "real wisdom" (23a5–6), which is the property of God, not human beings. The middle level is being "wisest among men" (23b2), which is the property of anyone who, like Socrates, "knows that he does not possess real wisdom of any value" (23b3–4). The lowest level is "not being wise, but seeming wise, especially to oneself" (21c6–7). Socrates is as wise as a mortal can be – *no one is wiser* – because only God possesses wisdom and because Socrates is significantly wiser than people who are ignorant even of their ignorance.

That the god who spoke at Delphi assigned him the full-time job of interrogation is the cornerstone of Socrates' defense: "The god gave me a station, as I believed and understood, with orders to spend my life in philosophy and in examining myself and others" (28e4–6), so that to cease to philosophize is "to disobey the god and therefore impossible" (37e6–7).

Socrates mentions being commanded "in oracles and dreams and in every way anyone was ever commanded by divine power to do anything" (33c5–7), but he takes his account of the Delphic oracle to establish his obligation to *philosophize*, that is, to cross-examine others in the way I showed him conversing with Ion.

The oracle gives no command, but simply states a fact: *no one is wiser*. Socrates' account of the meaning of this statement – that *human wisdom is worth little or nothing* – is also a simple statement of fact.

It may seem wild to members of the jury, as it has to many interpreters, that Socrates hears a command in either statement. In order to hear the command, the jury and we must recognize that *Socrates is reverent towards the gods of the city.* In other words, we must admit the falsity of the slander (mentioned at 18c) that Socrates does not believe in the gods. As soon as we admit that Socrates is reverent, it is possible to infer his obligation. It goes without saying that *the reverent recognize that their highest obligation is to serve the gods and hence to understand their words.* The assumption that Socrates is reverent explains his obligation to solve the riddle: "it seemed necessary to give highest priority to the god's meaning" (21e4–5).

The oracle's meaning, as Socrates interprets it, is at odds with the behavior that we observe in our cities, and that Socrates observed in his. In the *Laches,* for example (chapter 6), men seek advice from the distinguished citizens Laches and Nicias on how to raise children, evidently believing that Laches and Nicias have significant expertise. And Laches and Nicias give advice, taking themselves to know how to produce the human excellence of bravery. There is another example in the *Apology* itself: the success of Meletus in prosecuting Socrates shows that Meletus appears both to himself and others to know how to maintain reverence in the city.

Even after solving the riddle, Socrates believes that he continues to have an obligation to philosophize. Alluding to Hercules and his labors, Socrates asks the jury to view his work as "labors performed so that, because of me, the oracle would be irrefutable" (22a7–8). This is not an after-hours hobby for Socrates, but a full-time occupation, leaving him no time for conventional public or family life. "I have no leisure for any public or household affairs worth mentioning – I am in vast poverty on account of my service to the god" (23b8–c1). This raises a further interpretive question: once Socrates has figured out the god's word, why does he believe he has a continuing obligation to philosophize?

We can answer this question if we see how Socrates is similar to evangelical Christians. The oracle's meaning – that *human wisdom is worth little or nothing* – tells us that we are in danger and need to save ourselves. Socrates reverently assumes that God is benevolent and wants people to know their need for such salvation. And, being reverent, Socrates takes his highest obligation to be to serve God. These reasons explain why, having solved the riddle and figured out the meaning, Socrates says, "even now I continue to go about searching and investigating, *in obedience to God,* anyone I think is wise, citizen or foreigner, and when he does not seem so, I *help* God show him that he is not wise" (23b4–7). Each time Socrates unmasks a pretender, he spreads God's saving word a little further, the word that human wisdom is worth little or nothing.

Socrates gives two reasons why he must live as he does and why he cannot appease the jury by promising to live without defending the oracle.

> This is the hardest thing to make some of you believe. For if I say that to keep quiet is impossible because it is disobedient to the god, you will think I am being sarcastic and will not believe me. If I say that the greatest good for a human being is to reason every day about human excellence and the other things that you hear me examining in conversation, and that the unexamined life is not worth living for a human being, you will believe me still less. It is as I say, gentlemen, but it is not easy to make you believe it.
>
> 37e4–38a8

Socrates states that to live philosophizing is the greatest good and that any alternative life is worse than death: *the unexamined life is not worth living for a human being.* This is a wild statement. If we accept it, our lives will change. Our first priority in life would be to live as Socrates did, trying to figure out what human excellence is.

Can Socrates' wild statement be true? To answer this question, consider *playing with firearms* as an analogy to *living as a human being.* The decision to raise a child, to make friends with another person, or to go to college – any of these choices might lead to disaster for oneself or others. Like such activities of human life, the use of firearms might lead to serious harm. Because of the risks, everyone will agree that if I don't know how to use firearms, it is better for me not to use them at all than to play with them ignorantly. Of course, this analogy is limited. In the case of firearms, I can choose to have nothing at all to do with them, and simply leave them untouched. But in the case of human life, there is no analogous choice. Even the choice *not to act at all* is a choice I make as a human being, a choice with an obvious potential for disaster.

Is it possible to fix the disanalogy? We would need to imagine, somehow, that I am in a situation where there is no way for me to avoid using the firearms. This is so unrealistic that the only way for me to imagine such a situation is as the plot of a horror movie. The hero wakes up from a hospital bed surrounded by people. To his horror, he discovers that when he makes choices, he sometimes triggers gunfire in unpredictable directions. There are near misses and horrible carnage before he sees the cause of these frightening effects.

The question is: what ought the hero to do? Everyone will agree that the very first order of business for the hero is to try to figure out how to manage the disability. Certainly he should stop seeing his friends socially and postpone his professional career until then! His only blameless choice is to try to figure out his situation before he can ever try to do anything else. This is his only choice no matter how much he loves others, no matter how high his social aspirations. Even if the hero burns with the true love of Romeo or has the magnanimous soul of Othello, he still needs to make it his first priority simply to learn to live with his disability. The reason why the hero must postpone the other things he wants to do is not because he ceases to value those other things. It is precisely *because* he wants to get on with his life, as well as possible under the circumstances, that he makes a search for appropriate knowledge his first order of business. ✦ ☆

Assuming that the meaning of the oracle is true – that *human wisdom is worth little or nothing* – let me try to show that this bizarre movie plot is analogous to our human lives.[3] If it does speak the truth, then I dare not spend my time seeking the love of others or political power. I dare not take it upon myself to advise others as Laches and Nicias do, when I am so disabled by ignorance that I do not know whether those actions will destroy the very things I value. I begin by showing the truth of a related claim: *only living Socratically is guilt free*. To show this, I need to draw some distinctions about guilt. People find it easiest to recognize the distinctions in the case of homicide, though they apply to all actions good and bad.

Consider then, the following four degrees of guilt for homicide, the first two being voluntary and the second two involuntary.[4]

1 *Crime of premeditation* I plan the murder in advance, in cold blood. For example, I purchase poison and hide the fact that I administer it over a period of several months until the victim dies. While such murderers regret being caught, they are unlikely to feel remorse for their crime, unless they undergo some sort of moral conversion after the fact.

2 *Crime of passion* I commit murder on the spur of the moment. Although I act impulsively, in hot blood, nevertheless I know full well as I act that I am killing a person. For example, enraged, I grab a gun in a barroom brawl and shout as I pull the trigger, "I'm gonna kill you!" Remorse is typical in this sort of case, as soon as the murderer calms down.

3 *Crime of negligence* Unlike the first two degrees, there is no will to kill. For example, caught up in the enthusiasm of a hunting trip, I fire recklessly, without having a clear line of sight, and kill another hunter. Although such killing is unintentional, people judge the killer guilty of negligence.

4 *Accident (no crime)* The death is not blamed upon the killer, because what happens is, as Aristotle puts it, "contrary to reasonable expectation." For example, while hunting and conscientiously following all safety rules, it happens that I kill a suicidal animal-rights

protester cunningly disguised in a deer costume. Although I am likely to be traumatized by the discovery, no guilt attaches to me either for murder or negligence.

People tend to agree that the first degree of murder carries the highest degree of guilt and deserves the stiffest sentence, with less punishment merited in the second degree, and still less in the third. The distinction between the third and fourth degree – between *crime of negligence* and *accident* – is well developed in tort law. If you can show that I was in any way negligent – in other words, that a reasonable person in the same situation would have foreseen the possibility of harm to another – then you have established my culpability. On the other hand, if I am not negligent, I am guilt free in such a case.

Given these four degrees of responsibility, the divine word – that *human wisdom is worth little or nothing* – brings good news and bad news. The good news is that we are incapable of voluntary wrongdoing. There are voluntary crimes only to the same extent that there is significant knowledge, and according to the oracle only God has such knowledge. This means that, like the Hollywood hero who triggers mayhem with gunfire he cannot predict, human beings are not guilty of voluntary wrongdoing.[5]

The bad news is that we are guilty of involuntary wrongdoing due to our negligence. We are negligent – and therefore guilty – if the harm we do is not contrary to reasonable expectation. In the horror movie, for example, that the hero's mere thoughts and choices trigger gunfire around him is so contrary to reasonable expectation that no one would blame him for the carnage at the onset of his disability. It is only when, in this extraordinary situation, he and the audience reasonably recognize some connection between his choices and the gunfire that we might begin to assign blame to him. Suppose for instance, that after reaching the point of reasonable recognition the hero ignores the disability and instead pursues matrimony or seeks political office. Now we would properly blame him for the ensuing mayhem, however unintentional. He is worthy of blame because, given his disability, it is not contrary to reasonable expectation that he might harm others, just like a hunter shooting blindly.

And here is the lifesaving news: when the hero recognizes his disability, there is a guilt-free course of action. If he makes it his first priority *to examine how to do the best he can in his situation*, then he is not guilty for whatever harm he involuntarily causes in the course of his examination. And there is an obligation to tell those with the disability this saving news. If negligence leads the hero not to notice his horrible disability, his neighbors ought to bring his disability to his attention, let him know he is shooting blindly, and lead him to the only proper course

of action. Doing so ought to prevent him from further negligent wrong-doing. If the oracle is correct, we human beings have a disability. We are shooting blindly with our lives, and, like Laches or Nicias, we are negligent not to notice it. The only way for us to avoid further guilt is to make it our first priority to live Socratically, that is, to examine how to live excellently and to make others aware of their intellectual disability.

There is a further point. If you are hunting in the dark, there is an obligation not to shoot until you can see. If your vision never clears, you can never shoot without negligence. Likewise our Socratic lifestyle is obligatory until we discover the wisdom we seek. The likely outcome that we shall never make that discovery is no reason to cease either from the examination or from the missionary work we do, warning others of their culpable ignorance. In the case of involuntary wrongdoing, the most guilty are those who recognize their disability and act as if it makes no difference. Woe to us, then, who say, "Socrates is right; we are profoundly ignorant how to live well. But his insight does not tell us how we ought to live. So we need change nothing in our lives!" For us to continue to live as we have would be as if to go shooting in the dark after admitting that we cannot see what we are doing and might maim someone. Any unsocratic, that is, unexamining, life is guilty of wrongful negligence.

I take it, therefore, that if human beings lack wisdom how to live, any unexamining life will be guilty. Is it possible that, even if guilty, perhaps such a life could still be worth living? To answer this question Socrates needs an additional premise to show that the unexamined life, being guilty, is not worth living for a human being. The additional premise is about the value of righteousness.

Righteousness is a major concern of Socrates and hence of this book. If we human beings were crafted like buildings, righteousness would be the power that produces the right lines and angles in us. If we were vegetables, righteousness would be the power that causes us to grow upright in the right place in the garden. If we were athletic bodies, righteousness would be the power that gives us the right health and strength for the sport. If we have duties to perform as human beings, righteousness is the power enabling us to perform them. Athenians recognized righteousness as essential to human excellence.

The word *righteousness* is a better translation for the Greek *dikaiosunē* than the standard translation *justice*. Like *righteousness* but unlike *justice*, *dikaiosunē* refers primarily to a general human virtue, not a specific social condition. Unlike *justice*, the formation of the English word *righteousness* accurately represents the formation of the Greek word. The abstract noun *dikaiosunē* ("righteousness") stems from the adjective *dikaios* ("righteous"), from the root *dikē* ("right"). When the three forms occur together, as for example in the *Protagoras*,

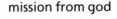

an English translation in terms of *justice, just,* and *right* hide the shared root from the reader. I understand that non-religious people sometimes have negative associations with the word *righteousness,* but such associations are no reason to avoid a word that conveys the religiosity of Socrates and his society. On the contrary, to translate so as to sanitize Socrates of religious connotations is inaccurate.

The additional premise Socrates needs is that *only a life that avoids perpetual unrighteousness is worth living for a human being.* Since Socrates is before a jury that is prepared to sentence him to death for unrighteousness, he can safely assume that the jury accepts this premise!

Collecting all the premises, I attribute the following argument to Socrates.

1 *Human beings lack wisdom* Our knowledge of righteousness is worth little or nothing; the most significant knowledge human beings can attain is recognition of their ignorance.
2 *Negligence is culpable* People who are ignorant about how to live as human beings, yet act presuming to know, are guilty of unrighteousness.
3 *Righteousness is supremely important* Only a life that avoids perpetual unrighteousness is worth living for a human being.
4 *Thus there is only one right way to live* Under the circumstances described by the oracle, the only life worth living for a human being is a life concerned above all else to examine how to live.

Socrates does not explicitly assemble these premises into an argument, but he does emphasize all four statements in his defense, and it is not hard to see the argument they form.

He emphasizes the first premise, the truth of the oracle, by telling the jury to view his life's work as *labors* – as if Socrates were a heroic Hercules – performed in order to prove the oracle "irrefutable" (22a7–8).

Socrates emphasizes the second premise as well, that unrighteousness due to negligence is culpable. He says, for example, that "to be afraid of death is only another form of thinking that one is wise when one is not; it is to think that one knows what one does not know, . . . and *this ignorance, which thinks that it knows what it does not,* must surely be culpable" (29a4–b2). Earlier Socrates accused Meletus of precisely this sort of negligence, saying Meletus is unrighteous because he "treats serious matters frivolously" (24c5–6). To treat serious matters frivolously – as we might say, *to play with fire* – is the form of wrongdoing of which all non-Socratic human beings are guilty. The particular form of fire-play of which Meletus is guilty is "lightly dragging people into court, and pretending to be earnest and to care about matters that he does not care about" (24c6–8). Later, Socrates describes his work in the city on behalf of the god, as to "question and examine and cross-examine" (29e4–5) those who claim to <u>care</u> about human excellence and righteousness before all else. In such cases, if Socrates discovers that the pretender "does not possess excellence but says he does" (29e5–30a1), Socrates "will blame him for scorning the things that are of most importance and caring more for what is of less worth" (30a1–2). That the unrighteousness of such scorn and misguided care is involuntary does not free the pretender from guilt. Finally, Socrates' accusers do not intend to act unrighteously. Yet Socrates warns that they ought to beware, because "the <u>real difficulty is to escape the condition of being wicked</u>, which is <u>quicker than death</u> . . . My accusers, who are clever and quick, have been <u>overtaken by the faster, by wickedness</u> . . . they will go away convicted by truth herself of depravity and unrighteousness" (39a7–b6).

Socrates emphasizes the third premise, about the value of righteousness and human excellence, in describing his characteristic activity in the city. He says, for example, "I go about doing nothing other than trying to persuade you, young and old, not to care for your bodies or your property more than, or even as much as, the excellence of your souls," (30a7–b2; reiterated at 29d–e, 31b, 36c–d). Earlier in the *Apology* Socrates precisely identifies the wisdom in question as *how to make a human being excellent*. And he reminds the jury that there are people, called *sophists*, who profess just such wisdom:

> I ran into a man who has paid more money to sophists than anyone else, Callias, the son of Hipponicus. So I asked him – for he has two sons – "Callias," I said, "if your two sons had happened to be colts or calves, we should be able to find and hire a supervisor to make them excellent and praiseworthy in the appropriate excellence – this would be some sort of horse trainer or farmer. Now, since the two are human beings, whom do you have in mind to get as supervisor? Who understands that kind of excellence, that of a human being and a citizen? For I suppose that you, being a parent, have looked into the matter. Is there anyone," I said, "or not?"
> "Certainly," he said.
> "Who," I said, "from what country, and what is his price as a teacher?"
> "Evenus," he said, "from Paros, five minae."
> And I called Evenus blessed, if he really had this expertise and taught so reasonably. I'd be proud myself and put on airs, if I understood these things – but I do not understand them.
>
> 20a4–c3

Socrates affirms that though this wisdom makes a man blessed, he lacks this wisdom himself.

Though he does not explicitly draw it as a conclusion from the other premises, Socrates also emphasizes the fourth premise, that his form of life is the best life, the only life worth living, and guilt free. In addition to the passage quoted above – "that the greatest good for a human being

is to reason every day about human excellence and the other things that you hear me examining in conversation, and that the unexamined life is not worth living for a human being" (38a2–6) – Socrates also says that "no greater good ever came to pass in the city than my service to the god" (30a5–7), his service, that is, of urging others to examine their lives. Socrates says that he is free of guilt, even unintentional guilt, and knows that his guilt-free condition is an even rarer achievement than that of an Olympic champion. This is why he proposes that the city provide him free meals in the Prytaneum, an honor reserved for champions and heroes, on the grounds that he "never intentionally wronged anyone" (37a5), an achievement that he also describes as "never wronging any one" (37b2–3). As I understand him, it is this lack of guilt that makes him a better man than Meletus or Anytus (30c–d).

Changed Lives

To accept Socratic philosophy is life changing. Like a religious conversion, it involves the recognition that one's previous life incurred guilt, that a change of priorities is needed, and that the change will save one's soul from guilt and make life worth living. One recognizes that one's previous actions were culpably negligent. As a result, one must postpone one's other concerns and make it the first priority to try to find out what human excellence is.

Yet Socrates himself did not withdraw from society. He fought in wars, fulfilled civic obligations, married, and raised children. We ought to interpret Socratic philosophy in such a way as to permit converts to do likewise. Again there is a similarity to Christianity. Many conventional social roles are possible for converts, consistent with leading a life of examination.

It would be silly to expect Socrates to help me to decide whether to make my home here or abroad, or whether to keep my day job or enroll as a full-time philosophy student. Socrates teaches me my first priority is to subordinate such mundane actions in life to the ultimate aim of seeking wisdom through Socratic conversation. Once I am converted, my subordinate choices are no-lose situations, my life having already been saved by Socrates' message.

notes

1   Socrates describes this kind of reaction at *Apology* 21d and 23a.
2   When Socrates speaks of "the god, the one at Delphi" at 20e8, he seems to distinguish this god from others he worships, such as Athena and Zeus. (Socrates

names these three gods as *his* gods at *Euthydemus* 302d3–6.) It is natural to take every reference Socrates makes to *ho theos*, "the god," in his references to the oracle (21b1–23c1 and 28e4–40b1) as a reference to *the god, the one at Delphi*. But at other times Socrates speaks as if there is only one God. For example, the last two words of the *Apology* are *ho theos*: "I go away now to die, while you go away to live, but which of us goes to the better thing is unknown to everyone except *ho theos*" (42a2–5). If these final words were a reference to *the god*, that is, *one among other gods*, Socrates would be saying that even among the gods *only* Apollo has knowledge of human well-being, *not* Athena, *not* even Zeus! Rather than accuse Socrates of an inconsistent theology, it is better to recognize that his culture permitted such numerical indeterminacy in speech about the gods (*Republic* 2, 379a–d, is an example). Thus English might translate the same two Greek words (*ho theos*) sometimes as *the god* and other times as *God* or *the Deity*, depending on context. I follow the same indeterminate practice in my interpretation of Socrates, sometimes referring to *the gods* and other times to *God*.

3 There are more realistic movie plots that are also analogous. Consider a war veteran who discovers that he is frequently and unpredictably subject to blackouts in which he goes on murderous rampages.

4 Aristotle identifies these four degrees in *Nicomachean Ethics* 5.8. The quotation in degree 4 below is from line 1135b16.

5 When Meletus accuses Socrates of voluntarily corrupting the young of the city, Socrates argues in reply that no one is likely voluntarily to corrupt another. Socrates' argument is different from mine. He argues that, in order to corrupt voluntarily, a man would need to be so ignorant that he would not know that to do so risks harming himself – an ignorance so extreme that "no one finds it possible" (25e5–6).

further reading

Thomas C. Brickhouse and Nicholas D. Smith, *Socrates on Trial*. Oxford: Oxford University Press and Princeton: Princeton University Press, 1989. The book examines philosophical and historical questions about Socrates' trial and Plato's *Apology*.

puzzling notoriety

Stages of Life

For some reason, Chaerephon went to the oracle at Delphi and asked whether anyone was wiser than Socrates. The oracle's answer was that *no one is wiser*. Socrates' account in the *Apology* of the oracle's answer divides his intellectual life into three stages. First is his life before he hears the oracle. The middle stage begins when he hears the oracle. Knowing his own ignorance, he tries to figure out the meaning of the oracle, finally testing it by cross-examining public figures. The last stage begins when he solves the riddle. He spends this stage of his life in defense of the oracle, on a religious mission to convert others to philosophy.

In the previous chapter I considered the question why Socrates takes himself, in the last two stages of his life, to have a religious obligation to convert others to philosophy. In this chapter I consider a different question, about Socrates' notoriety. To set out the question, I review the three stages in reverse order.

Socrates' last stage was a mission to the world. As Socrates describes it in the *Apology*, after he solves the riddle, his intellectual activity is "philosophizing," a kind of cross-examination that is not a sophist's display of expertise at teaching human excellence but a philosopher's display of *desire for* such wisdom. A philosophical display is a matter of "exhorting and reasoning" (29d5–6) such as the following.

> Most excellent man, are you not ashamed, as a citizen of Athens – the greatest of cities and the most famous for wisdom and power – to care about making as much *money* as possible – and reputation and prestige – when you neither care nor even *think* about practical wisdom and truth and your soul – how to make it as good as possible?
>
> 29d7–e3

The point of the exhortation is to elicit a protest: "I *do* care!" – and then the testing will begin, in the form of a cross-examination (29e3–5). The examination might result in an admission of ignorance and joint resolution to make it a first priority to try to discover wisdom.[1] On the other hand, Socrates says:

> If I find that he does not possess excellence, but says he does, I shall fault him for making the most important thing lowest priority and making worthless things high priority.
>
> 29e5–30a2

Such public faultfinding explains why for decades Socrates remained notorious as a civic nuisance, made enemies, and was put to death.

Socrates' middle stage tested divine word. Socrates begins the middle stage of his life when he hears about the oracle and is baffled.

> When I heard it, I wondered: "What in the world is the god saying, and what is he hinting at within the riddle? For I am well aware of being wise in nothing big or small. What is he saying when he states I am as wise as possible? He's not lying, of course – that's not his way." And for a long period of time I was at a loss as to what he meant.
>
> 21b2–7

Still baffled after the "long period of time," Socrates makes a momentous decision: "I turned my steps so as to investigate the god" (21b7–8).

Thus Socrates begins a systematic investigation of the citizens in Athens. His strategy is "to refute the oracle" (21b8–9), that is, to find someone with significant wisdom. He investigates representatives of three types of Athenians: public leaders, literary figures, and the working class (21b–22e). Were he to find a person with significant wisdom, he would "point him out to the oracle and say, 'This man is wiser than I, but *you* said *I* was wiser!'" (21c1–2).

Socrates describes three steps that typically occur in the middle stage. (1) He goes to a public man reputed wise, (2) talks with the man, establishing that he seems wise but is not, and (3) tries to show the man that he is not wise. The result of these three steps is that he becomes hated by the man and by many of those present:

> I went to a man with a reputation for wisdom . . . In conversation with him, he seemed to me to *seem* to be wise to many other people and especially to himself, but not to *be* wise. Then I tried to show him that, although he thought that he was wise, he was not. He hated me ever after and so did many bystanders.
>
> 21b9–d1

Socrates tells us that he repeated the process many times. Unable to find anyone with wisdom about human excellence, Socrates eventually solves the riddle:

With the oracle the god is saying: "The wisdom that human beings have is of little or no value." And it appears that the god mentions *Socrates* and uses my name to make me an example, as if he were to say: "Among you human beings, he is wisest who, like Socrates, recognizes that truly he has no wisdom of value.

23a6–b4

Socrates comes to the end of the middle stage of his life when he finds this solution.

The topic, form, and outcome of the conversations in the middle stage and the last stage are typically the same. In both, the topic is excellence at human life and our expertise at producing such excellence. As quoted above (29d5–6 and 29e4–5), Socrates' mission in his last stage takes the form of conversation, where he cross-examines and tries to demonstrate to people their ignorance of the expertise. His examination in the middle stage is the same. With public leaders, it consists of "examining" by "conversing" and "trying to demonstrate" ignorance (21c3–8). With literary figures, Socrates "took up what seemed to be the most carefully elaborated poems and cross-examined their poets" (22b2–4). Socrates does not give us any details of his conversations with the workers, other than that he "went to them" (22c9), but there is no doubt that the conversations had the same form. And the outcome is the same: he becomes hateful to those he examines in this way and to bystanders.

While the topic, form, and outcome of the conversations were the same at both stages, the systematic selection of three classes of people in the middle stage differs from the last stage, which has unsystematic chance meetings, directed at "any one of you whom I happen to meet" (29d6). There is also a difference in motive. The motive of the middle stage's investigation is to *solve the riddle* of the oracle, by finding someone with significant expertise at human life and therefore wiser than Socrates, who knows he is ignorant of this expertise. In contrast, Socrates' motive throughout the last stage of his life is to "serve the god by demonstrating to people their ignorance" (23b7), that is, to *convert others to philosophy* as their first priority (29e5–30a2).

The first stage of Socrates' life raises a puzzle about his notoriety. Socrates' defense at trial requires him to explain why he became notorious: "I must try in this short time to remove from your minds the slander that has been there for a long time" (18e5–19a2). To remove the slander, Socrates must answer the question: "Socrates, what is the trouble about you? Where did those slanders come from? Certainly your reputation and the stories about you did not come about from doing no more than other people, if you were doing nothing unconventional – so tell us what it is!" (20c4–d1). His answer is that the investigation of the oracle caused the unconventional behavior that led to the notoriety.

He became notorious because he *turned his steps* or *"changed direction so as to investigate the god"* (21b7–8).

This raises a question: where did Socrates turn his steps and what was his direction before he tested the oracle? In particular, what did Socrates do that gave Chaerephon a reason to ask the oracle whether anyone was wiser? Chaerephon must have known something extraordinary about Socrates *before* the oracle spoke. But Socrates' testimony at trial is that he gained notoriety by unconventional philosophical cross-examination only *after* the oracle spoke. There seems to be a contradiction in the testimony.[2]

It is possible that the testimony is false, that Socrates is either lying or confused. But there is a more charitable interpretation. In this chapter I pinpoint, within a month or two, when Socrates became notorious. I explain why his conversations before that time, in the first stage of his life, did not make him notorious and why Chaerephon had reason to go to the oracle before his notoriety. Finally, I conjecture within a year or two when Chaerephon went to Delphi.

When Socrates Became Notorious

Plato's dialogues contain more than Socrates' philosophical arguments. The arguments are embedded in a dramatic setting. By adding dramatic settings, which tell us when the dialogues took place, Plato shows us Socrates' activities from his teens until his death at 70.[3] In particular, the dramatic settings tell us when Socrates "changed direction so as to investigate the god" (21b7–8), the change that makes him notorious in Athens. These dates are consistent with the very little historical information we have about Socrates' life. One way to explain why Plato designed the dramatic setting as he did is that he wanted it to reflect historical facts, at least in some dialogues. But other explanations are possible. There is no certainty that the dramatic dates are historically accurate.

Dramatic details in the Laches *tell us that Socrates led a socially acceptable life to that time.* As the dialogue opens, Lysimachus and another old father have invited Laches and Nicias, two public leaders and generals in the army, to view a man advertising his martial arts course. After the man's display, when the old fathers ask for advice about how best to improve the characters of their two sons, Laches and Nicias each recommend that Socrates also be consulted:

LACHES: I am surprised that you invite Nicias and me to advise you on the education of young men but do not invite Socrates here. In the first place, he is of your *deme*.[4] Moreover, he is always spending his time where you find the sort of thing you're looking for – where there is teaching and training that is praiseworthy for young men.

LYSIMACHUS: Laches, are you saying that Socrates here has made this his concern?

LACHES: Very much so, Lysimachus.

NICIAS: I can recommend him as well as Laches. He just found my son a music teacher – Damon, pupil of Agathocles – who is not only most accomplished as a musician, but in every other way as worthy a companion as you could wish for young men of that age.

LYSIMACHUS: It is not possible, Socrates, Nicias, and Laches, for men at my age still to know those who are younger, since old age makes us spend most of our time at home. But if you, son of Sophroniscus, have any good advice for one who belongs to your own *deme*, you ought to share it. And it is only right that you should; for you happen to be our friend through your father. He and I were friends always together, and he died without ever having a single difference with me.

180b7–e4

In this exchange, Laches says that Socrates "is always spending his time" in places that provide intellectual and physical instruction. Nicias adds that, in the case of his own son, Socrates knew better than he the best teacher. Laches and Nicias are conventional upright citizens. Nothing in Socrates' behavior scandalizes them as inappropriate. Socrates at the time of this conversation spends his time somewhat like an academic adviser today in a liberal arts college. He advises people how to get a suitable education and recommends teachers for them. The difference is that Socrates works freely, not for a wage. Socrates might receive a gratuity for his services, though the dialogues nowhere say so. The important point is that Socrates' way of life is socially acceptable. In no way does it go beyond the bounds of conventional propriety.

The same exchange shows that Socrates at this time is not notorious. Socrates belongs to the same *deme* as both of the old fathers, Lysimachus and his elderly friend. Yet neither of the two old men, although spending their lives for decades in the same neighborhood, knows how Socrates spends his time. More than neighbors, Lysimachus and Socrates' father "were friends always together," and the two families are so closely related that Lysimachus will go on to say to Socrates (in the passage quoted below) that "your accomplishments reflect well on us as ours do on you." They are not strangers needing introduction; Lysimachus knows that "Socrates here" is "the son of Sophroniscus." With such a close connection, it is striking that Lysimachus does not know Socrates' way of life. These details show that, far from being notorious, Socrates' life is at this time unknown to the general public.

In the exchange, Lysimachus, as a kind of apology for his ignorance of Socrates' life, says, "Old age makes us spend most of our time at home." Lysimachus is not hereby claiming ignorance of famous people or public figures – on the contrary, he is actively researching people who publicly set themselves up as teachers, such as the man advertising martial arts. His apologetic remark explains why he does not know the occupations of his neighbors, even the son of a friend.

Additional details tell us Socrates' reputation among those who know him. Although by no means a public figure, Socrates' reputation among those who know him is honorable and there are at this time no scandals that his admirers feel obliged to explain away.

LYSIMACHUS: This conversation reminds me of something. The boys here, in talking with each other at home, frequently mention a Socrates and praise him highly. But I never asked whether they meant the son of Sophroniscus – so tell me, boys, is this the Socrates you were talking about?

SON: It certainly is, father.

LYSIMACHUS: In the name of all that is good for families, Socrates, it is good to know that you maintain the straight path of your father, who was the best of men. Apart from other reasons, it is good because your accomplishments reflect well on us as ours do on you.

181e4–181a6

Lysimachus is a conventional citizen of Athens. His reaction tells us that, done in a praiseworthy manner, Socrates' way of life – *spending his time where there is teaching and training praiseworthy for young men* – carries on his father's good name and reflects well on connected families. Even if widely known, such an occupation would not make Socrates notorious.

The next speech in the exchange gives a clue that tells when Socrates became notorious.

LACHES: Indeed, Lysimachus, don't let go of this man! I have watched him elsewhere maintaining not merely his father's but his country's straight path. He came back with me in the retreat from Delium, and I tell you: if the others had chosen to be like him, our city would be standing tall and would not then have had such a fall.

181a7–b4

The battle at Delium was waged in the fall of 424 BCE; so this dialogue, in which Socrates is *not* notorious, happened sometime after. Moreover, Aristophanes' *Clouds* premiered no later than March 423. In competition at the Dionysian festival, it placed behind the *Connus* of

Amipsias, which took second. The *Connus* is lost, but we know that it, like the *Clouds*, lampooned Socrates. Comedians would not have lampooned an anonymous, conventionally honorable citizen. Thus Socrates must have become notorious in the early winter of 424, inspiring two comedians to feature him as they composed their entries for the March 423 festival.

What Socrates says in the *Apology* is consistent with this date. Socrates says that the slander in question is old (19a), so old that most of the jurors – who are likely to be men past the prime age for physical labor and so in their forties at least – heard it in their childhood (18b): hence 25 years or more ago, when Socrates was 45 or younger. Socrates was 45 in 423; so the slanders began to appear prior to then but after his return from Delium in the fall of 424.

Why Socrates Became Notorious

The *Laches* shows us a 45-year-old Socrates before he becomes notorious. There are two relevant dialogues with dramatic dates earlier than the *Laches*, the *Charmides* and the *Protagoras*. The *Charmides* opens with Socrates returning to Athens from combat duty at Potidaea. This sets the dialogue in 429 and means Socrates is 40 years old. The *Protagoras*, set in Athens, opens with remarks on the age of Alcibiades, who has just grown his first beard. In 432 Alcibiades will leave Athens as an adult soldier – 18-year-olds were too young – going to Potidaea for three years with Socrates. Alcibiades will be long past his first beard by the time he returns. Thus the dramatic date of the *Protagoras* is before 432. And it cannot be long before 432, or Alcibiades would be too young to have his beard. Thus Socrates must be about 36 or 37.

Dramatic details in the *Protagoras* show that at this time – in his thirties – *Socrates already has a name for himself in intellectual circles in the first stage of his life, although not notorious in the city.* Protagoras moves in intellectual circles of the cities he visits, attracting paying students. Hippocrates is a young man eager to study with him. He tells Socrates two reasons that keep him from approaching Protagoras by himself. He says, "for one thing, I am too young to do it myself; and for another, I have never yet seen Protagoras nor heard him speak a word – I was but a child when he paid us his previous visit." For these reasons he asks Socrates to talk to him on his behalf (310e2–5). Now Protagoras has just arrived two days ago, and Hippocrates has assumed that Socrates hadn't seen him yet on this visit (310b). It follows that Socrates already made the acquaintance of Protagoras 10 years ago on his previous visit (310e), when Socrates would have been in his twenties. Indeed Socrates is familiar enough with Protagoras to know that he spends most of his time indoors (311a). At the end of the dialogue, Protagoras confirms that Socrates has a reputation when he says, "I have said to many that I admire you greatly of those whom I meet, especially those of your age" (361e2–3). Protagoras goes on to predict that Socrates *will* "become famous for wisdom" (361e4–5). Socrates, although known to the sophist and mentioned in his circles, is *not yet* famous in the city for wisdom and cannot yet be notorious.

The *Protagoras*, *Charmides*, and *Laches* show us Socrates in the first stage of his life before he becomes notorious. He philosophizes in all three dialogues. In many important ways, his philosophizing is the same as in the later stages. But there is also an essential difference, a difference that explains why such philosophizing does not make him notorious as a public nuisance. I begin by showing the similarities.

Socrates' philosophizing in the first stage is similar to the later stages in many important ways. The topic and form of conversation are the same. The topic is excellence at human life and the expertise that produces such excellence. The form in the first stage is the same as in Socrates' investigation of the oracle, namely establishing that a man pretends to wisdom and trying to show the man that he is not wise.

For instance, in the *Protagoras*, Socrates establishes seeming wisdom with the following exchange.

"Do I follow you?" I said. "You seem to be describing civic expertise, and promising to make men good citizens."
"That is the very thing, Socrates," Protagoras said, "that I profess to do."

393a3–7

In the *Charmides*, he takes this step with Critias.

"Critias," I said. "I suppose *you* are likely to know what soundness of mind is, on account of your age and studies. If you agree that soundness of mind is what he says and accept the definition, I would much prefer to consider with you whether the definition is true or not."
"Certainly I agree," he said. "I accept the definition."

162d7–e6

The same step occurs in the *Laches*.

SOCRATES: In that case, don't *we* need to know what human excellence is? If we were ignorant what excellence happens to be, how could we advise anyone how best to get it?
LACHES: In no way, Socrates.
SOCRATES: Then we say, Laches, that we know what it is.
LACHES: Of course we do.

190b7–c5

There is also a demonstration of ignorance in all three dialogues. This step takes place at the end of the *Protagoras*.

> "One more question: does it still seem to you, as at first, that there are men who are supremely ignorant yet supremely brave?"
>
> "In making me give the answer, Socrates," he said, "you seem to me to be acting like a person who has to win. And so I will oblige you and say that from what we have agreed it seems to be impossible."
>
> "I am asking all these questions," I said, "for no other reason than a desire to find out the nature of human excellence and what it is. For I know that if this were to become evident, then the matter we have considered at great length would become evident."
>
> 360e1–361a2

In the *Charmides*, the demonstration of Critias's ignorance is clear to the bystander Charmides.

> Charmides said, "By Zeus, Socrates, I don't even know whether I have or lack soundness of mind – for how could I know when you and Critias haven't been able to figure out what it is, as you say!"
>
> 176a7–b1

Nicias sees that two people are demonstrated ignorant in the *Laches*.

> NICIAS: You [Laches] and I know nothing of the knowledge appropriate to a self-respecting man."
>
> 200a7–8

Socrates, despite the discomfort he causes to the men he questions in the first stage of his life, does not become hateful to those present. In the *Protagoras*, for instance, the great sophist, despite his displeasure at being bested by Socrates, praises Socrates' "spirit for and method of discussion" and says he would be "the last person to bear Socrates ill will" (361d7–e2). In the *Charmides*, Critias, after Socrates demonstrates that he is ignorant, endorses young Charmides' desire to spend time with Socrates (176a–b). In the *Laches*, both Laches and Nicias, after they are shown ignorant, withdraw their claim to be advisers and recommend Socrates as the best instructor for young men (200c–d).

I propose that *Socrates does not become hateful in these conversations because he has behaved in a socially appropriate manner.* In particular, despite the pointed cross-examinations with which he tests others, he follows social conventions in the places where and the people whom he cross-examines.

In the *Protagoras*, Socrates goes to the private estate of Callias in order to cross-examine Protagoras, a public figure. He goes not to test the oracle, but in order to assist Hippocrates, the young man seeking self-improvement (310e). Protagoras, as a professional teacher in Athens to drum up business, welcomes people to come to him in just the way Socrates does (316b–c). There is nothing inappropriate in the way Socrates joins conversation with Protagoras.

In the *Charmides*, Socrates goes to the private gym of Taureas, his favorite place for conversation with his friends (153a–c). While at the gym, Socrates cross-examines Critias, but he does not go to Critias with any such design. On the contrary, it is Chaerephon who seats Socrates next to Critias (153c). Socrates' interest is "the present state of philosophy and the young men, if any are distinguished for wisdom or beauty" (153d3–4), which leads Critias to describe his cousin, the young man Charmides. It is this young man, by no means a public figure, with whom Socrates wishes to speak (155a). There are social proprieties to observe in such a conversation, and Socrates follows them. In particular, it might be unseemly for an older man to approach and converse with a young man in such a setting. But "even if Charmides happened to be younger than he is, there would be no disgrace" for Socrates to talk to him in the presence of Critias, who as his adult cousin is an appropriate guardian (155a4–7).

In the *Laches*, Socrates happens to be present at a public demonstration by a martial arts teacher when Laches draws him into conversation to help advise a pair of fathers (180c). Although Laches and Nicias are public figures, and although in this dialogue Socrates cross-examines them in a public place, Socrates does not go to Laches and Nicias. After being invited to advise, Socrates defers to social propriety, using a word that equates *propriety* with *righteous action*: "I will try to advise so far as I am able . . . but as I am younger and have less experience than Laches and Nicias it seems most appropriate [literally, "most righteous"] for me first to listen and learn from them" (181d1–5). No one can accuse Socrates of impropriety in joining this conversation.

An essential change in Socrates' behavior when he investigates the oracle explains his hatefulness. According to the *Apology*, when Socrates "after a long time, reluctantly turned his steps" to investigate the oracle (21b7–8), he described his conversations as following a three-step pattern. He would (1) go to a public man reputed wise, (2) examine the man, establishing that he seemed wise but was not, and (3) try to show the man that he was not wise. As a result, Socrates would become hateful to the man and many of those present. As the *Protagoras, Charmides,* and *Laches* show, the second and third steps mark no change in his behavior from the beginning stage of his life. What is different is that, instead of confining his cross-examinations to places and people appropriate for such conversation, Socrates begins to *go to* public figures. This change explains why he becomes hateful to those he cross-examines.

I propose that there is impropriety in going to public figures, impropriety that explains how he might have suddenly achieved public notoriety after many years of philosophizing without scandal. My proposal is that for the ancient Athenians, just as for us, it would be inappropriate to go to a man in a public setting and accost him as Socrates describes in the *Apology*:

> "Most excellent man, are you not ashamed, as a citizen of Athens – the greatest of cities and the most famous for wisdom and power – to care about making as much *money* as possible – and reputation and prestige – when you neither care nor even *think* about practical wisdom and truth and your soul – how to make it as good as possible?" And if any of you argues the point, and says he does care, I shall not let him go or leave him, but I shall question and examine and cross-examine him. If I find that he does not possess excellence, but says he does, I shall fault him for making the most important thing lowest priority and making worthless things high priority.
>
> 29d7–30a2

The demand to consent to cross-examination, with the threat of public shaming as a result, repeated again and again in society, easily explains the sudden hatred and notoriety Socrates acquired in the winter of 424.

I am assuming that social norms do not differ in this respect between ancient Athens and contemporary times. As a philosopher in a university, I know from my own experience that it is appropriate in a college classroom today to engage in pointed cross-examination that drives students, when they take themselves to know, to an admission of ignorance. There is no scandal; many such students become philosophy majors as a result, and many parents and guardians of those students approve of such instruction. But it would be inappropriate for me, a philosophy professor, to accost the president of my university outside the classroom at some public event in the terms Socrates uses above. Onlookers would perceive me as using shame to try to extort a conversation from the public figure, and they would be indignant at my accusation of immorality at the end of the conversation.

As I said, Socrates' way of life was somewhat like a liberal arts adviser to the young. Evidently in such an occupation his cross-examinations were as respectable as a university professor's are today. Moreover, although I love to spend my time in cross-examination with students in the classroom, I would be as reluctant as Socrates was to turn my steps to the path of accosting public figures and trying to induce them to consent to cross-examination. It is easy to understand why Socrates, who was concerned with the social propriety of his conversations, says in the *Apology* that he turned to such a path only "with deep reluctance" as a last resort to try to solve the riddle of the oracle (21b8).

Why Chaerephon Went to the Oracle

As Socrates says at trial, he did not become notorious until after the oracle induced him to turn his steps to examine public figures. This raises the question: what reason did Chaerephon have to ask the oracle whether anyone was wiser than Socrates? The *Protagoras* gives a reason.

Socrates is most famous among philosophers, ancient and modern, for arguing that human excellence is nothing more than a branch of knowledge. Such a view makes morality merely a matter of intellectual understanding with no additional requirements about personal character. Such intellectualism flies in the face of conventional thinking about morality. The conventional moralist objects: "Surely mere intellectual understanding without a good heart, a good will – without proper desires and pleasures – is not enough for human excellence!" The assumption behind the objection is that a person's knowledge of what is good often conflicts with other desires in the soul, and sometimes such knowledge may be impotent in the grip of such desires.

With a remarkable argument (see chapter 5), Socrates demonstrates that this conventional assumption is false. On the contrary, as he shows, knowledge of human well-being must rule when present in the soul. Plato chose to put this remarkable argument into the *Protagoras*. With this choice Plato is telling us that Socrates by age 37 already both understood that knowledge rules and understood the extraordinary consequence:

> It seems to me that the outcome of our argument . . . if it had a voice, would say, "How extraordinary you are, Socrates . . . attempting to demonstrate that everything we've been discussing – righteousness, soundness of mind, and bravery – is knowledge in such a way that human excellence would evidently be teachable."
>
> 361a3–b3

Socrates in seeing this consequence shows himself wiser than Protagoras. Protagoras agreed with Socrates' claim that knowledge always rules when present in the soul (352c–d). But Protagoras agrees from professional pride as an avowed teacher of human excellence – "to say otherwise would be a disgrace" (352d1). Protagoras lacks theoretical understanding of the claim, because he does not see that it undermines his conventional belief that bravery is different from wisdom (349d). Protagoras cannot lead the world to see the truth of the claim that knowledge rules, but only follows as Socrates makes the demonstration (352e–357b).

Protagoras enjoyed a reputation as the wisest man in Greece, a fact the dialogue emphasizes in the way it introduces his name. The dialogue opens with a metaphor of *hunting with dogs* to show the irresistible sex appeal of Alcibiades, who was for Athens – among many other things – the equivalent of its hottest supermodel. Dramatically, it is the moment of the very peak of his beauty: "Where have you come from, Socrates? No doubt from running your dogs after Alcibiades at his finest time of life," asks a close friend of Socrates (309a1–2). Socrates replies with a surprising comparison of value. He agrees, on the authority of Homer, that Alcibiades is at his most beautiful just now (309a6–7). But, although he was with Alcibiades, Socrates says that he forgot all about him, because of someone "much more beautiful" (309c4). The close friend is astonished: "You cannot come upon anyone more beautiful, at least not in Athens" (309c2–3). All this drama builds up to Socrates' dénouement: "The greatest wisdom is evidently more beautiful" than physical beauty (309c11–12), and Socrates has just been with "the wisest man now living, if Protagoras seems to you to be wisest" (309d1–2).

Socrates' close friend does not dispute the superlative when he hears it. But by the end of the dialogue, after Socrates relates to him his dialogue with Protagoras, it is clear that Socrates is wiser than Protagoras. Therefore this very dialogue gives Chaerephon reason to ask the oracle: "Is *anyone* wiser than Socrates?" – if we can assume that Chaerephon knew about Socrates' dialogue with Protagoras.

I conjecture that the unnamed "close friend," to whom Socrates tells the conversation with Protagoras, is none other than Chaerephon, and that Plato means for us to make this conjecture. Plato shows us with the dramatic date of the *Protagoras* that Socrates is about to leave for a three-year military deployment; Plato shows us in the opening details of the *Charmides* that the most enthusiastic of Socrates' friends in Athens at the time of that deployment is Chaerephon. In the *Apology*, describing how Chaerephon went to the oracle, Socrates calls him his "*close friend* since youth," using the same word (*hetairos*, 21a1) as in the *Protagoras*.

The close friend to whom Socrates speaks at the beginning of the *Protagoras* does not dispute that Protagoras is the wisest man in the world. And so this close friend will have reason after hearing the dialogue to wonder whether anyone in the world is wiser than Socrates. Plato regularly names the speakers in his dialogues, so I take it that Plato means to set us a riddle by leaving this companion unnamed. The most elegant solution to the riddle is that it is Chaerephon.

When Chaerephon Went to the Oracle

Knowing from the *Apology* "how intense he was about whatever he started" (21a3), I conjecture that Chaerephon made the journey from

Athens to Delphi to consult the oracle as soon as possible after he heard Socrates' conversation with Protagoras, which would be in the spring or summer of 432. At about the same time, Socrates leaves on military deployment. There is no certainty here, but what we know of the history of war and disease in ancient Greece permits such a date. Athens was still at peace that year, but not for long, because war with Sparta began in 431. Athenians, crowded within the city walls, lost between a fourth and a third of their population in 430 to a plague that returned in 429.

Having heard the oracle, impetuous Chaerephon would have wanted his close friend Socrates to know the oracle's pronouncement as soon as possible. Socrates' deployment took him to Potidaea for three years. Because Potidaea was far from Athens, he was unlikely to have been able to return on winter leave to Athens. But it is possible that there were opportunities to send messages from Athens to the deployed troops, and hence it is possible that Socrates first heard the oracle's answer while on deployment.

Such a date is mere conjecture, but it does connect a few dots. First, Socrates would according to this date wrestle unsuccessfully with the riddle for about seven years. This is consistent with his statement that he puzzled over the oracle's statement "for a long time" before he began to accost public figures late in 424.

Second, such a date explains the extraordinary vigil Socrates kept on the very same deployment. In the *Symposium*, Alcibiades describes Socrates on this deployment:

> A thought having occurred to him, Socrates stood from daybreak considering something, and when nothing came to him he didn't let go but stood there seeking an answer. By midday men had noticed. Amazed, they told one another how Socrates had stood there from daybreak in reflection. Finally some of the Ionians brought out their bedding after supper when it was evening – it was summertime – partly to sleep out in the cooler air and partly to keep an eye on him to see whether he'd stand there all night. And he did stand there until dawn came and the sun rose. Then he said his prayers to the sun and went off on his way.
>
> 220c3–d5

I take it that Plato, writing these words, knew it would be impossible for us to read them and not wonder what Socrates found so extraordinarily puzzling. If Plato meant with these words to set *us* a puzzle, there is no more elegant solution than that Socrates had at this time heard the oracle and was unsuccessfully pondering it.

Third, such a date explains a change in Socrates' behavior between the *Protagoras* and the *Charmides*. In the *Protagoras*, before the three years of deployment, Socrates, as ever, professes his own lack of expertise about human excellence (361b). Nonetheless, his self-confidence is striking in this dialogue. He claims that he is able to "teach the world" that knowledge rules (352e5–6). In the *Charmides*, by contrast, Socrates' self-deprecation, rather than his self-confidence, is striking. Socrates takes more pains in the *Charmides* than in any other dialogue to emphasize his own ignorance. He says he is ignorant even how to inquire about human excellence, "a fool who is never able to reason out anything" (176a3–4). The *Charmides* is Socrates' very first conversation upon returning from his three years of deployment. Plato takes pains with the dramatic setting to tell us how Socrates surprised Chaerephon and his other friends with his appearance at their favorite club, while they feared him dead in the bloody battle that ended the deployment (153a–b). We know that the oracle's pronouncement that Socrates is wisest produced in him this reaction: "I am well aware of being wise in nothing big or small" (21b4–5). Such a reaction explains the change in Socrates' behavior between the time before and the time immediately after his deployment. The date I have conjectured lets us read the *Charmides* as if Socrates there is taking pains to point out his own woeful ignorance to the god who spoke at Delphi, even as he points it out to Chaerephon and the other bystanders to his conversation.

My conjectured date when Socrates learns of the oracle explains why he says that he puzzled over the oracle's statement for a long time. It explains his extraordinary vigil, witnessed by Alcibiades on deployment in Potidaea. And it explains Socrates' new emphasis upon his own abject ignorance after the deployment.

Conclusion

Plato put dramatic details as well as philosophical arguments into the dialogues he wrote. Those details call for explanation. I have selected some of the details and made a conjecture that gives them an elegant and therefore charitable explanation. The conjecture explains and dates the three stages of Socrates' life. About 433, when he is about 36, Socrates tells Chaerephon about a dialogue he had with Protagoras. Socrates' achievement in that dialogue gives Chaerephon reason to wonder whether anyone could be wiser. Notoriously impetuous, Chaerephon asks the oracle whether anyone is wiser than Socrates as soon as possible after he hears of Socrates' conversation with Protagoras, perhaps as early as the spring or summer of 432.

I conjecture that Socrates hears about the oracle at some point during the three-year period he is deployed, 432–429 BCE. He finds it to be a riddle that he cannot solve, even after the extraordinarily intense thought that Alcibiades witnesses. Socrates ponders the riddle for a long time, through repeated wartime emergencies, until he returns in 424 to Athens. Although his life of philosophical conversation is not known at that time to the general public – not even among family friends in his own *deme* – he suddenly gains notoriety for his conversations in the winter of 424 by going to public figures to cross-examine them.

It is not the act of cross-examination that scandalizes people; for Socrates has privately spent his free time in that activity for perhaps 20 years in relative anonymity. What scandalizes is the socially inappropriate way that he now induces people to submit to cross-examination. Socrates is reluctant to offend against the norms of propriety in this way, but his reverence leaves him no alternative other than such a test of the god's word that *no one is wiser*.

Within a couple months, his inappropriate behavior makes him so notorious throughout Athens that comedians like Aristophanes stage his character for laughs in city-wide performances. Even after solving the riddle – that is, in the third stage of his life – Socrates continues his notorious activity as a religious obligation until his trial and death at age 70. But, as the *Apology* tells, in this third stage he no longer methodically seeks out conversation partners, but converses with "any one of you whom I happen to meet" (29d6). In this final stage, his motive is not to *solve the riddle* of the oracle, since he knows the solution. Socrates' motive throughout the last stage of his life is to "serve the god by demonstrating to people their ignorance" (23b7), in other words, to *convert others to philosophy* as their overriding priority in life (29e5–30a2).

I turn next to Socrates' remarkable achievement in the *Protagoras*, where he demonstrates his superiority over the man deemed wisest.

notes

1 We see an example of this outcome at the end of the *Laches*:

> SOCRATES: Perhaps you will allow me to give you a piece of advice. What I say to you – in confidence, gentlemen! – is that we ought all together to look for the best teacher we can get, first for ourselves – for *we* need one – and then for the young men, sparing no expense at all. I suggest we *not* leave ourselves in our present condition . . .
>
> LYSIMACHUS: I'm happy to accept your words, Socrates. As I am the oldest, I am the most eager to have lessons with the young ones.
>
> 201a1–b8

2 I am in debt to forthcoming work by C. C. W. Taylor for a pointed statement of this contradiction.

3 In the *Parmenides* Socrates is a teenage prodigy, concerned there not with ethics but the metaphysics of separated Forms. On such Forms and the relation between the metaphysician Socrates and Plato, see the epilogue.

4 Athens had a population very roughly of a quarter million, divided into 139 political districts, called *demes*, with an average size of only a couple thousand. *Demes* held their own religious festivals, collected and spent revenue, and contained families that had shared the neighborhood for generations.

further reading

Debra Nails, *The People of Plato*. Indianapolis: Hackett, 2002. There are biographical entries on each character appearing in Plato's work. Appendix 1 considers dramatic dates for the dialogues.

the *protagoras*

bravery

Teaching Excellence

In the *Protagoras*, a Socrates in his late thirties relates a conversation he has just had with Protagoras, then nearing 60 and regarded as the wisest man in Greece. Socrates narrates to an unidentified "close friend" (309a1) how Protagoras professed to teach human excellence:

> "My subject is proper management of personal and family matters, so that one might best manage one's homelife, and proper management of civic matters, so that one might be most powerful to act and speak about what has to do with the city."
> "I'm following what you say," I said. "You seem to me to be describing civic expertise and to be promising to make men good citizens."
> "That is exactly what I profess to do," he said.
> 318e5–319a7

Protagoras's profession of expertise causes conflict for Socrates. On the one hand, Socrates gives reasons why he does not believe human excellence is "teachable" (319a10): Athenians let any citizen, regardless of expertise, speak about the civic good – yet in all technical matters they consult only experts. Moreover, those reputed to be excellent leaders and human beings are unable to teach others how to be excellent, an ability we expect experts to have. On the other hand, Socrates says he is "not in a position to doubt" that the renowned Protagoras, a man much his senior, can teach excellence (319b1).

Protagoras explains away Socrates' reasons for disbelief in what has become known as his "Great Speech" (320c–328d). To this day people celebrate Protagoras's Great Speech as a classic statement of democratic values. As Protagoras explains, in cases of *medical* treatment, a city requires only one person with know-how for many who are ignorant, and likewise for all but one other kind of expertise. The exception is the case of treating others *as human beings*. A city cannot survive unless "all have a share" of this expertise and know how to treat each other "respectfully and right" (322c1–d4). Indeed it is Zeus's will that anyone unable to learn how to treat others respectfully and right ought to be put to death "as a plague to the city" (322d5). Thus although only a few citizens in each city are experts in medicine and the other kinds of expertise, all know how to treat each other respectfully and right as human beings. And so a democracy is justified in seeking advice from only a few experts in technical questions, such as medicine, while seeking advice from all its citizens about political questions.

Moreover, Protagoras says, the general human ability to treat others right is "not inborn" but "acquired by education" (323c5–7). For whereas we do not "get indignant with, or admonish or teach or scold" people for their birth defects (323d1–2), we do "get indignant, and we do admonish unrighteousness and irreverence and everything opposed to excellence in human community," which shows that human excellence is "acquired by learning" (323e3–6). This is also why communities emphasize above all else that the youth learn from infancy how to be as righteous and good as possible. As soon as a child understands speech, his parents tell him, "Do this! Don't do that!" and his teachers at school put more emphasis on good behavior than on the curriculum. The point of the students' literature is to give examples that inspire good behavior, while musical instruction teaches them self-control and harmony of soul, and the point of physical education is to enhance the confidence to endure the ordeals of life (325c–326c). It is in this way that "all of us are teachers of human excellence" (327e1–2). As to himself, Protagoras claims not to be a solitary expert with the rest of us being ignorant about human excellence. He differs from the rest of us in being "a little better" at helping people improve their excellence (328a8).

Nor is it surprising, Protagoras says, that exceptionally good men are often unable to train their sons to be as good: it is the same as any other expertise. For example, the sons of exceptional flute players, no matter how well trained, are often mediocre as flute players (326e–327c). Exceptional mastery of any subject matter requires inborn talent in addition to instruction.

When Protagoras finishes, Socrates thanks him for the speech. He says that it has convinced him to change his mind and to admit that what Protagoras professes to do is possible – "*Except*," he says, "for one small point that holds me back" (328e3–4). Socrates says that he was "surprised" (329c1) to hear Protagoras in his speech talk about human excellence as if it is a whole consisting of parts like righteousness, soundness of mind, reverence, and the like (at for example 323e3–6, quoted above). He asks Protagoras to answer whether excellence is indeed such a whole with parts, as opposed to the alternative that Socrates suggests, that *righteousness, soundness of mind, reverence, bravery,* and *wisdom* are "all names for one and the same thing"

(329d1). Protagoras confidently replies that Socrates' question is "easy to answer" (329d3): human excellence is one whole, with the parts Socrates mentioned.

Then, with a quick pair of arguments, Socrates demonstrates first that "righteousness and reverence are either the same or most similar" (331b4–5) and then that "soundness of mind is wisdom" (333b4–6). Socrates appears to be on the way to compelling Protagoras to retract the easy answer. But disagreement arises about the proper method of inquiry into the question (333e–335b). The two drop the thread of Socrates' argument for some time (335b–349a). When they pick it up again, Protagoras modifies his earlier answer to Socrates' "easy" question. He says that the five terms under discussion – *wisdom, soundness of mind, bravery, righteousness,* and *reverence*" (349b1–2) – all refer to "parts of human excellence, and four of them are similar in nature, but bravery is completely different from the rest. And here is how you can see that I'm right: *You will find many people who are most ignorant but most brave*" (349d3–8).

Socrates' Subtle Argument

Socrates proceeds to refute Protagoras's modified answer. The refutation is difficult to follow, especially if it is only heard in conversation. Plato, putting the argument in writing, allows the reader to examine it closely. The effect of the writing is like that of a video frame-by-frame replay of an athletic competition, revealing prowess otherwise undetected by the average viewer.

Socrates elicits as a first premise from Protagoras the distinctive feature of brave people, namely their *readiness to do what most people fear*. Like Socrates and Protagoras, we can agree to call this feature *confidence*. As Socrates narrates:

> "Hold on," I said, "It is worth considering what you say. Do you say that the brave are confident, or something else?"
> "Yes, and ready to go," he replied, "where most people fear to go."
> 349e1–3

Socrates' second premise is an equally obvious point about what is distinctive about human excellence, namely that it is praiseworthy. If it has parts, as Protagoras believes, every part of it is praiseworthy.[1]

> "Well now, do you say that human excellence is something praise-worthy, and do you offer to teach it as something praiseworthy?"
> "It is most praiseworthy," he said, "unless I am crazy."

"Then," I said, "is one part of it shameful and another part praiseworthy, or is the whole praiseworthy?"

"Surely the whole is praiseworthy in the highest possible degree."

349e3–8

The thesis under examination is that two parts of human excellence, wisdom and bravery, are distinct: *you can find people who are ignorant yet brave.* This is why Socrates will examine only the relation of wisdom (that is, expertise at human excellence) to bravery.

Socrates uses examples and appeals to observations to establish the third premise, that, on the one hand, the cause of some people's confidence is knowledge of one sort or another, while, on the other hand, you can also find confident people who are ignorant.

"Do you know those who dive confidently into wells?"[2]

"I do; divers."

"Do they dive with confidence because they have knowledge or for some other reason?"

"Because they have knowledge."

"And who are confident to fight on horseback – trained riders or non-riders?"

"Trained riders . . . and so with all other cases," he went on, "if that is your point. Those who have knowledge are more confident than those who lack it, and people are more confident after they've learned than before."

"But have you also seen people," I said, "who are without knowledge of any of these things, yet confident in each of them?"

"I have," he said, "much too confident."

349e8–350b4

Knowledge of something – like well diving or military riding – is *expertise.* Protagoras and Socrates are right to agree that *expertise causes confidence.* That is, well-diving expertise causes confidence in well diving; riding expertise causes confidence on horseback, and so on. In addition, the lack of expertise – when the lack is so complete that it is ignorant even of its ignorance – also causes confidence. (Protagoras and Socrates ignore here a level of ignorance that Socrates distinguishes in the *Apology,* an ignorance that knows its ignorance – see chapter 2. Such intermediate ignorance does not cause confidence.)

Diagrams help keep track of the argument. The Premise 3 diagram (figure 4.1) shows how Socrates and Protagoras have divided those who are confident in acts of human excellence into two kinds, wise and ignorant.

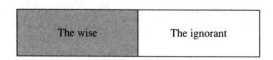

Figure 4.1 Premise 3 diagram of those who are confident in acts of human excellence

With the fourth premise, Protagoras admits that ignorant confidence is something shameful, because it indicates an unsound mind:

"Then are *these* confident people [that is, the confident people who are ignorant] also brave?"
"That would make bravery a shameful thing," he said, "since such people are crazy."

350b4–6

Protagoras already has recognized (second premise, above) that all who are wise, including therefore the confident who are wise, are praiseworthy. The consequence of the present admission – that *the ignorantly confident are shameful* – is a division of the confident into the praiseworthy and the shameful, a division along the very same line as the division of confidence into wise and ignorant in the Premise 3 diagram. Confident people are praiseworthy just in case they are wise, and they are shameful just in case they are ignorant. As the Premise 4 diagram (figure 4.2) represents it, these pairs of terms cover the very same area (hence the equal signs in the diagram).

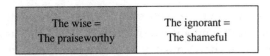

Figure 4.2 Premise 4 diagram of those who are confident in acts of human excellence

Since the brave are confident in acts of human excellence (first premise) they must be *somewhere* in the Premise 4 diagram. This is the point of Socrates' fifth premise:

"Then whom," I said, "do you say to be the brave? Surely not the confident?"
"I *still* say yes," he said.[3]

350b6–7

The Premise 5 diagram (figure 4.3) represents this added information.

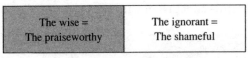

– The brave must be somewhere here!

Figure 4.3 Premise 5 diagram of those who are confident in acts of human excellence

Socrates' sixth question asks Protagoras to recognize that the brave cannot be anywhere in the unshaded box.

> "Haven't we found in the latter case [that is, the case of the ignorantly confident]," I went on, "that such people, although confident, are not brave but crazy?"

350c1–2

Let me answer for Protagoras: We have indeed found that no ignorantly confident person is brave, since that would make bravery, a human excellence, something shameful. The Premise 6 diagram (figure 4.4) represents this correct answer.

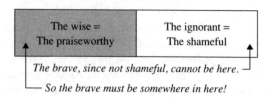

Figure 4.4 Premise 6 diagram of the confident in acts of human excellence

The Premise 6 diagram refutes Protagoras's thesis. You will not find *any* people who are most ignorant but most brave. Moreover, as the Premise 6 diagram shows, the brave must be *at least a part of* the wise.

Having refuted Protagoras's thesis and shown that the brave are at least part of the wise, Socrates with his next question tries to elicit that *the wise* are at least part of *the brave*. He does this by recalling the first premise, that confidence is the distinctive feature of bravery.

> In the former case – where the most wise are most confident – isn't it true that, being most confident, they are most brave?

350c3–4

In other words, since *the wise in acts of human excellence are confident in those acts*, we ought to agree that *the wise are at least part of the brave* – what else could wisely confident people be but brave!

Logically, since it is now established that the brave and the wise are *parts of each other*, they must cover the exact same area in the diagram. That is, not only are the brave wise, the brave *and only the brave* are wise. I represent this conclusion with the Premise 7 diagram (figure 4.5).

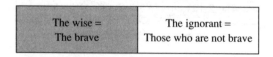

Figure 4.5 Premise 7 diagram of the confident in acts of human excellence

To say that *the brave are the wise* is to say that whoever is one is the other. In terms of the diagram, each extends over the very same area. But this co-extension of brave people and wise people is not sufficient reason to identify *bravery* (namely, that power, whatever it is, that causes praiseworthy confidence in acts of human excellence) with *wisdom* (namely, the power that causes people to act wisely).

To see that co-extension is insufficient in general for identity, consider this parallel: any species of animal has a heart just in case it has a kidney. As we might say, *the hearted are the kidneyed:* whoever is one is the other. But this co-extension does not give sufficient reason to identify *heart* with *kidney*. Thus to say that *the hearted are the kidneyed* or that *the brave are the wise* merely makes a claim that heart and kidney (or bravery and wisdom) are *inseparable*, that is, any species that has one will have the other (or any person who has one will have the other). In contrast, to say that *bravery is wisdom* makes a claim that the two names refer to one and the same thing.

I have just shown that the inseparability of wisdom and bravery is insufficient grounds for their identity. Nonetheless, as soon as Socrates shows their inseparability, without further ado he asks Protagoras to infer the identity of wisdom and bravery. This is the last question of his argument:

> And so, isn't it the case according to this reasoning that wisdom would *be* bravery?
>
> 350c4–5

The correct answer to Socrates' question is *yes*. The key premise justifying the inference is their earlier agreement identifying the cause of confidence (at 349e8–350b4, quoted above). When expert well divers, as opposed to crazy people, dive confidently, it is *"because* they have knowledge" (350a2). And Protagoras rightly agrees that knowledge is the cause of confidence also in "all other cases" of wise confidence (350a6). It follows that *wisdom (that is, expertise at human excellence) is the cause of confidence, in acts of human excellence, of brave people* – unless we can name an expertise other than wisdom that all and only brave people have!

And it goes without saying that *bravery is the cause of confidence of brave people*. Such a premise is unremarkable. Indeed, earlier in the *Protagoras*, Socrates and Protagoras evidently made a similar unstated assumption, that *reverence is that which causes things to be reverent.* They made this assumption as part of a larger argument, when they agreed that *reverence itself is reverent,* on the grounds that *"there is such a thing as reverence"* and *"nothing else could manage to be reverent if reverence itself won't be reverent!"* (330d8–e1). In Plato's *Phaedo,* similar causal statements – such as *beauty is that which causes things to be beautiful*

(100d7–8), *largeness is that which causes things to be large* (100e5), and *heat is that which causes things to be hot* (105b9–c1) – are called "safe but showing no expertise" (105c1), that is, such statements are the sorts of things that are so obviously true – given the existence of beauty, largeness, and heat – that it takes no expertise to know them.

Since wisdom and bravery play one and the same causal role, it follows that *wisdom is bravery*. Is it valid to reason in this way from *same cause* to *identity?* Consider the form of argument often used by crime scene investigators:

1 The perpetrator of the crime is the cause of this evidence (a fingerprint, a strand of hair, or whatever).
2 Horatio (say) is the cause of this evidence.
3 Thus Horatio *is* the perpetrator.

Such arguments from cause to identity are so obviously valid that we rarely spell them out in the natural flow of human speech.

Socrates' argument refutes Protagoras's thesis and establishes the identity of bravery and wisdom. But the argument is subtle. I think it is harder to follow than any other argument in this book. By comparison, for example, Socrates' equally surprising demonstration that *luck is wisdom* is childishly simple (chapter 9) – that argument, too, is from *same cause* to *identity*, but elicited from a child and novice. Socrates is justified in testing Protagoras with this difficult argument, since Protagoras is neither child nor novice but proclaims himself an expert in human excellence and has a reputation as the wisest man. Having elicited the necessary premises from Protagoras, therefore, Socrates invites Protagoras to see that the identity of wisdom and bravery is a consequence of the agreed premises. His invitation is a test of Protagoras's wisdom.

Protagoras Replies

Protagoras does not assent to Socrates' final questions. His dissent adds spice to the dialogue and challenges the reader. He accuses Socrates of doing wrong with the agreed premises, "calling them to mind in a way that is not praiseworthy" (350c6).

In explaining the wrongdoing, Protagoras makes several correct points about the argument. First:

> When you asked me whether *the brave are confident,* I admitted it: I was not asked whether *the confident are brave.* Had you asked me this before, I should have said, "Not all."
>
> 350c7–d1

Protagoras's memory of Socrates' first premise is correct, and we ought also to endorse as true his further statement that *not all the confident are brave* (see the Premise 7 diagram, figure 4.5, above).

Protagoras adds a second point:

> And about the brave – in what way they are *not* confident – you have nowhere demonstrated that I was wrong in agreeing.
>
> 350d1–2

Protagoras did agree (at 350b4–6) that the brave are not confident *in an ignorant way*. Indeed he was right to agree. If we interpret Protagoras here to be referring to that prior agreement, we ought to endorse this point, too.

Protagoras continues:

> Then you show that the same people are more confident after they have knowledge than they were before and more confident than others lacking knowledge, and on the basis of this you suppose that bravery and wisdom are the same.
>
> 350d3–5

Again Protagoras is correctly recalling both a part of the argument (used to establish Socrates' third premise, admitted at 350a6–b1) and the conclusion that Socrates tried to elicit at 350c4–5.

Having made these points, Protagoras explains why he said Socrates' move in the argument was "not praiseworthy" (350c6). He claims that Socrates' argument proceeds in the same invalid way as the following argument that absurdly proves physical strength to be wisdom.

> Using the same course of reasoning, you might conclude that physical strength is wisdom! Reasoning this way you might begin by asking me whether *the physically strong are powerful* – and I'd say yes – next, whether those who know how to wrestle are more powerful than those who do not know how to wrestle, and whether the same people are more confident after learning than before [in short, whether *the wise are powerful*] – and I'd say yes. And on my admitting these points you might take it, using the same inference, that according to my admissions *wisdom is physical strength.*
>
> 350d5–e6

Protagoras has in this passage correctly evaluated a certain line of reasoning as fallacious. The two premises of the fallacious argument are as follows:

1 The physically strong are powerful.
2 The wise are powerful.

As Protagoras rightly judges, Premises 1 and 2 do not prove the absurd conclusion that *wisdom is physical strength*. Protagoras might safely admit Premises 1 and 2 and still deny the absurd conclusion. For it is true, as he asserts, that:

> Power and physical strength are not the same. One of them, power, comes from wisdom or from madness or passion, whereas physical strength comes from the nature and training of the body.
>
> 351a1–4

Protagoras also correctly identifies the missing premise needed to produce an argument for the absurd conclusion.

1   The wise are powerful.
*2   The powerful are physically strong.
3   Thus the wise are physically strong.

As Protagoras sees, although this argument is valid, Premise *2 is false: "By no means do *I* admit, nor would I, that *the powerful are physically strong*, only that *the physically strong are powerful*" (350e6–7).

Protagoras asserts that the fallacious argument that wisdom is physical strength is similar to Socrates' argument that wisdom is bravery:

> It is similar to your argument that confidence and bravery are not the same, with the result that your argument proves that the brave are confident, but not that the confident are all brave; for confidence, like power, comes to people from expertise, and from passion and from madness, whereas bravery comes from the nature and training of the soul.
>
> 351a4–b2

The alleged parallel between the two arguments explains why Protagoras accuses Socrates of doing wrong with the agreed premises, "calling them to mind in a way that is not praiseworthy" (350c6).

Protagoras's Ignorance

Protagoras's criticism seems to carry the day. Neither Socrates nor any of the audience defends Socrates' argument. It is easy to understand why the audience does not object. Socrates' argument is hard to follow, especially to one who only hears it. But Plato put the allegedly parallel arguments into writing. Readers can examine the alleged parallel more carefully than hearers.[4] If we set the two arguments side by side, as in table 4.1, it is easy to see disanalogies between them.

Table 4.1 The disanalogies

Socrates' argument	Protagoras's alleged parallel
1 The brave are confident (349e2–3).	The physically strong are powerful (350d7–e1).
2 Excellence (all of it, including bravery and wisdom) is praiseworthy (349e4–8).	
3 Experts at an action (for example, diving) are confident in that action because of their knowledge (349e8–a5).	
4 Those with the relevant knowledge are more confident in action than those without and are more confident after they've learned than before (350a6–b1).	Those with the relevant knowledge are more powerful in action than those without and are more powerful after they've learned than before (350e1–3).
5 Some ignorant people are confident (350b1–4).	
6 No ignorantly confident people are brave (350b4–6).	
7 Being confident, the wise are brave (350c3–4).	
8 Thus bravery is wisdom (350c4–5).	Thus wisdom is physical strength (350e5–6).

As table 4.1 shows, Protagoras in his alleged parallel states no premises corresponding to rows 2, 3, 5, 6, or 7 of Socrates' argument.

We can supply, on behalf of Protagoras, some of the missing rows in his parallel. Parallel to Socrates' row 3, we might agree that *experts at action (for example, wrestling) are powerful because of their knowledge*. Parallel to Socrates' row 5, we might agree that *some ignorant people are powerful*.

But we cannot supply all of the missing rows; we cannot remedy all the disanalogies. For example, we ought to agree to row 6 of Socrates' argument that *no ignorantly confident people are brave*, on the grounds, as Protagoras said, that any such ignorant confidence would be a shameful thing indicating an unsound mind (350b5–6). But we cannot agree to the parallel statement that *no ignorantly powerful people are physically strong*. For, as Protagoras himself points out, power does not have to come from knowledge; it can come "as well from madness or passion" in an ignorant person (351a2–3).

The disanalogy at row 6 is itself caused by a more fundamental disanalogy at row 2. We ought to agree that *excellence (all of it, including bravery and wisdom) is praiseworthy*. But we ought not agree to the parallel statement that *all physical strength is praiseworthy*. Indeed there is nothing to praise about physical strength, unless it is used wisely. Foolishly used it indicates an unsound mind and is shameful.

Above, I have already displayed Socrates' prowess in securing the premises needed to refute Protagoras's thesis (that *you can find ignorant brave people*) and to establish the Socratic thesis that *bravery is wisdom*. Protagoras was wrong in his thesis that bravery is different from wisdom, and he was wrong to impute shame to Socrates' argument. Protagoras did not appreciate the beauty of Socrates' argument and put up a crude and unlovely construction as parallel. Protagoras remains ignorant of the identity of wisdom and bravery and unable to follow correct reasoning on the subject. Yet Protagoras has spoken with striking confidence in this dialogue, first in his Great Speech and then in alleging Socrates' argument to be shameful. Protagoras appears wise to himself, to his audience, and to many readers down to the present day. Yet in reality he is condemned by his own words. It is not Socrates' argument but Protagoras's ignorant confidence that is shameful, indicating an unsound mind.

Socrates is Extraordinary

Unlike Protagoras, Socrates does not pretend to be a teacher of human excellence. Indeed he says the subject "continually perplexes" him (348c6) and asks only that Protagoras "join in inquiry" with him (349a8). Although Socrates' argument is ingenious, the premises are ordinary (rows 1–7 of table 4.1). It does not take any special expertise to judge their truth. Socrates does not take his ability to know such ordinary truths as evidence that he possesses expertise about human excellence. Unlike Protagoras, he is not guilty of recklessness.

The dramatic setting of Socrates' beautiful argument charms me. With aristocratic propriety, Socrates declines to defend his reasoning from Protagoras's attack. When a human being feels misunderstood it is extraordinary, in the heat of argument, *not* to try to explain how the audience missed the point. Moreover, after the event of the conversation, in retelling it to his close friend, Socrates is again extraordinary not to point out how brilliant his unappreciated argument is. Evidently Socrates already knew in his thirties what he says in the *Crito* at the end of his life: "Why should we care about the opinion of the many? The most competent people, who are worthy of consideration, will have an accurate idea how we acted" (44c6–9).

It is not helpful to belabor a subtle argument to a skeptical and perhaps incompetent audience. Socrates, without a word of complaint or comment on his unsuccessful pedagogy, immediately begins the next argument with the words, "Protagoras, do you speak of some people living well and others badly?" (351b3–4). Socrates' next argument will prove to be pedagogically successful. Protagoras and the audience will prove able to follow that decisive and final argument of the dialogue, to which I now turn.

notes

1   I translate the Greek word *kalos* throughout this chapter as *praiseworthy*. Other possible translations of *kalos* are *beautiful*, *noble*, or *good*. The opposite of *kalos* is *aischros*, that is, *shameful* (as I translate it in this chapter), or *ugly*, *ignoble*, or *base*. Because they are opposites, throughout the argument it goes without saying that the praiseworthy are not shameful.
2   Well divers pulled themselves headfirst down a rope underwater into a well, working in numbing cold in the dark on the bottom for minutes at a time, typically to load baskets with silt in order to clear the well's water entry. A city like Athens depended upon well water and hence upon such divers for their water supply.
3   There is a detail here, having to do with the word *the*. In ancient Greek as in English, to ask if *the brave are <u>the</u> confident* is subtly different from asking if *the brave are confident*. To say that *the brave are confident* is to say everyone who is brave is confident, but there may be confident people who are not brave. In terms of parts and wholes (as at *Euthyphro* 12a–c), it is to say that bravery is a part of confidence. Answering Socrates' first question, Protagoras has already agreed that *the brave are confident*. Socrates' question here – whether *the brave are <u>the</u> confident* – asks something else. It asks, in terms of the Premise 4 diagram, whether the brave and the confident cover the very same area. Socrates has not asked this question before.
       Protagoras's answer – "I *still* say yes" – shows that he thinks Socrates is repeating his earlier question, which shows that he has confused the two questions. His next speech (350c6–351a2) confirms that he has lost the thread of the argument, as I go on to show.
4   Socrates' argument is subtle enough, even when written down, that scholars to this day find fallacies in it (see this chapter's further reading list for references). In the 1970s, Terry Penner pointed out to me why Protagoras's analogy fails.

further reading

C. C. W. Taylor, *Plato: Protagoras*. 2nd edn., Oxford: Oxford University Press, 1991. This book, part of the Clarendon Plato series, discusses Socrates' argument (pp. 150–61). (Another book with the same title and author, published in 2002 as part of Oxford's World's Classics series, lacks this discussion.)

knowledge rules

Odysseus's Iron Soul

The "most sickening thing" Odysseus saw on his voyage home from Troy was Scylla eating six of his sailors alive, while "they shrieked and stretched out their hands in horrible destruction" (*Odyssey* 12.256–9). After this horror, he faces a choice. He can keep sailing through the dangerous night or find shelter on the Sun God's desert island with its taboo cattle. Odysseus gives the order to keep sailing, but his crew complains: "Odysseus, you are hardened. There is a mighty power in you. Nothing wears you out. At this moment you must be entirely made of iron!" (12.279–80). They mutiny and force him to the island.

Trapped by bad weather on the island, Odysseus again shows he is made of iron when he and his crew begin to starve amid the bounty of taboo cattle. They all know it will be death for them to harm the cattle. Facing this choice, Odysseus never considers eating the cattle. He simply goes to high ground and prays (12.333–4). Suffering the same hunger, the all-too-human crew breaks its vow and slaughters and feasts upon the cattle (12.320–65).

Yet not even iron Odysseus can resist the call of the Sirens. He knows it is death to stay to listen to them sing. As the goddess Circe warned him beforehand, the Sirens sing while "sitting in a green field, on both sides a great dune – from bones of rotting men" (12.45–6). Odysseus describes how in this case his heart overcomes his knowledge: "They sang, casting beautiful words. *Despite all, my heart willed me to listen*" (12.193–4). Odysseus's heart would have led him to destruction had he not been forewarned to have his crew plug *their* ears with wax and bind him to the mast. Although "with the eyebrows he signals his comrades to release him," they respond by binding him more tightly and rowing on (12.194–5).

Socrates' Wild Claim

The Sirens' musical performance is fabulous. But it illustrates the seeming impotence (the Greek word is *akrasia*) of knowledge, the knowledge of *the best course of action*, and how that knowledge seems sometimes to lose control to some other part of the soul. Socrates begins his final argument in the *Protagoras* by reminding his audience of the common view that knowledge often is impotent.

> It seems to most people that knowledge is nothing strong or guiding or controlling. They do not think it is anything of that kind. They suppose that, though present in a man, often not knowledge but something else is in control – now high spirits, now pleasure, now pain, sometimes sexual desire, and often fear. They simply think that knowledge is like a slave, dragged about by anything else.
>
> 352b3–c2

As Plato points out in Book 4 of the *Republic*, two truths seem to support the common view.[1] The first truth is that, as thirst is just for drink and hunger is just for food, *in general any desire is for nothing but the object that satisfies it*. The second truth is that *the soul finds itself drawn towards its objects of desire*. Aversions are analogous to desires: they too have their objects, but they propel the soul away from the object instead of drawing the soul towards it (437c–e). These two truths explain why we feel torn between conflicting desires. The common view is that knowledge alone is not enough to save a human being from ruinous choices: whenever a desire is strong enough, like Odysseus's desire to hear the Sirens, it will overpower knowledge. This is why, on the common view, an excellent soul needs, in addition to knowledge, an iron-like character.

Socrates, questioning Protagoras, shows that neither accepts the common view:

> "Come, Protagoras, open up your thoughts on this . . . Do you consider that knowledge is something noble and able to rule a human being – that whoever learns what is good and bad will never be overpowered by anything else so as to do other than what knowledge commands – that practical wisdom is all it takes to save a human being?"
>
> "My view, Socrates," he replied, "is exactly what you are saying. It would be a disgrace for me more than anyone else to say that wisdom and knowledge were any but the most powerful of all human things."
>
> "Well and truly spoken," I said.
>
> 352a8–d4

The two recognize, of course, that human beings are frequently led by the experience of pleasure or pain to ruin their lives. But Socrates proposes, with striking self-confidence, "*to teach the world* what this experience is, which they call *knowing but not doing what is best on account of being overcome by pleasure*" (352e5–353a2). Socrates' teaching to the world will be that an experience such as Odysseus's hearing the Sirens is not a case of impotent knowledge but simple ignorance. Socrates will claim that human beings need only to be able to compare the value of different things insofar as they contribute, more or less, to the best life. An excellent soul does not need anything else.

The Treasure Parable

A parable of Jesus illustrates Socrates' claim.

> The kingdom of heaven is like a treasure hidden in the field, which a man found and hid again; and from joy over it he goes and sells all that he has and buys that field.[2]

> Matt. 13:44

In the parable, the only operative value is profit. For the treasure finder, the decision is to liquidate and spend, say, one talent's worth of land in order to purchase property with a treasury value of, say, a thousand talents. The decision involves nothing more than an easy intellectual calculation. Jesus describes the man in such a case as experiencing no conflict in his soul, only joy. There is no conflict, because the decision involves a simple exchange of very little for vastly more.

The treasure parable teaches that – for anyone able to make the calculation of value – there is no conflict, only joy, in the choice to live a heavenly life. Is this doctrine about the choice between better and worse lives true? One might object on the grounds that *the monetary man is not true to life*. There is no one whose only desires, fears, pleasures, and pains are monetary. The man in the parable must sell all his other property – even his home, with all its memories and attachments. Perhaps the man grew up playing under *this tree*, brought his bride home to *this room*, watched his children grow up in *this yard*, and buried his parents in *that field*. Only a monster would have no conflict, no regret at selling a place with such attachments! No human being reduces all life to pure monetary profit.

This objection misses the point of the parable. Jesus claims not that a purely monetary man exists, but that such a man, whether he exists or not, would be analogous to a man who has discovered heavenly life buried, as it were, in ordinary life. The discoverer of heavenly life, with nothing but joy, trades in his previous non-heavenly life for the heavenly. In the way that the hypothetical monetary man easily calculates the relative value of fields without buried treasure to a field with buried treasure, so Jesus claims that actual human beings would calculate the insignificant value of non-heavenly to the huge value of heavenly life.

In replying to the objection, I have admitted and disarmed the point that actual human beings desire other things besides money. Consider now a revised objection: *perhaps actual human beings desire other things besides heavenly life.* Perhaps actual human beings have non-heavenly concerns that conflict with the heavenly. For example, Augustine, as he describes his conversion to Christianity, does not share the unmixed joy of the man in the parable. The tortured eighth book of the *Confessions* tells how he becomes "certain of God's eternal life" (8.1.1) and takes himself to know the best course of action, but "day after day" (8.6.13) he holds back from acting on his knowledge, in the grip of sordid sexual desires that are, as he judges them in comparison to heavenly life, "trifles of trifles and emptiness of emptiness" (8.11.26).

The revised objection can take two forms. First, we might desire other than heavenly life because there are in fact non-heavenly as well as heavenly values in life, and these values are *incommensurable*, that is, they cannot all be measured on one scale of better and worse in the way that monetary man weighs all business transactions. According to this form of the objection, Augustine is wrong to assess sordid sexual pleasure as trifling, that is, as an infinitely small amount of heavenly life. On the contrary such pleasure would be a value *entirely different from* heavenly life, not *a tiny amount of* heavenly life.

There is a second form the objection can take. Even if there is a single scale of better or worse in human life, it may be that my soul contains *brute desires* for other things besides the best human life, and these desires fight each other in my soul. According to this form of the objection, Augustine might be right that sordid sexual pleasure is infinitely small in terms of heavenly life. But the infinite difference in magnitude of the same value does not make it easy for him to avoid the sex, because he has a brute desire for it, regardless of its value.

After presenting Socrates' teaching that knowledge rules, I shall consider in separate sections both forms of the objection: the *incommensurable* objection and the *brute-desire* objection. I also shall propose an explanation why the choice, as it seemed, between an infinitesimal as opposed to an infinite amount of heavenly life could have tormented Augustine.

How Socrates Teaches the World

The first step of Socrates' teaching shows the world that they are *hedonists,* that the *only* operative values in their lives are pleasure and pain.

As soon as Socrates has the world's agreement that the good and bad are nothing other than pleasure and pain, he announces that he is able to demonstrate the absurdity of knowledge ever being impotent.

> The absurdity will be clear if we keep from using a number of terms at once, such as pleasant, painful, good, and bad; but since these appeared to be two, let us call them by two names – first, *good* and *bad*, and then later on, *pleasure* and *pain*.
>
> 355b3–c1

In fact the argument against impotence does not need the premise of hedonism. As I will show, the argument needs only the less controversial premise that the good consists of *positive* factors while the bad consists of *negative* factors. Socrates proceeds to state the target that he will reduce to absurdity:

> Let us then lay it down as our statement, that *a man might do something bad in spite of knowing that it is bad.*
>
> 355c1–2

In terms of Jesus' example, the target is that *the monetary man might refuse to exchange his fields for the field with buried treasure in spite of knowing that this act will keep him from becoming rich.* Socrates derives the absurdity of the target statement from its conventional explanation, as follows.

> Suppose that someone asks us, "Why does he do the bad thing?"
> We shall answer, "Because he is overcome."
> "By what?" the questioner will ask.
> This time we shall be unable to reply, "By pleasure" – for this has exchanged its name for the good.
>
> 355c2–6

At this point of the argument, Socrates assumes that the good is nothing but *pleasure*. For the sake of non-hedonists, let us avoid this assumption, as I promised. Let us assume only that the good consists of some *positive factor* or factors, perhaps including pleasure. In that case, when the questioner asks us, "By what?" – we shall reply not with any positive factor (be it pleasure or anything else). For the positive factor has exchanged its name for *the good.*

> So we must answer only with the words, "Because he is overcome."
> The questioner will ask, "By what?"
> We must reply, "By the good."
> Now if the questioner happens to be an insolent person he will laugh and say, "What a ridiculous statement, that a man does bad things, knowing

that they are bad, and not bound to do it, because he is overcome by the good!"

355c6–d3

For example, suppose that the monetary man refuses to trade his fields for the field with buried treasure, knowing that this act will keep him from becoming rich. It would be ridiculous to explain his refusal on the grounds that *he is overcome by the monetary value of his fields*!

The "insolent questioner" elaborates the absurdity with a dilemma:

> "Is this," he will ask, "a case where the good things *are not* worth it for him to conquer the bad, or because they *are* worth it?"
>
> 355d3–4

In Jesus' example, the two choices are either that the fields he owns *are not worth as much* as the field with buried treasure, or else that they *are equal or greater in value*.

Socrates immediately rules out the second alternative.

> Clearly we must reply, "Because they are not worth it" – Otherwise he whom we speak of as overcome by pleasures would not have erred.
>
> 355d4–6

In Jesus' example, if the fields the man already owned were equal or greater in value to the field with buried treasure, the man would not err in refusing to exchange his fields for it. This would be a case of properly functioning knowledge, not impotent knowledge!

So we are driven onto the first horn of the dilemma: it must be the case that the fields he owns are not worth as much as the field with buried treasure.

> "But in what way," he might ask us, "are the good things not worth the bad, or the bad not worth the good?" – This can only be when the one is greater and the other smaller, or when there are more on the one side and fewer on the other. We shall not find any other reason to give.
>
> 355d6–e2

In terms of Jesus' example, to say that *the fields he owns are not worth as much as the field with buried treasure* can only mean that the cash value retained by continuing to own his present fields is less than the cash value lost by not exchanging them for the field with buried treasure.

> "So it is clear," the insolent questioner will say, "that by *being overcome* you mean accepting greater bad in exchange for less good." That must be agreed.
>
> 355e2–4

And this is precisely the absurdity: a man whose one motive is to maximize profit refuses to exchange his fields for the field with buried treasure in spite of knowing that this act will keep him from becoming rich, *because he – knowingly – accepts a big financial loss precisely in order to achieve a small financial gain.* It is as if you offer to give me one dollar for every ten dollars I give you, and I accept your trade, and the reason I accept is *because I only want to make money and I know that I shall lose it on this deal.* Absurd indeed.

The Incommensurable Objection

To Jesus' treasure parable, I raised the objection that *perhaps actual human beings are concerned with more than heavenly life.* I can consider one form of that objection here. The objection is that Socrates must assume that in actual human life there is but one value – he calls it *pleasure* – that measures every other value, but there is no single such value: not pleasure, not heavenliness, not money. I do not escape this objection by substituting the broader value *positive factors in life* for Socrates' value *pleasure.* The substitution assumes that there is a *single scale* of positive factors. But, according to the objection, in real life our choices are between apples and oranges, that is, between *incommensurable* values.

Odysseus and his crew illustrate incommensurable values in the choice they faced between on the one hand discomfort and possible death from a stormy night on the open sea and, on the other hand, an island where they might be tempted to slaughter taboo cattle – this is a choice between apples and oranges. Incommensurable values appear again when, starving on the island, one of the crew described their grim choice this way: either "to drink salt water once for all and have done with it" (after feasting now upon the taboo cattle and being punished later at sea) or to continue to fast and "to be starved to death by inches on a desert island" (12.350–1) – apples and oranges. Again, bound to the mast, Odysseus at each moment before the Sirens faced something like a drug addict's choice between turning away in pain to go on with life or postponing that turn for just one more minute of pleasure – more apples and oranges. These choices are representative of human life, and in these choices there seems to be no single scale of more and less.

The incommensurable objection escapes the horns of Socrates' dilemma. The dilemma assumed there are only two choices, that the good either *was* or *was not* worth the bad. This objection finds a third choice: sometimes there is *no way to measure* the worth of good against bad.

Although this objection escapes one dilemma, it falls upon the horns of a new dilemma. The new dilemma asks *why* there is no way to measure the worth of good against bad. The answer must be *either* because we humans are unable to measure the real values of more against less, or because there simply is no more against less in reality. As it happens, on either horn it is impossible for knowledge to be impotent.

On the first alternative, the inability to measure a real more or less is a case of ignorance not impotent knowledge. In Jesus' example, this would be a case where an appraiser, unaware that one field had buried treasure, is unable to determine which field is worth more. Perhaps one field is more fertile, but the other is closer to town. Not knowing that buried treasure makes one field more valuable, and unable to weigh fertility against location, the appraiser might be unable to decide that one field is worth more. A wrong choice of fields under these circumstances is not a case of knowledge at all and so not a case of impotent knowledge.

On the second alternative, the good and the bad in reality are not a case of more against less. In Jesus' example, this would be a case where there is no buried treasure, and the appraiser wisely sees that neither field is worth more. Wisely, the appraiser might say: "This one is more fertile, but the other one is closer to town, and there simply is no real monetary advantage to discover, when I weigh one against the other." In such a case, since *neither* field has a greater monetary worth compared to the other, there is no monetary error in either choice. This alternative, like the first, fails to be a case where *a man does bad things in spite of knowing that they are bad* – for neither choice is bad in such a case.

Socrates Restates the Absurdity

Although one absurdity is enough to show the impossibility of impotent knowledge, Socrates goes on to restate the absurdity, this time in terms of pleasure and pain. The restatement provokes in many people the brute-desire objection, which I consider below. Socrates says:

> Let us now switch to the names *pleasant* and *painful* for these things and say that a man does – what we previously called *bad* things, but now call *painful* – knowing that they are painful, because he is overcome by pleasant things that, it is clear, overcome him while not worth it.
>
> 355e4–356a1

Again in this second version of Socrates' argument it will not affect the argument to substitute *positive* and *negative factors* for *pleasure* and *pain*. Socrates restates in terms of pleasure and pain the rhetorical question he asked at 355d6–e2 (quoted above). When a man is *overcome by pleasure*:

> How can pleasure not be worth it in comparison to pain, except by surpassing or falling short of the other? And this is a matter of one being larger and

the other smaller, or of there being more and fewer, or of a greater and lesser degree.

356a1–5

The answer to Socrates' rhetorical question is indisputable: *The only way that a positive is not worth a negative factor is by one surpassing or falling short of the other, and this is a matter of one being larger and the other smaller, or of there being more and fewer, or of a greater and lesser degree.* The absurdity is, for example, that of a hedonist choosing the less pleasant *because it is less pleasant!*

Next Socrates considers an objection about the role that time plays in weighing positive and negative factors: "But, Socrates, there is a big difference between pleasure *right now* and pleasure and pain *at some later time!*" (356a5–7). Likewise financial experts are familiar with the difference between money now and money later. When banks loan money, for example, they rely upon financial expertise to calculate how much more money is needed at some point in the future to make the present loss in the form of a loan financially worthwhile. The point is that *the nearness and remoteness can be put into the scales* when weighing a monetary choice: the more remote the monetary prospect, the more money needed to offset a present loan.

Socrates makes this very point in his reply to the objection about time:

> I would reply, "Do they differ in anything other than pleasure and pain? For there is nothing else. So, like someone good at weighing things, put together in the scales the pleasant and painful, and with them put the nearness and the remoteness, and tell me which count for more."

356a7–b3

Thus Socrates confirms the answer to his rhetorical question above: *The only way that a positive is not worth a negative factor is by one surpassing or falling short of the other* – an answer that shows the absurdity of the common point of view. Socrates has shown the truth of Jesus' account of the man who chooses heavenly over non-heavenly life: if the positive obviously outweighs the negative, the choice is obvious. The choice of the buried treasure of heavenly life is made with joy and no psychological conflict.

> For if you weigh pleasant things against pleasant, you will always take the greater and the more, and if painful against painful, then always the fewer and smaller. If you weigh pleasant against painful, and find that the pleasant surpasses the painful – whether nearness by remoteness or remoteness by nearness – you will do what brings the most pleasure. And if you find that the painful surpasses the pleasant, you won't do it. "Can the case be otherwise?" I would ask the people. I know they could say nothing else.

356b3–c3

Augustine's Tormented Decision

Why, then, did Augustine feel conflict when he stood at the entrance to heavenly life? Why could he not without torment leave behind the sordid sexual pleasures whose positive factors were "trifles of trifles and emptiness of emptiness" in comparison with the infinitely superior positive factors of heavenly life? The answer is that Augustine's choice was not the obvious choice of an infinitely large amount weighed against a negligibly small amount. His choice, as he understood it, was *either* an eternity of heavenly life, losing "from this present moment to eternity" the chance of sordid sexual pleasure (*Confessions* 8.11.26) *or* sordid sex for a little longer *and* the eternity of heavenly life later. Once again, the common view that knowledge can be impotent faces a dilemma: *either* Augustine was wise to delay, since each day of sordid sex added a positive amount, albeit very small, to the huge positive factor of heavenly life, *or* his way of looking at the losses and gains of heavenly life was distorted and inaccurate. On the first horn of this dilemma, Augustine's knowledge functioned well and was not impotent; on the second horn, Augustine's inaccurate calculation was a case of ignorance, not knowledge, and hence not a case of impotent knowledge.

The Brute-Desire Objection

Socrates in his discussion with Protagoras never considers the two truths that Plato states in Book 4 of the *Republic* (437c–e) and uses to establish the common point of view that knowledge can be impotent. Let me conclude this chapter by considering those two truths as an objection to Socrates. First, it is true that hunger is desire just for *food* and not for *food-as-a-positive-factor*. Second, it is true that *the soul finds itself drawn towards its objects of desire*. From these two truths, it seems to follow that brute hunger all by itself will draw the soul towards food, and if that desire is strong enough, it will override one's rational ability to calculate positive and negative factors.

This objection fails because it confuses *blind* hunger with *cognitive* hunger. The example of the taboo cattle illustrates the error. The first truth is that the crew, starving on the island, was hungry, which was a desire *just for food*. Notice, however, that there is no such thing as *just food* on the island. The cattle, for example, are not *just food*, but also beef, and a god's property, and forbidden, and many other things. The other crew members are not *just food*, but also human flesh, and companions, and many other things. One's own body on the island is not *just food* but also arms and legs, and needed for survival, and many other things. As *a blind drive*, the hunger of the crew is no more for cattle than for their companions, for their own bodies, or for any other food on the island. Indeed, as a blind drive, the hunger is no more for the food on the island than for non-food on the island! For, if something deluded the crew into believing, for instance, that the clay on the island was meat, they would have eaten it as readily as they ate the cattle. In a word, blind drives are *for nothing in particular*. And so the blind drive hunger cannot *all by itself* draw the crew towards the taboo cattle rather than towards each other or towards their own bodies or even towards dirt.

Now, in contrast to the blind drive, there is a second, cognitive, hunger that draws the crew towards some particular object on the island. The second truth behind the objection refers to cognitive hunger. Cognitive hunger goes two steps beyond the blind drive, a step of perception and a step of judgment. First, the crew needs to *perceive* the particular object. Second, the crew needs to *judge* that the particular object is edible, that is, *good for hunger*. So the cognitive desire for *this* object is for it *as a good*. Therefore when the crew acts, the judgment of goodness will after all be one good weighed among the others in choosing. As quoted above, this is in fact how Homer's *Odyssey* portrays the crew. They assume a worst-case scenario and deliberate about which is less painful: *either* feasting now and later, drowned at sea by the angry Sun God, "to drink salt water once for all and have done with it" *or* to fast now and continue "to be starved to death by inches on a desert island" (12.350–1).

The two steps make the second stage of hunger *cognitive*, but cognition can be ignorant as well as knowledgeable. For example, if the crew perceived some clay, and delusion brought them to judge that it was edible, they would have cognitive hunger for that clay, but they would be judging ignorantly.

It is now clear why the brute-desire objection fails. Although there are blind drives just for food, a blind drive cannot by itself drive one towards any particular object. On the other hand, to have a cognitive desire for any particular object requires the judgment that it is something good for a blind drive. The objection argues from two truths about desire, but the first truth refers to blind drives as desires while the second refers to cognitive desires. The brute-desire objection confuses these two different stages of desire.

It is false that desire can drag knowledge about like a slave: a blind drive is for nothing in particular, while cognitive desire is subordinate to the weighing that one does, whether ignorantly or expertly. Thus expertise at weighing does not need any further iron-like power in the soul to carry out its conclusions about what is best. Although Socrates' argument assumes that pleasure is the only value in human life, he does not need so strong a premise. Human beings are bound to take that course of action to which they see the most positive or fewest negative factors attached (356b). If present in our souls, all by itself knowledge will rule us and save our lives from ruinous choices.

Eight years later, Socrates again will discuss bravery, the human excellence seemingly most compatible with ignorance. Again he will make the same point about the saving power of knowledge – but with a twist. Instead of showing that bravery is knowledge, in the *Laches* he will show that bravery is *not* knowledge. The argument is the topic of the next chapter.

notes

1 My distinction between Plato and Socrates is guided by Aristotle, who said that Plato saw that an excellent soul requires more than knowledge, while Socrates thought that knowledge alone makes a soul excellent. On Aristotle as a guide, see the epilogue.
2 The treasure or treasury would be a hidden underground room containing precious objects. In the following two verses Jesus makes a similar point with a parable about a pearl of great value.

further reading

Naomi Reshotko, *Socratic Virtue*. Cambridge: Cambridge University Press, 2006. Part 1 examines Socrates' theory of human motivation.
The *Protagoras* is in many ways a companion to Plato's *Gorgias*. I discuss that dialogue in *Socrates, Pleasure, and Value*. Oxford: Oxford University Press, 1999.

the *laches*

bravery again

Advising Parents

In the *Laches*, two fathers, Lysimachus and Melesias, are intimate friends. Each father is the son of a well-known civic leader and war hero, but neither has any comparable achievements of his own. The men blame their middle-aged mediocrity on their renowned fathers, "for leaving us to indulge ourselves when we were entering adulthood, while they looked after the affairs of others" (179c7–d2). The two want their two sons, now teenagers, to succeed where they failed at becoming men of note. And so the two are "considering what teaching or training will make the sons as good as possible" (179d6–7). Appropriately, Lysimachus and Melesias consult two heroes and leaders of their own generation, Nicias and Laches.

There is a teacher in Athens advertising fancy techniques for fighting in armor. Will Nicias and Laches recommend that the sons enroll for lessons? Socrates, in this dialogue age 44, happens to be present at the conversation. Both Nicias and Laches are willing to give advice, and both recommend that Socrates give advice, too, for the following reasons. Nicias knows first-hand from the case of his own son that Socrates is good at recommending teachers for children, and Laches was eyewitness to bravery Socrates displayed on a battlefield under his command.[1]

Unfortunately, Nicias and Laches give opposite advice to the two fathers about the value of the fighting lessons for developing the character of young men. And so the advisees, facing this dilemma, ask Socrates to cast the deciding vote. Socrates demurs. Rather than simply stating his opinion, he elicits it by a train of questions: "Good decisions need to be made on the basis of expertise, not majority vote" (184e8–9). The expertise "concerns the two sons, how to make their souls as good as possible" (186a5–6), a subject of ultimate importance to the fathers, for the sons are their "greatest possessions" upon which each family's success depends (185a5).

Perseverance

In order to resolve the practical dilemma about how to advise the two fathers, Nicias and Laches both consent to be questioned by Socrates. Socrates begins with Laches, who professes to know what human excellence is (190c). And so Socrates makes his philosophical challenge:

> "Let us not ask about the *whole* of human excellence – perhaps that is more work – but let's see whether we have sufficient knowledge about some *part* of it – which is likely to be an easier question."
> "Yes, Socrates, let's do as you propose."
> "Which one of the parts of human excellence? Clearly, whatever part lessons in fighting in armor seem to develop! – and most people think such lessons develop bravery, don't they?"
> "Yes."
> "Then let us try to say what bravery is."
>
> 190c8–d8

Laches first tries to meet the challenge by giving a sign of bravery: "If someone were willing to stay at his post to fight against the enemy and did not run away, you can be sure that he'd be brave" (190e5–6). Socrates agrees, at least for the sake of argument: "I suppose this man to whom you refer, staying at his post to fight the enemy, is brave" (191a1–3). Socrates gives much the same example himself a quarter century later in the *Apology*: "Wherever someone takes a post himself, thinking it best, or is posted by a commander, it seems to me that he ought to stay there to face danger" (28d6–8).

Should *we* agree with the example? I myself have doubts about endorsing as brave a man who acts for insufficient or incorrect reasons. Perhaps the battle against this enemy is unjustifiable; perhaps this man has been given inconsistent orders, or has been ordered to commit a war crime. Elsewhere Socrates himself recognizes the possibility of inconsistent orders (*Republic* 1 337a–b) and absolutely prohibits acts of unrighteousness (*Crito* 49a–c). Before I can agree to this example, then, I must assume that the war itself is not a crime and that one's orders do not enjoin a war crime. I suppose if I were to ask Socrates and Laches about these assumptions, they would reply, "But of course! Those things go without saying."[2] It is a feature of ordinary language to speak in this implicitly open-ended way, because it is tiresome and often impossible to try to make every relevant condition explicit in our statements.

Unfortunately, even if we generously accept Laches' statement as true, it does not in practice help us identify what bravery is. The problem is that in some cavalry and chariot fighting men who do *not* stay in place and *do* run away while fighting are also brave, as Socrates points out (191a–b). Laches had been thinking only of the fighting of armored foot soldiers, but even in this case men who behave opposite to Laches' statement can be brave, as the Spartans famously were at Plataea. "They say that the Spartans, up against troops with wicker shields, chose not to stand and fight them but to run away – and when the Persians broke rank to pursue them, they turned upon them like cavalry and by fighting this way won the battle" (191b8–c5).

While accepting Laches' statement for some cases, Socrates has shown that the opposite statement is equally true in other cases. Thus Laches' statement is not general enough to define the bravery at issue in the discussion. The bravery at issue is the human excellence parents want their children to have. *That* bravery, as Laches agrees, includes "not only those brave in armored infantry, but also in cavalry and every form of warfare, and not only in warfare, but also those brave in dangers at sea, and against disease, and against poverty, and in government" (191d1–6). All of these cases come under the heading of "bravery *against pain or fear*" (191d6–7). In addition to pain and fear, Socrates and Laches further agree that "there are also those brave *against desire or pleasure*" (191d7).

There is a problem about the way Socrates and Laches have broadened their account of bravery. Can we expect to find any uniform definition that holds throughout such a variety of cases? It may reassure us that Socrates shows how there can be one definition in the case of *quickness*. Quickness shows as much variability as bravery. "We find it in running and harping, in speaking and learning, and in many other activities" (192a2–4). Yet Socrates easily defines quickness as a single power, "the power that does much in little time" (192b1). So we ought to admit the possibility of a unified definition. Nonetheless, the unity of the definition does not guarantee that the definition is *embodied in a single human power* to act quickly in all things. For example, the power that enables us to run quickly does not enable us to play the harp quickly, since someone might be able to run quickly yet be able to play the harp only slowly. Likewise, even if there is a single *definition* of bravery, it may not be *embodied as a single power* to act correctly in the face of pleasure and desire as well as fear and pain. Indeed, even if we restrict ourselves to cases of fear and pain, there may be no single power to act correctly. As Aristotle observes in the *Nicomachean Ethics*, "some men, who are generous and face loss of wealth bravely, are nonetheless cowards in war" (3.6 1115a20–22). Aristotle's example appears to show that a man with the power to act correctly in the face of poverty might lack what is needed to act correctly in the face of death on a battlefield. Just as human excellence consists of different parts, which was the first premise of the whole discussion (190c8–d8, quoted above), so also bravery may be a collection of different parts. Laches and Socrates, in their pursuit of a practical good for fathers to give sons, may be taking a wrong turn by assuming that bravery is one power rather than a collection of many distinct powers. Let me save for later this worry about the unity of the power of bravery, that there may be no *single embodied power* of bravery that can master every fear and desire, even if the dialogue arrives at a *single definition* of bravery.

Laches, guided by Socrates' example of bravery, gives a second definition of bravery: "A kind of perseverance of the soul" (192b9). This definition, unlike Laches' first, is general enough for all cases of bravery, not only in fear and pain but also against desire and pleasure. However, Socrates rules out perseverance on the ground that perseverance, unlike bravery, is not always good (192d).

No one doubts Socrates' reasoning that perseverance, joined with folly, can be harmful. But many people object to the assumption that bravery is always good. Perhaps bravery as well as perseverance can be harmful when joined with folly. It is easy to think of examples of criminal or self-destructive acts that seem to require bravery. Let me put the objection this way: *since there is more than one definition of bravery, how do Laches and Socrates justify their assumption that bravery is always and everywhere good?*

The existential goal governing the inquiry disarms this objection. If Laches and Socrates had the academic goal of writing a dictionary, certainly they ought to note the variety of ways people use the word *bravery*, sometimes to refer to a human excellence, other times to refer to a character trait that in itself is no more good than bad. But the goal governing this dialogue is to advise fathers how best to produce excellence in their sons. Laches and Socrates have agreed to identify the bravery that is good for a human being to possess. Thus they are right to assume that this thing they seek to identify – which they call *bravery* – is a human excellence, that is, something always and everywhere good. And so they are right to reject perseverance of the soul, which itself is no more a human excellence than a human defect, depending on whether or not it is guided by wisdom.

Since Laches wants to identify the bravery that is a human excellence, and since he has identified it as a kind of perseverance of the soul, it is reasonable for Socrates to infer that, on Laches' account, bravery is *wise* perseverance (192d). However, as Socrates' examples show, bravery is not wise perseverance at just anything. A man who perseveres in spending money because of his wisdom in recognizing a good investment is not in that act brave, nor is a doctor who perseveres in a treatment for a patient brave because of his healing wisdom (192e). Evidently, bravery is not expertise at moneymaking or healing. So Socrates is right to ask Laches to specify, "*In what* is bravery wise?" (192e1).

Socrates and Laches go on to agree that it takes more bravery to fight against *expert* military strategy than to fight against *inexpert* strategy. Likewise it takes more bravery to fight against expert cavalry, slingshots, or archers than against inexpert, and more bravery to descend into a well inexpertly than to descend expertly (193a–c). Of course, not every case of fighting against the odds, or against superior skill, or facing dangers without appropriate expertise is a case of bravery. We need not (and so ought not) interpret Socrates and Laches to say so. But in such cases where it is brave not foolhardy to act inexpertly, "such persons are actually more foolish in running risks and persevering than those who do these things [that is, *strategy, riding, slingshots, archery,* or *diving*] with skill" (193c9–11).

There is an air of paradox here. It seems as if the same act will be both foolish and not foolish! Moreover, Socrates and Laches earlier "observed that foolish boldness and perseverance are harmful," and that "bravery was an excellence," but now they are saying "this shameful thing, foolish perseverance, is bravery" (193d1–7).

We can resolve the paradox by answering Socrates' question: "*In what is bravery wise?*" (192e1). A mother might be ignorant of diving and inexpert at how to descend to the bottom of a well, yet wisely understand that the well-being of her family requires in a particular case that she make an inexpert descent. In this case, the mother perseveres foolishly *in well diving* and does so precisely because she is persevering expertly *as a mother.* The paradox is resolved when we recognize that inexpert well diving in some cases might be expert action for a human being to take. According to this resolution, we meet Socrates' challenge by specifying in the first place that bravery is not any perseverance but only *wise* perseverance, and in the second place not any kind of wisdom in enduring but only wisdom *in human well-being.*

I have just now imagined a case where a mother would be wise to risk her life to persevere in diving inexpertly into a well. Obviously, there are also many cases where a mother would be foolish to risk her life with such perseverance. This variability leads me to abandon Laches' original definition: *perseverance* no more than *non-perseverance* characterizes bravery; evidently it is *wisdom at human well-being* that is essential to the bravery we seek. As it happens, my conclusion agrees with Socrates' conclusion about bravery in chapter 4 and mirrors what Nicias is about to propose in this dialogue.

While I find a way to meet Socrates' challenge, Laches does not. Oral conversation happens quickly, and it is not surprising that Laches momentarily feels perplexed and unable to give a successful account (194a–b). If Laches had a chance to read and ponder the things said, I suppose he might see how to resolve the paradox as well as I do. He might even decide to abandon perseverance in favor of a wisdom-based definition. Let us recognize, though, the human nature he shares with us: it is hard *not* to persevere in a position we have publicly defended – to abandon our words sometimes takes bravery!

Wisdom

Nicias, unlike Laches (188d), has heard Socrates' conversational challenges before (188a), and has remembered Socrates' often-repeated statement that "each of us is good where we are wise and bad where we are ignorant" (194d1–2: chapter 8 examines a nearly identical argument, that each of us is *beloved* where wise). Nicias endorses Socrates' statement and abandons Laches' definition. Just as Socrates' considerations led me, they also lead Nicias to a wisdom-based definition of bravery: "The knowledge of what is to be dreaded and dared both on and off the battlefield" (194e11–195a1).

Laches intelligently objects to Nicias's definition. Doctors know what is to be dreaded and what is to be dared in treating disease. For example, in the case of gangrene, doctors know in each case what to fear and what to accept with confidence: amputation or blood poisoning. But brave people need not know such medical things, and such knowledge does not make a doctor brave. Laches makes the same point about farmers and every kind of craftworker (195b–c).

Nicias's successful reply is to discriminate the doctor's knowledge from the knowledge of human well-being, much as I did above. Doctors by their knowledge know "concerning sick people what is healthy and what is diseased," but not "whether it is better to rise from the sickbed" (195c7–10). Laches is right to agree with Nicias that in some cases it is "better to die than to live" (195d1–2). For example, if Shakespeare's Othello had fallen deathly ill after his wedding to Desdemona, dying before losing his trust in her love, he would never have murdered her nor killed himself in despair. Alas, such tragedy is all too real: in the United States there are hundreds of romantic murder–suicides each year. An even grimmer example is, perhaps, Nicias himself. Had he gone home from this discussion to a sickbed and died there while a hero in the eyes of Athens, he would have avoided being a cause of catastrophe for his city and a far more wretched death, not counting years of misery from the excruciating pain of kidney stones.[3] The knowledge of *when human life may be more terrible than death* is different from the doctor's knowledge *how to heal*.

My judgments about Othello and Nicias assume that the hypothetical alternative deaths from illness would *not* have led to tragedies even more grievous than murder–suicide or civic destruction. Only magical knowledge of the future might tell whether my assumption is true. It is with reference to such seer's knowledge that Laches raises a new and plausible dilemma: "It seems to be the seers that he is calling brave! . . . And yet, Nicias, do you admit to being a seer, or – not being a seer – do you deny being brave?" (195e1–4). Laches is right: it is preposterous to suppose that a seer's knowledge is bravery.

Although Laches is right that a seer's knowledge is not bravery, Nicias gives another successful reply, this time drawing a distinction between knowledge of what *will* happen and knowledge of what will be *best* to happen.

> The seer need only know the signs of what *will* come – future death or disease or loss of property, or victory or defeat in war or some other contest. But is it *better* for a person to go through any of these things? – The seer is no better at deciding *that* question than anyone else.
>
> 195e9–196a3

For example, a seer might foretell that Juliet will soon see Romeo dead and kill herself. But the seer's knowledge is unable to tell Juliet whether life without Romeo is worse than suicide. Nicias calls *bravery* not the seer's knowledge but the knowledge that can tell Juliet which is better – life without Romeo or suicide.

It is my confident judgment that the typical adolescent would be wrong to kill herself in response to her lover's death. I suppose (though I would not mention this to a grief-stricken teenager!) that it is – barely – conceivable that Juliet had such extraordinary passion that she was right to kill herself in response to Romeo's death. This raises the troubling question, *Who's to say what's right and wrong in such a case?* Nicias is right that it is not for the doctor or even a seer to have such knowledge of what is right. But Laches' frustration is understandable, when he complains that he has no idea what sort of expert Nicias is talking about, "unless he is saying it is some god" (196a6–7). It is shocking that *human* excellence should turn out to be a sort of wisdom that only a *god* can actually possess! (And yet Socrates, speaking in his own voice at *Apology* 23a–b, asserts this very thing – see chapter 2.)

Socrates makes a suggestion how to act when one hears a wild idea. "Let's find out more clearly what he thinks. If he shows that he has a good point, we'll agree. If not, we'll instruct him" (196c1–4). Earlier, Socrates recommended the same method to Laches: we should "instruct, not abuse," those who speak in gross error (195a7). Socrates' suggestion applies to us as well as to Laches: if we recognize the error in the thought of others, we should be able to teach them the error.

Socrates takes over the cross-examination from the frustrated Laches, and draws attention to a preposterous consequence of Nicias's claim:

> It is necessary for him who states this theory to refuse bravery to any wild beast, or else to admit that a beast like a lion or a leopard or even a boar is so wise as to know what only a few men know because it is so hard to perceive. Why, he who subscribes to your account of bravery must agree that a lion and a *deer*, a bull and a *bunny rabbit* all have an equal share of bravery in their nature!
>
> 196e3–9

Nicias disarms this objection by distinguishing rational bravery from brute rashness, boldness, and fearlessness. Although animals, like human beings, do not know when it is best to live and when best to risk death or other evils, Nicias can nonetheless account for the marked difference in temperament among different animals: deer and bunnies are fearful in contrast to fearless lions and bulls. Although Nicias goes against a common human practice of attributing bravery and cowardice to animals, he is right to make this distinction. As I said before, the present inquiry is governed by a practical human concern, not the academic concern of cataloguing the way most people use words. Fathers want sons to have the bravery that is a form of human excellence, not a brute character trait, like fearlessness or fearfulness, that can be either good or bad.

Socrates has one more line of questions for Nicias, in which he raises a puzzle that Nicias cannot solve. Socrates begins by getting Nicias's explicit agreement to the first premise of the inquiry, the premise that bravery is but a part of human excellence.

> "You know that we investigated bravery from the beginning of the argument as a part of human excellence?"
> "Certainly."
> "And do *you* affirm it as a part among other parts, all of which together are called human excellence?"
> "Of course!"
> "Now *I* call the other parts besides bravery such things as *soundness of mind* and *righteousness* – is that what *you're* saying, too?"
> "Certainly."
> "Hold that thought! We agree to this."
>
> 198a1–b2

Is human excellence as a whole a collection of different parts? Socrates argued for a different answer in the *Protagoras*, that *righteousness, soundness of mind, reverence, bravery,* and *wisdom* are "all names for one and the same thing" (329d1), namely, that "they are all knowledge" of human well-being (361b1–2, see chapter 4). I return to this puzzle at the end of the chapter.

In any case, Socrates next gets Nicias to agree that the dreadful is nothing but what causes fear, which in turn is not past or present but *expected future* evils. And the opposite of dreadful – that which is to be dared – is the opposite of what causes fear, that is, an expected future *good* (198b–c). For example, when Juliet finds Romeo dead, she must expect either future life without Romeo or suicide, and she must decide which of these to dread and which, in contrast, to dare. I take it that *the dreaded and dared* are what is dreaded and dared *all things considered, in the case at hand.* Had Juliet never met Romeo, future life without him would in no way be dreadful, nor would it have been possible for her to dare suicide. It is only when she is faced with the death of her beloved that she judges life without him dreadful and dares to embrace suicide as a relative good under the circumstances.

Accepting this account of the dreadful and its opposite, Nicias accepts this restatement of his definition: *bravery is the knowledge of the good and bad things that one might expect in the future.* As the example of Juliet shows, the goods and evils that Nicias and Socrates have in mind are so only in comparison, weighed one against the other. The knowledge at issue is a knowledge not merely how to produce either alternative but also how to compare them, by determining which is best and which is worst all things considered in terms of human well-being.

And Socrates is right to point out that if one knows how to make all-things-considered judgments of relative value about future goods, then that same knowledge empowers one to make judgments about present and past goods as well (199b–c). It would be absurd for me, contemplating Juliet's choice, to claim to know which was good and which bad only so long as the choice remained in the future, but to be at a loss when the choice is present or past! Thus Nicias must accept that the real meaning of his definition of bravery is the knowledge of the comparative value of all good and bad things (all, that is, relative to human well-being) *past, present, or future.*

Now at last I can consider the worry that bravery is not a single embodied power but a collection of distinct parts. The worry is that there might be a distinct part of bravery that is only the knowledge of battlefield good and evil, not of goods and evils of seafaring, disease, or poverty. Bravery might only be knowledge of goods and evils that arise in connection with armored infantry, or indeed, to defend Laches' original example, not *all* armored infantry (for example, not the fancy Spartan technique involving running and turning), but just plain old-fashioned Athenian armored infantry, staying in position. According to this objection, Nicias's problem was that he did not distinguish that different situations call for different kinds of knowledge, a problem that leaves him unable to distinguish bravery from the rest of human excellence.

This objection fails. As a plain armored soldier, I have to choose between either deserting my position or facing death. My reason for facing death might be to save the city, but it might also be to save my family, to defend my religion, to win back Helen from Troy, to gain honor, to enjoy the dark pleasures of city sacking, to avoid a seafaring route, or to make money (for any variety of reasons). If I wanted my son to know how to make the correct choice *as a plain armored soldier,* there are no human values I could safely leave him ignorant how to weigh. I made the point in terms of plain armored infantry, but the point applies in general. Any allegedly specialized part of bravery requires the general knowledge how to compare *all* human goods and evils in producing its decision and the good it realizes.

Thus Socrates can fairly ask us all:

> Does such a man of human excellence seem to you to be missing anything, if he were to know [how to compare] all good and bad things past, present, and future? Do you think this man would lack soundness of mind, righteousness, and reverence – a man who alone knows how to take due precaution in dealings with gods and men, so as to get a good outcome in the face of what is to be dreaded and dared, by knowing the right way to associate with them?

> 199d4–e1

Nicias, with his definition, must admit that his bravery will be not part but all of human excellence, which contradicts the starting point of the inquiry, that bravery is but a part of human excellence.

Interpretive Puzzle

In defining bravery, Laches begins with the thought that bravery is a non-intellectual character trait like perseverance or fearlessness or confidence. But that thought leads to a dead end. Socrates makes obvious that any non-intellectual character trait will be bad for a human being when joined with foolishness. Moreover, persuaded by the *Protagoras*, we see that wisdom all by itself will cause perseverance in the same way it causes confidence (chapter 4). Like Nicias, we ought to be willing to define the bravery that is human excellence as nothing but a kind of knowledge.

It is surprising, then, that Socrates does not endorse Nicias's suggestion but refutes it. And the way Socrates refutes it is even more surprising. Socrates suggests to Nicias, as he did to Laches, that bravery is *but a part* of human excellence. Yet in the *Protagoras* his argument proved that bravery is nothing less than the wisdom that is *the whole* of human excellence, the wisdom that saves our lives.

The surprise calls for an explanation. If Socrates himself thinks that *bravery* is nothing less than *the whole of human excellence*, then why does he not directly tell Laches and Nicias but suggest the opposite? Many explanations are possible. Perhaps Socrates changed his mind in the span of eight years. Perhaps it is a mistake to think that the character *Socrates* represents the same man in different dialogues. Perhaps Socrates is not a serious moral teacher but amuses himself by toying with others in conversation. Perhaps Socrates is serious in the *Laches* but deceptive in the *Protagoras*. My existential interest in finding wisdom in Socrates leads me to a different explanation. I give this explanation in the next chapter.

notes

1 Alcibiades gives more details about Socrates' battlefield heroism at *Symposium* 221. It is the same speech where he describes Socrates' extraordinary vigil (see chapter 3). Socrates describes his war service more modestly at *Apology* 21e1–4.
2 Xenophon, a contemporary of Socrates, lists a few examples of war crimes in his *Anabasis* (5.7), calling them "crimes" (5.7.33.2).
3 The dialogue is set after the Peace of Nicias (described in Thucydides' *History* 5.16–20), before Nicias's reluctant expedition to Sicily (6.8–14, 6.19–24). Thucydides describes Nicias's lamentable deference of military expertise to seers (7.50.4 with horrible sequel 7.51–87), as well as Laches' mishap with a Spartan army worse in skill but superior in bravery (5.72.2). Plato wrote the dialogue at a time when his audience knew the prominent lives and deaths of Laches and Nicias. The contrast between the overcautious Nicias and man of action Laches is reflected in the dialogue at 197c.

further reading

Gregory Vlastos, *Socratic Studies*, ed. Miles Burnyeat. Cambridge: Cambridge University Press, 1994. Chapter 5 compares the *Protagoras* and the *Laches* on bravery.

puzzling pedagogy

n the *Apology*, Socrates solved the riddle of the oracle by distinguishing three levels of wisdom. The highest level is "real wisdom" (23a5–
6), which is the property only of God. The middle level is "wisest
among men" (23b2), which is the property of anyone who, like Socrates,
"knows that he does not possess real wisdom of any value" (23b3–4).
The lowest level is "not being wise, but seeming wise, especially to
oneself" (21c6–7). If the oracle is right, living at the highest level is
not something human beings can achieve, and of the remaining two
lives available to us, only the middle level is guilt free.

Recognizing the supreme value of wisdom and understanding the
oracle to be saying that such wisdom is not possessed by human beings
(23a5–b4), Socrates values and recommends only one sort of activity
for a person at the middle level: "Each day to make arguments, engage
in dialogue, and carefully examine human excellence and related topics
– this is the very best thing for a human being" (38a1–5). Indeed, as
I have argued (chapter 2), an unexamining life is not worth living for
a human being.

But there is a problem with the interpretation I am giving of Socrates
as a serious moral philosopher. In the *Protagoras* Socrates proved that
bravery is nothing less than the *whole* of human excellence. Yet in the
Laches he suggests that it is *but a part* of human excellence, and explicitly relies on that premise in his argument. Again, in the *Protagoras*
Socrates says, "I myself would say, on my own behalf, that righteousness is a reverent thing and reverence is a righteous thing . . . and
I would say that these are surely either the same thing or else righteousness is as similar as can be to reverence" (331b1–5). Thus reverence is
not a mere part of righteousness. Yet in the *Euthyphro*, Socrates gets
Euthyphro to agree that all that is reverent is righteous. (I discuss the
Euthyphro, reverence, and righteousness in chapter 14.) Then Socrates
asks him, "And is all righteousness reverent, too?" (11e7–12a1). Socrates
explains how reverence is *but a part* of fear, suggesting thereby that reverence is *but a part* of righteousness. Certainly Euthyphro understands
Socrates to be making this suggestion, because when Euthyphro replies

that reverence is *but a part*, he says, "For you, Socrates, appear to speak rightly" in suggesting that it is but a part (12d4).

Socrates' misleading behavior – either in the *Protagoras* or in both the *Laches* and the *Euthyphro* – makes him appear either dishonest or inconsistent. If Socrates really believes that reverence and righteousness are the same, why does he pester Euthyphro with misleading questions instead of speaking honestly with him? Likewise, if Socrates himself thinks that *bravery* is nothing less than *the whole of human excellence*, then why does he not directly tell Laches and Nicias? Why does Socrates seem to toy with Laches, Nicias, and Euthyphro? Why would a serious moral philosopher seem to amuse himself at the expense of others? Scholars have given many different interpretations to explain Socrates' surprising behavior. In this chapter my existential interest in Socrates leads me to interpret Socrates' misleading behavior as a way, often the best possible way, to lead human beings from the lowest to the middle level of wisdom.

From Lowest to Middle Level

Socrates knows that, being ignorant, he is unable to give people wisdom. As doctors benefit bodies by making them healthy, so might *sages*, that is, experts at human well-being – if any existed – benefit human beings by making their souls wise. Socrates wants to be but is not such a sage. And just as someone who wants to be but is not a doctor is incapable of healing others, so likewise Socrates is incapable of healing the souls of others so as to make them capable of human excellence. Socrates is capable of compelling others to admit in conversation such things as that human excellence is nothing but a kind of expertise. But it is obvious that one might master many such lines of argument and still be unable to weigh the choices facing an Odysseus, an Augustine, or any human being, so as to determine better and worse (see chapter 5).

Nevertheless, at the middle level, Socrates is capable of a pedagogy that is in a sense beneficial, reverent, and righteous, as he explains in the *Apology*. To be at the lowest level, ignorant but seeming wise, is an error damaging enough to negate any value in the wisdom of any other craft one may possess (22d–e). Socrates attempts to move his fellow citizens out of this lowest level into the middle level by combining "exhortation" with "demonstration" (29d5–6), "questioning and examining and testing" one by one those who consent (29e4–5). This activity of Socrates is not the true beneficence of the sage, who would have the power to move people to the highest level. Nonetheless Socrates' activity is as great a good as any that the Athenians have ever received (30a), for Socrates is changing them from *bad* to *not bad* as they reach the middle level. This very same activity of Socrates, although not true reverence – which is expertise at perfecting human beings in goodness by moving them to the highest level (see chapter 14) – nonetheless is a kind of "service to the god" in obedience to what "the god commands" (30a5–7). And this same activity of Socrates, although not true righteousness, which has the power to make us righteous, nonetheless is in a sense righteousness, for it is "really fighting for righteousness" (32a1) by replacing our culpably ignorant activities with an ignorant but guilt-free activity, namely *seeking wisdom*. Although Socratic pedagogy is inexpertly done and not strictly speaking beneficent, reverent, or righteous, it is at least guilt free (see chapter 2).

False-Lead Pedagogy

As Socrates says in the *Apology*, his pedagogy consists among other things in "testing" (29e5). The testing we find in the dialogues takes at least three different forms. The first form of testing is simply a matter of asking for a justification or explanation. Socrates describes this sort of test at the beginning of the *Protagoras*.

> To test Hippocrates' grit, I began examining him with a question, "Tell me, Hippocrates," I said, "What sort of service do you expect to get – and who do you expect to become – by going to Protagoras and paying money to hire him for yourself?"
>
> 311a8–b5

The youth Hippocrates, in seeking a teacher, seems willing to recognize ignorance in himself. Certainly he lacks the pretenses seen in Ion, Protagoras, Laches, and Nicias. Nonetheless, he begins by taking himself at least to know what a *sophist* is: "I think I know," he says (312c4). Yet Socrates finds it relatively easy to bring Hippocrates to the middle level where he is aware of his ignorance as to what a sophist is:

> "Tell me what you think a sophist [literally *wisdom-man*] is."
> "For me," he replied, "as the name says, he is one who knows wise things."
> "Well," I said, "it is possible to speak this way of painters and carpenters – that they are people who know wise things. See, if someone asked us, 'What are the wise things that painters know?' we'd tell him that they know wise things about, say, *how to make images*, and we could find such an answer for the carpenter, too. But if he asked in the same way, 'What are the wise things that sophists know?' then what might we answer? What sort of thing does he know how to make?"
> "What else could we say, Socrates, but that he knows how to make someone a skilful speaker?"

"Perhaps," I said, "we'd be speaking the truth, yet even so not saying enough. Our answer requires a further question. The sophist makes one a skilful speaker – *about what?* As for instance a harp player makes one a skilful speaker about what he knows, namely harp playing – do you agree?"
"Yes."
"Well, about what does the sophist make one a skilful speaker?"
"It must be that of which he gives one knowledge."
"That's likely. And what *is* this thing, of which the sophist himself has knowledge and gives knowledge to his student?"
"By Zeus," he said, "I no longer have anything to say . . ."
"And although you are about to put yourself in the hands of a sophist, you show that you do not know what one is."
"That is likely, Socrates, from what you have said."

312c1–313c

Notice that in this exchange Socrates did not need to show a contradiction in Hippocrates' beliefs, because Hippocrates is quick to recognize his own ignorance.

A second form of test faces Socrates himself, whenever he meets someone with radically different views, as when he meets Callicles in the *Gorgias* (486d, 487a, 487e), and must try to produce that person as a witness for the truth of his own view (as he promises to do with Polus in the same dialogue at 474a).

Neither of these tests explains the misleading behavior in the *Laches* and the *Euthyphro*. But a third sort of test does explain Socrates' misleading behavior. The third way to test a person's claim to knowledge is to say something false in order to see whether the person catches the error. Socrates mentions examples of such tests. In the *Apology*, he says that Meletus looks as if he is "making a test" in his indictment of Socrates "to see whether Socrates, the 'wise man', will recognize the contradiction" (27a1–4, again at 27e3–4). In the *Protagoras*, he says that Prodicus is "testing" Protagoras (341d8) when Prodicus falsely (falsely, that is, as Socrates sees it) says that Simonides in his poem used the word *hard* to mean *bad* not *difficult*. He says that Prodicus made this test "in order to see whether Protagoras can support his statement" (341d8–9). In the same dialogue, he says that Protagoras was likely to have been "testing" Socrates when Protagoras falsely (again, as Socrates sees it) said that human excellence had parts (349c8–d1).

There is good reason for Socrates to use this sort of test in his pedagogy. We know from the *Apology* that Socrates does not believe that any but God know what human excellence is (23a, 42a). Thus by falsely claiming or suggesting that his interlocutors have such knowledge, he can determine whether they take themselves to be knowledgeable. If his interlocutors pretend to knowledge, an additional false lead accepted by them will make it possible for Socrates to drive them into contradiction, which in turn might lead them to awareness of their ignorance.

I can think of no better way than this *false-lead pedagogy* to help those who are not as ready as Hippocrates to recognize their ignorance. It is not an infallible technique, but I take it to be more effective than the widely-used alternative of simply telling the other person: "You're ignorant!" The person subject to the alternative technique, in my experience, usually becomes aware only of the speaker's lack of charity. Many readers are frustrated when Socrates does not elicit positive doctrines from his interlocutors. To alleviate their frustration, I say that interlocutors at the lowest level of wisdom need to reach the middle level much more than they need to enhance their conceit of wisdom with a few positive premises and conclusions!

In what follows, I show that Socrates uses and re-uses four pedagogical steps with interlocutors at the lowest level of attainment of wisdom:

1 *Question*: Socrates asks the question.
2 *False lead*: If necessary, he prompts the interlocutor with a suggestion that is false, but seems true to those who are ignorant.
3 *Accepted*: The interlocutor accepts Socrates' suggestion.
4 *Refuted*: Socrates refutes the interlocutor's answer.

If Socrates succeeds in refuting the interlocutor, he repeats his original question and the process is repeated, as often as necessary, until the interlocutor either breaks off the discussion or admits ignorance.

Meno's Slave

Socrates' discussion with a slave in the *Meno* (82a–86c) illustrates these four steps. Socrates' knowledge of geometry in that dialogue and his interest in proving a doctrine of reincarnation are not characteristic of the Socrates of the *Apology*, and so the traditional interpretation (which I accept) of the slave-boy passage is that it represents Plato's own interests rather than being a portrait of the historical Socrates. I use the passage not to claim that Socrates had such mathematical knowledge or interest in reincarnation, but only to illustrate false-lead pedagogy. The boy, Socrates points out, begins at the lowest level of knowledge about the square, thinking he knows when he does not know (82e). We find the expected steps of the testing process:

Question   Given a square of area 4, "Try to tell me how long each side of the square of area 8 will be" (82d8–e2).

False lead	"The side of *this* square is 2 feet. What will be the side of the twice-as-big square?" (82e1–2). Socrates' suggestion to look to the *side* of the square of area 4, rather than its *diagonal*, is misleading, as is his suggestion that the length of that square's side, 2, is relevant to the twice-as-big-area problem.
Accepted	"Obviously, Socrates, twice as big" (82e2–3).
Refuted	Socrates questions the boy step by step until the boy retracts his answer (82e–83c).
Question	Socrates repeats the original question (82c).
False lead	Socrates points out that doubling the side of the 4-foot square produces a 16-foot square, that the desired 8-foot square is double the 4-foot square but half the 16-foot square, and that the 8-foot square will have a side bigger than 2, but smaller than 4 (83c–d). Socrates misleads by continuing to direct the boy's attention to the *sides* of the squares of area 4 and area 16, and by suggesting that some rational relationship between those sides is relevant to the solution.
Accepted	The boy seems influenced by Socrates' suggestion, saying that the 8-foot square will have a side of 3 feet (83e).
Refuted	Socrates again cross-examines until the boy retracts his answer (83e).
Question	Socrates again repeats his original question (83e).

At this point, the boy describes himself unequivocally as ignorant: "By Zeus, Socrates, I do not know" (84a1–2). He has reached the middle level, knowing his own ignorance and "happy to look" (84b10) for knowledge. Socrates thereupon questions the boy further, with a positive rather than negative effect, demonstrating that the square of area 4 has a side equal to the diagonal of the square of area 2 (84d–85b). He denies that the boy has yet achieved knowledge, describing him as now in a "dreamlike" state (86d). Socrates says that "if the same questions were put to him on many occasions and in different ways [by someone who knows geometry], in the end he would have as much knowledge as anyone on the subject" (85c9–d1).

We ought not to expect this further step – eliciting positive doctrine – to occur with Laches, Nicias, or Euthyphro, since none of these ever reaches the middle level in his dialogue with Socrates. The subject in the *Laches* and the *Euthyphro* is human excellence, not geometry. If we accept the hypotheses that reverence is nothing but righteousness and that bravery is the whole of human excellence, then we find parallels between these dialogues and the slave-boy passage of the *Meno*.

The *Laches*

Consider the *Laches*, where Socrates tests both Laches and Nicias (see chapter 6). When Socrates begins to cross-examine, Nicias tells of his familiarity with Socrates' techniques and predicts that Socrates "will not let them go until he *tests* them well" (188a3). All agree that the question is "how human excellence may come to the souls of their children and make them better" (190b4–5). Thus Socrates elicits agreement that "we need to know what human excellence is" (190b7–8) – "because, I suppose, if we did not thoroughly know what human excellence actually is" (190b8–9), we could not be advisers about the best way to acquire it. After Laches agrees to this, Socrates makes the assertion, "Therefore we claim to know what human excellence is" (190c4).

The false-lead hypothesis, according to which Socrates for pedagogical reasons sometimes makes false leads to test his interlocutors' pretenses to wisdom, can explain his claim to know at 190c4: he is testing Laches and Nicias, as Nicias predicted and as the illustrative dialogue with the slave boy in the *Meno* would lead us to expect, with just the sort of test that Socrates has described others as making.

It is uncharitable to interpret Socrates as telling a lie when he tests Laches in this manner. Socrates points out to Laches that implicit in the act of advising is a claim to know (190b7–c2). Laches agrees that there is such an implication in the act of advising and does not express any reservations about the advising he has done or proposes to do (190c3). From this fact Socrates infers ("therefore") what must follow from Laches' agreement: "[Since we are going to be advisors,] therefore we say that we know what human excellence is." Laches agrees: "Of course we say so" (190c4). We need not take Socrates' statement of group knowledge ("we") to be a lie about his own state of conscious ignorance but rather the first inference to which he secures Laches' agreement and from which he will derive a contradiction.

The false-lead hypothesis explains another statement of Socrates, where he suggests that Nicias and Laches must be wise: "If Nicias or Laches has discovered or learned it, I would not be surprised; for they are wealthier than I am, and may therefore have learned of others, and they are older too, so that they have had more time to make the discovery. They do seem able to educate a man, for unless they had been confident in their own knowledge, they would never have spoken thus unhesitatingly of the pursuits which are advantageous or hurtful to a young man" (186c5–d3). It is uncharitable to take this speech to be mean-spirited sarcasm. On the contrary, it is evidence of good manners, which are governed by the general principle of charity, in this particular case requiring Socrates to assume the best of others and hence to interpret their knowledge claims in the best possible light. Moreover, although

Socrates' suggestion that there is a likelihood of wisdom in his companions is courteous, the suggestion also serves as a test, giving his companions an opportunity to accept or reject the suggestion of their wisdom.

There are alternatives to the false-lead interpretation. Perhaps Socrates was carelessly inconsistent or intellectually dishonest. Perhaps he wanted to toy with people rather than serve God. But if the texts permit, we should reject such alternatives as uncharitable to Socrates. The false-lead interpretation is the only way to provide a coherent account of Socratic moral theory, not only between the *Laches* and the *Apology*, but within the *Laches* itself. Even in the *Laches* Socrates makes his characteristic denial of knowledge of human excellence – both at 186b8–c5 and at the conclusion of the dialogue, 200e2–6 – which conflicts with the statement, "we know what human excellence is" (190c4).

It is clear that Laches is at the lowest level of wisdom from his confident statements: "Yes [we know what human excellence is]" (190c5); "It is easy to say what bravery is" (190e4). Thus his dialogue with Socrates fits the pattern of false-lead pedagogy:

False lead	"I would not have us begin with the whole, . . . let us begin with a part [of human excellence, bravery]" (190d8–10).
Accepted	Laches says, "Yes, certainly" (190d6).
Question	What is bravery? (190e3). Laches needs no prompting from Socrates, and begins by giving a specific instance of bravery: *Bravery is staying at one's post.*
Refuted	Socrates gets Laches to see that his answer fails to define bravery (190e–191e).
Question	Again, "Try to say what bravery is!" (192b5–6). Laches again takes no prompting: *Bravery is endurance of soul* (192b).
Refuted	Socrates gets Laches to revise his definition to *Bravery is wise endurance of soul* (192d), which he goes on to refute (192e–193e).

At this point in the dialogue, Laches has contradicted himself. In striking contrast to the self-aware slave boy, Laches blames the puzzle in the discussion upon something other than his own ignorance: "I am unused to this sort of inquiry . . . I am really grieved at being unable to express my meaning, for I think I do know the nature of bravery" (194a6–b2).

Socrates next turns to Nicias, and we find the same steps of the testing process:

Question	"Tell us, Nicias, what you think bravery is!" (194c).

False lead	Laches proceeds to question Nicias until Socrates takes over, and Socrates begins with a false lead: "You yourself said that bravery was a part, and there were many other parts, all of which taken together are called *human excellence* . . . In that case, do you say the same as I? In addition to bravery, *I* call soundness of mind, righteousness, and the like *human excellence*. Would you not say the same?" (198a4–9).
Accepted	"Certainly" (198b1).
Refuted	Socrates refutes Nicias (198a–199e).

Socrates does not get a chance to repeat his question to Nicias, for Laches interrupts with abusive remarks. Nicias in reply quits the testing process: "Enough has been said on the subject" (200b2–3). Nicias admits no ignorance.

The *Euthyphro*

Consider, finally, the *Euthyphro*. Like Laches and Nicias, Euthyphro also begins at the lowest level, thinking himself wise about the nature of reverence (4e–5a, 5c). Again we find the predictable pedagogical pattern:

Question	"What is reverence?" (5c9). Euthyphro needs no prompting but gives specific instances instead of a general definition of reverence (5d–6d).
Refuted	Socrates gets Euthyphro to see that his instances of reverence do not give a general definition (6d–e).
Question	"Teach me what the form [of reverence] is!" (6e3–4). Euthyphro again needs no prompting: *Reverence is what is pleasing to the gods* (6e–7a).
Refuted	Socrates gets Euthyphro to revise his definition to *Reverence is what is pleasing to all the gods* (7b–8a), then gets him to agree that the revised definition fails (9c–11a).
Question	"Begin again: say what the reverent is" (11b4).

At this point, Euthyphro is unable to answer. Unlike the slave boy, he does not reach the middle level of coming to see his own ignorance. Instead, he blames Socrates for his own failure to answer: "Socrates, I'm not able to tell you what I have in mind . . . you are a Daedalus [making the assertions move out of place]" (11b6–d1). Accordingly, our model of Socratic pedagogy predicts he will keep giving false leads to Euthyphro until, if ever, Euthyphro reaches the middle level. This is exactly what we find:

False lead	When Euthyphro agrees that all that is reverent is righteous, Socrates asks him, "And is all righteousness reverent, too?" (11e7). Then Socrates makes an analogy with fear and reverence, suggesting that the relation of righteousness to reverence is like the relation of fear to reverence, that is, of whole to part (12d).
Accepted	Euthyphro takes himself to be agreeing with Socrates' own view: "Just so – for you, Socrates, appear to speak rightly" (12d4).
Refuted	Socrates attempts but does not complete a refutation (12e–14b).

Socrates is frustrated by Euthyphro's evasive and vacuous answer to his question "What is the greatest result that the gods produce when they employ human beings in their service?" (14b–c). Euthyphro has a tendency to assimilate reverence with righteousness: his paradigm of reverence is "opposing unrighteous people" (5d). And Euthyphro's assimilation must have been natural for Greeks, for Socrates relied upon it in the *Protagoras* in his argument identifying reverence and righteousness (330a–331b). Given this tendency, Socrates might well have expected Euthyphro to have answered the question how we serve the gods by saying, "We serve the gods not by acts of shipbuilding, winning victory in war, or growing food, but by acts of righteousness." This answer would have enabled Socrates to go on to reach a contradiction with his earlier false suggestion that reverence is but a part of righteousness. Instead, Euthyphro jumps to a new answer: "[Reverence is] knowing . . . how to pray and sacrifice" (14b). Then the pattern repeats itself:

False lead	"And to give properly to the gods is to give them those things which they happen to need to receive from us?" (14e1–2: I call this suggestive question a false lead because they agreed just earlier at 13c that the gods can gain no benefits from us).
Accepted	"True, Socrates" (14e5).
Refuted	Reverence becomes a business transaction, in which humans provide advantage to the gods – an account that Euthyphro rejects: "What! – Socrates, do you suppose that the gods gain anything by what they get from us?" (14a5–6).

Socrates can now raise again the question – "What, then, are the gifts we give to the gods?" (15a7–8) – to which we might expect a Greek such as Euthyphro to answer, "Our proper gift to the gods consists of our human acts of righteousness to each other." This answer would allow Socrates to use his earlier false lead, that reverence is but a part of righteousness, to refute Euthyphro and try to bring him to the middle level. Euthyphro does not find this answer, but goes in a different direction to a different refutation (15b–c). And so Socrates begins another cycle of the testing process with the question: "So we must go back again, and start from the beginning to find out what the reverent is" (15c11–12). Euthyphro here breaks off the conversation and hurries off (15d–e), never admitting his ignorance or reaching the middle level, despite Socrates' efforts.

Interpretive Skepticism

The false-lead hypothesis gives us a Socrates engaged in the pedagogy of helping move others from the lowest to the middle level of human goodness or wisdom. Those at the lowest level seem to know, though they are ignorant. Socrates describes himself as testing such people, and he is aware of the sort of test where one suggests a false lead to see whether the other will recognize its falsity. The false-lead hypothesis explains Socrates' seemingly inconsistent behavior. The hypothesis explains why, although Socrates himself might think that reverence is nothing but righteousness and that bravery is nothing less than the whole of human excellence, he suggests the opposite to Euthyphro, Laches, and Nicias. Instead of seeing Socrates as toying with these men, we can see him doing God's work, that is, trying to get them to recognize their own ignorance. By recognizing his pedagogical method, we can attribute consistent beliefs to him about human excellence and at the same time accept his claim to be devoted to saving the souls of human beings from their culpable ignorance.

Let me consider one final objection. The objection is that the false-lead hypothesis is self-defeating. For, it might seem, the only reasonable conclusion to draw from the false-lead hypothesis is complete skepticism about the views of the Socrates of these dialogues, that is, a rejection of *any* interpretive hypothesis!

In reply, I admit that no statement taken in isolation from these dialogues can serve as evidence. What saves me from interpretive skepticism are not *isolated statements* but *compelling lines of argument*. As I interpret him in this book, Socrates gives lines of argument that lead to wildly unconventional conclusions. Since, as I evaluate them, these lines of argument are sound, then the most charitable interpretation of Socrates is that he recognizes their soundness and accepts, at least provisionally, their conclusions.

Our task, then, to avoid skepticism about Socrates' moral theory, is to continue to examine his arguments to see whether they are as laughable as they seem on the outside or whether, when examined and taken apart, they prove to be compelling. The consequence of this approach is that the knowledge how to interpret Socratic texts is the very same as the knowledge of the truth about human excellence, a doctrine Socrates himself defends (chapter 1). As part of this project, the next chapter interprets Socrates' arguments on human love.

further reading

Hugh H. Benson, *Socratic Wisdom*. Oxford: Oxford University Press, 2000. Part 1 examines Socrates' method of cross-examination.

the *lysis*

love

Scandal

As the public saw him, Socrates taught his young followers, who admired and emulated him, that the good will of loved ones was worthless if they did not have the expertise to produce a pay-off, and that people ought to replace sentimental attachments to family and loved ones with love for those able to make cold calculations of maximum advantage. Such doctrines would seem as heartless and shallow in Socrates' time as in our own. The Greeks of that time had a variety of words for love, and we can find in Greek literature and philosophy examples and discussion of the ranges of human relations we refer to today as love: *needy* love (for example, in romantic or erotic love), *giving* love (for example, in parental love for children), and the *equality* love that exists between best friends.

It is no surprise that Athenians ridiculed Socrates for his views. Aristophanes' popular comedy *The Clouds* satirizes Socrates on several grounds, but the climax – the point of highest comical absurdity – has one of Socrates' students repeatedly strike his father, justifying the beating with an argument that "to strike is to love" (line 1412). The parody is fair: Socrates says in the *Euthydemus* that he is willing to let loved ones be destroyed – *if* it would make them "useful" (285a7). It is no wonder that Socrates' words were made into formal charges against him at trial, including the charge that, since Socrates professes to make sons wiser than their fathers, sons may abuse their fathers.[1] For Socrates' heartless arguments seemed to threaten the traditional authority of fathers over sons, an authority based upon procreativity not expertise.

It is likely that Socrates' arguments about love were one reason why he was found guilty and sentenced to death on the charge of corrupting the young. The other important charge brought against him at trial was that, like the new scientists of nature, he disparaged belief in the traditional gods. This charge was easy to refute, as both Xenophon's *Memorabilia* (1.1) and Plato's *Apology* record (26b–28a). But neither Xenophon nor Plato denies that Socrates led his followers to scandalous conclusions about love. In the *Memorabilia*, Xenophon bluntly admits: "I know that he did say these things about fathers, family, and loved ones" (1.2.53). In Plato's *Apology* Socrates draws attention to the decades-old public perception produced by parodies such as Aristophanes' as being more likely to convict him than the actual courtroom charges (18a–19c), but he never mentions or tries to defend his scandalous account of love.

In the *Lysis* (210b–d) Plato attributes the same account of love to Socrates as Xenophon and Aristophanes do. That account explains the two historically distinctive loves of Socrates' life, a *needy* love and a *giving* love. Socrates' greatest needy love was for the practical wisdom that enables a human being to live well, the only thing, according to Socrates, that was of unconditional importance:

> For every man who knows not how to make use of his soul it is better to have his soul at rest and not to live, than to live acting according to his own caprice; but if it is necessary for him to live, it is better after all for such a one to spend his life as a slave rather than a free man.[2]

In addition to Socrates' needy love for wisdom – that is, *philosophy* – his greatest giving love was a religious benevolence towards other human beings. According to Socrates, the god who spoke at Delphi commanded him to convert non-philosophers to the life of philosophy. Such conversions, Socrates believed, are unsurpassed among the goods one human being can give another (*Apology* 29d–30a, see chapter 2).

The *Lysis* gives us a picture of a Socrates at age 60 defending precisely the scandalous doctrines for which the historical Socrates was put to death. There are other Platonic dialogues in which Socrates speaks of love, at greatest length in the *Symposium* and *Phaedrus*. The *Symposium* describes the ultimate object of love as a mystically known, abstract Beauty, while the *Phaedrus* gives an image of the lover as an everlasting, reincarnating chariot. These accounts, although to some extent consistent with the doctrines of the *Lysis*, are not direct defenses of the reported doctrines of the historical Socrates. The account of love Socrates elicits in the *Lysis*, unlike the *Symposium* and *Phaedrus*, is corroborated by Xenophon's report and Aristophanes' parody of Socrates. Scholars are probably justified in regarding the *Symposium* and the *Phaedrus* as more Platonic than Socratic (see epilogue).

Leaving aside the mystical and supernatural accounts of love in the *Symposium* and *Phaedrus*, one might ask why anyone would study the Socratic eccentricity of the *Lysis*. My answer is not academic but existential: as I interpret him, Socrates' arguments, however eccentric, give us a compelling account of love. In this chapter I first show that Socrates explicitly states his doctrine of love in the *Lysis*, a doctrine in terms of nothing but needy desire for beneficent wisdom. Next I show that this doctrine is identical with an implicit conclusion about love that Socrates also argues for in the *Lysis*. I call it an *implicit conclusion* because, although Socrates does not state it, his argument states the premises that entail it. The identity of the explicit doctrine with the implicit conclusion supports my interpretation of the *Lysis*. I provide further support for my interpretation by showing how it harmonizes on important points with related Socratic doctrines and arguments in other works by Plato and Xenophon.

Although Socrates' account is unconventional, I defend it by showing the force of Socrates' reasoning and by replying to the main objections against it. The *standard* objection is that Socrates gives us an account only of needy love and ignores giving love, which leaves his account inadequate. This objection, I show, is based upon a misreading of the *Lysis*, which gives us an account of giving love as well as needy love. The *best* objection to the *Lysis* – it is Aristotle's objection – is that it ignores an important type of love, the equality love between best friends. Such love seems irreducible to either needy or giving love. This objection, unlike the standard objection, is based upon an accurate reading of the text, and in reply I try to show how Socrates might plausibly explain equality love in terms of profound mutual needs.

Explicit Doctrine

In the *Lysis* Socrates speaks with Hippothales, a youth in love with the younger boy Lysis.[3] Socrates claims to have received from a god the ability "to identify both the lover and beloved" (204c2). He speaks with apparent knowledge of the actions of those "wise in matters of such love" (206a1), and, when asked how "to win the love of boys" (206c3), admits to having the ability "to demonstrate how to speak" (206c5–6) to win the love of such a boy. (In terms of chapter 7, Socrates knows a pedagogy to turn non-lovers into lovers, that is, to move people from self-ignorance to the level of the philosopher, the lover of wisdom.) In that demonstration, with the boy Lysis, Socrates develops an explicit though unconventional doctrine of what causes love, namely wisdom.

We should take this demonstration at face value to give us Socrates' account of love for the following reasons. First, as shown above, there are corroborating reports that Socrates was notorious for just such an account of love. Second, there is the evidence within Plato's *Lysis* itself. Socrates confidently gives the demonstration as a self-described expert on love. Lysis certainly takes it seriously: he gives it his closest attention, wants to recollect it as well as he can so that later he can share it with his best friend, Menexenus, and will ask Socrates about any part of it that he might forget (211a–b). Socrates wants Lysis to take it seriously:

he urges Lysis to recollect it as well as he can, to tell the whole of it clearly to Menexenus, and to ask him about any part he might forget (211a–b). Moreover, within the demonstration, Lysis assents to Socrates only when Socrates' conclusions fit his own experience. Lysis disagrees with Socrates' suggestions when they strike him as contrary to his experience. For example, Lysis vigorously disagrees when Socrates tries to infer that Lysis's parents never stop him from doing what he pleases (207e8–9). Therefore, Lysis's assent within the demonstration is further evidence that he takes Socrates seriously and thus that Socrates seriously intends the demonstration and its conclusion.

Socrates begins his demonstration with a valid inference and obvious premise. The valid inference is that, since Lysis's father and mother "love him very much" (207d6), they wish him "to be as happy as possible" (207d7). Evidently this inference uses the word *love* in the sense of *giving love*. In the course of the *Lysis* Socrates switches back and forth between giving love and needy love, using the same Greek word for both as if they were reciprocal and part of a single love relationship. As I show below, Socrates proves precisely this necessary reciprocity in his argument that love is requited.

Next the two agree to the obvious premise that happiness requires that one be "free and able to do whatever one wants" (207e). Given the valid inference and obvious premise, the two require an explanation of characteristic parental behavior: Lysis's parents do not let him do whatever he wants but prevent and subordinate his action to the will of others in the case of all his possessions, even in the case of his own body (208a–209a). Lysis's first explanation, that he is not old enough to be free to do what he wants, fails: for he is free after all in his actions with some possessions: in reading, writing, and lyre playing (209a–b). They find a successful explanation why Lysis's parents give him freedom in some matters but not others: his parents allow him freedom insofar as he "has knowledge" (209c2).

Since Lysis's parents want to make him free and happy, not as a mule-carter, weaver, or lyre player, but as a human being, they must make him wise not at the skill of carting, weaving, or playing, but at the skill of living well as a human being. Socrates' argument supports this inference, and even though he does not explicitly draw it here, he does draw it in the *Euthydemus* (282a–b). The theme that the characteristic behavior of parents is to provide such expertise at human well-being to children is familiar in other Socratic dialogues such as the *Apology* (20a–c) and the *Laches* (185e–190b) and is explicit in a simile Socrates himself uses later in the *Lysis* as well: poets are like fathers insofar as they are "conductors of wisdom" (214a1–2, trans. Lamb). The fact that Lysis lacks that expertise at human well-being explains why his parents can at the same time be "eager to secure his happiness" (207e5) yet hinder and subordinate his actions as a human being. The function of parents – that is, what their giving love consists in – is to give to their children not carting, weaving, or playing skills, but expertise at human well-being.

Conventional thought might agree with Socrates' account so far, assuming that parental love explains why a parent gives freedom and control to a child who is wise. Socrates' next examples go beyond conventional thinking. Not just loving parents, but also neighbors, indifferent strangers, and even traditional enemies who are powerful rulers will give freedom and control to the wise. On the day when Lysis's father considers him to have greater expertise than himself, the father "will entrust" (209c5) the son with all that belongs to the father, as will Lysis's neighbor (209c–d). Heads of households are the same today, we must admit, in choosing those with whom they entrust their investment portfolios. Moreover, the Athenians "will entrust" (209d4) Lysis with what is theirs, when they consider him sufficiently intelligent. Today this remains the goal of democratic political systems. And the Great King of Persia, rather than his own firstborn son, heir of all Asia, "would entrust" (209d7–8) Lysis with, say, cooking or healing, if the king thought Lysis had a superior intelligence about these things. He would trust Lysis even to the extent of letting him throw fistfuls of salt into his stew or apply ashes to his own son's eyes, while not allowing his heir to put the least thing into the soup or touch his own eyes (209d–210a). Seasoning large pots of stew with fistfuls of salt is correct culinary technique, though not predictable by one ignorant of cooking (ancient salt was a malodorous grit). Likewise wood ash, because of its antiseptic properties, was a standard treatment in ancient times for eye infection, though this would be surprising to a non-expert. A contemporary parallel might be that the king would never permit his own son but would allow Lysis – if he were an expert dentist – to treat the son's toothache by putting a high-speed steel drill in his mouth.

There is a limit to Socrates' conclusion about what causes people to entrust their possessions to another: not everyone but only the ignorant – indeed, only those who know their own ignorance – will entrust their possessions to others with knowledge. And there are objections. You might not be trustworthy if you do not have a good will toward me. If you hate me or you are ruthlessly selfish, I will not trust you no matter how much you know – call this the Good Will Objection (for a reply, see chapter 11). There is also the Impotent Knowledge Objection. You might not be trustworthy if your passion keeps you from acting wisely. If greed, fear, anger, or lust can make your knowledge impotent, I will not entrust things I value to you no matter how much you know (for a reply, see chapter 5). In general, there is the Problem of Unrequited Love: your expertise in some area does not seem to ensure that you will act to requite the needy love of non-experts for you.

Socrates, astonishingly, will argue later in the *Lysis* that, if I ever find human expertise in another, that expertise will always requite my soul's needy love for it with giving love! But Lysis does not limit or object to Socrates' examples of household wealth, civic matters, cooking, and healing. He agrees with Socrates' generalization, and, on the basis of the examples, the two agree that our wisdom will cause others to trust and needily love us, a love we shall requite with giving love that makes us powerful and free. This is Socrates' explicit Love Doctrine.

> "Everyone – Greeks and barbarians, men and women – will entrust to us those things about which we are wise. We shall do whatever we like with those things. No one will willingly impede us. We shall be free in those things, and in those things we shall rule others. And those things will be *ours*, for we shall have the use of them. But no one will entrust to us, to do what seems best, the things about which we are ignorant. In those things everyone – not only those who have no connection to us, but even our father and mother and anyone closer to us than our parents (if there were anyone closer) – will impede us as far as possible. And in these things we shall have to listen to others. We shall have no ownership of these things, for we shall have no use of them. Do you agree this is how things are?"
> "I agree."
> "Will we be loved in anything – will anyone love us in anything in which we are without benefit?"
> "Surely not," he said.
> "Then no one, not even your father, will love you in anything, insofar as you are useless."
> "It would not be fitting," he said.
> "If you are wise, everyone will be lover and family to you, for you will be useful and good. If you are not wise, neither your father nor mother nor family nor anyone else will be your lover.
>
> 210a9–d4

Socrates' examples have illustrated this doctrine. We ought to view this doctrine as unproved until Socrates solves the Problem of Unrequited Love. According to this doctrine, if you are expert in some matter of importance, your wisdom causes "all" – *all*, as I limit it, who lack expertise in that matter and recognize their lack – to become your needy lovers. They will seek to put you in charge of that matter, whatever it is, giving you free use and effective ownership of the things involved.

Implicit Conclusion

Immediately following the statement of the Love Doctrine, Lysis asks Socrates for a favor, namely that Socrates talk with Lysis's best friend,

Menexenus. Socrates agrees, but says Lysis must join the conversation if Socrates needs help (211b). The conversation with Menexenus provides an independent examination of love, an examination that ends in a puzzle rather than an explicit doctrine of love. I take it that Socrates, as one who knows how "to identify lover and beloved," is not himself puzzled but sets the puzzle as a test to his audience for pedagogic reasons. I propose a solution, finding an implicit conclusion about love. My solution makes the second account complementary to the first. While the examples of the first conversation suggest but do not prove the Love Doctrine, the theoretical considerations of the second conversation lead to the same doctrine and solve the Problem of Unrequited Love.

Socrates frames the second conversation with the question: "In what way does one become a friend of another?" (212a5–6), in other words, what is the cause of friendship? The conversation first rules out that *the loving* – that is, "whenever one loves another" (212a8) – causes one or both parties to become a friend on the grounds that the loving need not be requited and that it is "irrational and impossible" (213b2–3) for a friend "to be friend to a non-friend or enemy" (213c1–2). Second, the conversation rules out that likeness is the cause (214a–215a), on the grounds that, insofar as one is like another, one can render no benefit to that other. Third, it rules out that good can be friend to good – not insofar as they are like but insofar as they are good – on the grounds that insofar as one is good one has no need and hence no love of another (215a–c). Fourth, it rules out opposition as the cause of love on the grounds, already used, that it is impossible for one to be friend to a non-friend or enemy (215c–216b).

These four arguments limit love to cases of either needing or conferring benefits – that is, to needy love or giving love – and, accordingly, Socrates will proceed to consider a model that provides both. He begins with the premise that there are three kinds of things: the good, the bad, and the neither-good-nor-bad. This three-part distinction is fundamental to Socrates' mission in life (see chapter 2). From this premise and the preceding four results, by process of elimination, Socrates infers that "only the neither-good-nor-bad can be a friend, and only to the good" (216e7–217a2). Unlike the four previously rejected causal models of love, Socrates presents this model as an inference from a process of theoretical elimination. This model will never be refuted and is able to serve as the framework for Socrates as he develops his causal explanation of love in the remainder of the dialogue. In addition to its place in the structure of Socrates' argument, this model is in harmony with Socrates' doctrine in other dialogues that all desire is for the good (chapter 10). The structure of the argument in the *Lysis* and the harmony of both premise and conclusion with other Socratic arguments indicate that this model is indeed Socrates' own.

The first causal explanation Socrates proposes for his model is that it is the *bad* that causes the neither-good-nor-bad to love the good. For example, he says, "a body on account of illness loves medical expertise" (217b3–4). Here disease is the bad, medicine a benefit and thus good, and "a body, considered as a body, neither-good-nor-bad " (217b2–3). Socrates goes on to distinguish one sort of case, when illness is merely a "presence" (217b6) to a body so that it becomes needy but retains its status as neither-good-nor-bad, from another sort of case, when illness has so corrupted a body that it cannot profit from medicine and loses its status as neither-good-nor-bad, "having become bad" (217b6–7).

A problem Socrates notices with his model is that it does not distinguish what we might call *intrinsically* from *extrinsically* beloved objects. He gives three examples of extrinsically loved objects: (1) a sick man loves "a medical doctor for the sake of health" (218e4); (2) a father loves an antidote, and the vessel that holds it, for the sake of his son who has drunk poison (219d–e); and (3) silver and gold are loved for the sake of whatever they buy (220a). Socrates does not say, but his models illustrate, that this distinction applies to both needy and giving love. Socrates infers from the existence of any series of extrinsically beloved objects that the series must end in an intrinsically beloved object, a "beginning" (219c6) or "first friend" (219d1). He recognizes that in ordinary language we call both extrinsic and intrinsic beloveds alike "loved ones" (220a7). The appearance of language notwithstanding, Socrates concludes that the only "real friend" (220b4) is the intrinsically beloved. (In the *Gorgias* Socrates elicits the harmonizing thesis that we desire only the intrinsically good, 468b–c.) One might have thought that the intrinsically valuable causes our love of and friendship for extrinsically valuable objects. By denying that extrinsically beloved objects are loved at all, Socrates has forestalled such an account. Socrates does not explicitly revise his model to state that the neither-good-nor-bad loves the *intrinsic* good only, on account of the presence of something bad, but his argument justifies such an interpretation.

There is a problem with the cause Socrates first proposed for his model, namely, that *bad things* cause the neither-good-nor-bad things to love the good. Socrates next explicitly rejects such a causal proposal on the grounds that (1) some desires are neither-good-nor-bad and would exist even if there were no bad things; (2) what one desires, one loves; and (3) if bad things were the cause of love, then if there were no bad things, there would be no love (221b–c). Premise (2) of this argument states Socrates' new proposal for the "cause of love: desire" (221d3) and I therefore attribute to Socrates a revised model of love: the neither-good-nor-bad loves the good because it desires the good.

There remains another, potentially fatal, problem facing this revised model of love. Socrates consistently discarded other causal models –

namely the first, "loving," and the fourth, "opposition," as shown above – whenever they entailed the impossible result that there is love between friend and non-friend. According to the revised model, the neither-good-nor-bad is a friend to the good – but will the good be a friend in return? If not, the neither-good-nor-bad would be a friend to a non-friend, which would be fatal to the revised model.

Socrates does not explicitly raise this problem for his revised model, but his statement of the model is tentative (221d2, 221d6). In order to be consistent with his argument's assumptions, Socrates needs to establish that love will be requited according to this model. Hence, on my interpretation, it comes as no surprise that Socrates next establishes this very result. There is also, at the dramatic level, interest in this result. In context the boy Lysis is compelled to admit that he must requite the love of his lovers, including, it would seem, the amorous Hippothales. The dramatic level of interest mirrors the theoretical level of inquiry.

The strategy of Socrates' argument to prove that love is requited is as follows. *Desire* is not a symmetric relation: A can desire B without B desiring A. But the relation of *belonging with* is symmetrical: if A belongs with B, obviously B belongs with A. Accordingly, from the postulate that desire is the cause of friendship, Socrates argues that, whenever there is *desire* and hence love and friendship, the cause of the desire is lack and *deprivation*. As a chess set can be deprived only of items that belong with it (the white queen, say, but not the queen of hearts), and as likewise a human family can be deprived only of family, not non-family members, so in general A can be deprived of B only if B belongs together with A (221d–e). Then, from the symmetry of belonging, Socrates draws the needed conclusion: if A loves B, B will love A (222a). In illustrating this argument, the chess set is my own interpretation, but the family membership illustration is implicit in Greek vocabulary: the noun *oikos* "household" or "family" is cognate with the adjective *oikeion* "belonging with" or "akin to." The English noun *family* has a similar cognate adjective in the slang expression, "He's family," meaning *he belongs with us* or *treat him as our kin*.

The love-requited argument, if sound, would remove the otherwise fatal problem with Socrates' model and would justify the following revised statement I make of it: *If the neither-good-nor-bad A desires and hence loves the good B, then B will respond with giving love and care for A.* If we apply this model to human beings or human souls, who are as such neither-good-nor-bad, and supply Socrates' account of goodness as expertise at human well-being, we get the same formulation stated in the Socratic Love Doctrine (210d1–3): Insofar as you are wise (= good), all who are not wise (= the neither-good-nor-bad) will be lovers of you, for you shall be useful and good to all (= you shall requite that needy love with beneficent care or giving love).

But the love-requited argument flies in the face of conventional thinking. Of the many objections the reader might well raise, let me consider only one (for others, see this chapter's further reading list). Let us grant that needy, neither-good-nor-bad lovers are incomplete and that in some sense they belong with the beloved good. The objection asks why the good, merely because they belong with the neither-good-nor-bad, must therefore requite their needy love. Perhaps the good have better things to do!

Socrates does not explicitly address this objection. But I find a reply in his first conversation with Lysis. Socrates and Lysis agreed how the good would requite the needy love of the neither-good-nor-bad, namely by taking charge of their lives. The reply is that being in charge *is* the best thing for the good to do: being in charge is what makes the good happy. Being in charge is happiness because (1) happiness consists in freely doing whatever we wish (207e) and (2) being good enables us to do as we wish; no one will voluntarily impede us and we shall be free and rule over others (as stated in the Love Doctrine, 210b2–5).

In order to test the reply, consider two of Socrates' examples of the needy: the sick and the ignorant. A doctor and a teacher might in some sense *belong with* the sick and the ignorant, but in the real world doctors and teachers will not necessarily *requite* these needs: all too often they require pay. Such doctors and teachers do not requite with a friend's benevolence but with a mercenary calculation. To explain such mercenary cases, Socrates needs to consider if the good must be benevolent and how they are free (chapters 11 and 13).

In any case, having developed his account of love, Socrates concludes the dialogue by testing the boys' understanding of *that which belongs or is kindred*. This concluding passage has the logical form of three *disjunction eliminations*. A disjunction is a statement of alternatives: *either a or b*. In disjunction elimination one alternative is ruled out (*eliminated*) and the remaining possibility is inferred to be true. The first disjunction is:

Either (a_1) there is or (b_1) there is not a difference between what is kindred and what is alike (222b3–6).

Socrates eliminates alternative b_1 on the grounds that if it is true, the kindred, being alike, would be useless, leading as before to a failed model of friendship (222b6–c1).
The second disjunction is:

Either (a_2) the good is kindred to all and bad kindred to nothing or (b_2) good is kindred to good; bad to bad; and what is neither good nor bad to what is neither good nor bad (222c3–7).[4]

Socrates eliminates alternative b_2 by showing that if it is true, again "we have fallen into a previously rejected" model of friendship, making the bad be a friend to bad (222d1–3).

The third disjunction is:

Premise a_2 – that the good is kindred to all and the bad to nothing – either (a_3) does not or (b_3) does entail that none are friendly with the good but the good (222d5–6).

When the boys choose alternative b_3, Socrates eliminates it by recalling that it is a model refuted earlier, impossibly making the good a friend only to the good (222d7–8).

Upon establishing the premises for these three disjunction eliminations, Socrates does not draw the conclusions but merely asks the boys: "What further use might the argument have?" (222e1). The boys cannot answer and the dialogue ends in perplexity. But it is only a tiny interpretive step to notice the consequences entailed by these three disjunction-elimination arguments:

a_1 There is a difference between what is kindred and what is like.
a_2 The good is kindred to all.
a_3 The fact that the good is kindred to all does not entail that none are friendly with the good but the good.

We find confirmation that Socrates accepts consequences a_1, a_2, and a_3 in Socrates' Love Doctrine:

If you become wise, everyone will be your [needy] friend and be kindred to you; for you will be useful and good; if you do not become wise, no one – not even your father, mother, or other kin – will be your friend; for you will not be useful and good.

210d1–4

Accordingly, all are kindred to the wise, which entails that (a_2) the good is kindred to all, and hence that (a_1) the kindred is different from likeness (since the good is not like all, in particular not like the neither-good-nor-bad nor the bad). Furthermore, all – that is, all who lack wisdom and know their lack – are friendly to the wise; hence some who are not good are friendly with the good; hence conclusion a_3 is also true.

Objections

Before my conclusion about Socratic love, I consider two objections. First is the standard contemporary objection to Socrates' account – by those who are not too shocked to take it at face value – that it reduces all friendship and love to needy love, ignores giving love, and thus is crude. This objection fails, since it is based upon a misreading of the text. Socrates, as I have shown, provides an account of giving love as well as needy love. But readers ought nonetheless to worry that Socrates' account is incomplete. Although it explains both needy and giving love, it gives no account of *equality love* as a third type of love distinct from the giving and needy love in inequality relationships. I give credit to Aristotle for raising this second objection. Although he does not state it as an objection to the account in the *Lysis*, many scholars consider that he wrote his account of love and friendship (*Nicomachean Ethics* 8–9), in which he emphasizes equality love as the only true friendship or love, with the *Lysis* in mind.

Equality love, as we seem to experience it between *best friends*, is a love such that neither friend's love is motivated by the need for goods or by a will to improve the other by bestowing goods: rather than getting or giving, the goal of both friends is *co-operation* in a shared life that in some sense requires an equality of character between the two friends. For example, in the *Euthydemus* Crito and Socrates engage to become, not students *of* each other, but students *together* (272c–d): their engagement as co-students, including the conversation in which they make the engagement, constitutes a part of their shared life as equality friends.

There are cases where an equality friend may also act as a giving teacher and therapist or as a needy student and client of another. For example, Crito at times takes it upon himself to admonish Socrates for being foolish (*Euthydemus* 304a–b) or unrighteous (*Crito* 45c), attempting to give to Socrates some of his own understanding and character. Such examples show that actual human beings are involved in relationships with each other that are compounds of both equality and inequality love, but they leave equality love distinct as a third type of love. If the character of the beloved becomes depraved, an equality love must end (as Aristotle points out, *Nicomachean Ethics* 9.3.3), although a giving love might begin. For example, the infidelity and betrayal that could end a best friend's equality love might mark the beginning of a therapist's giving love, where the therapist seeks to remedy the defects in the character of the client – and the best friend and therapist in such a case might be the same person. Since equality love can exist only towards one of good or at least satisfactory character, it is selective and thus distinct from giving love, which is beneficent to all (as stated in the Love Doctrine, 210d2–3). Since equality love does not try to acquire the character of the other, it is selective in a way that distinguishes it from needy love.

Socrates nowhere undertakes to analyze Crito's equality love for Socrates, but before developing his theory of love in the *Lysis* he does emphasize the equality between the boyhood friends Lysis and Menexenus: neither one accepts the other as elder, nobler, more beautiful, or wealthier (207b–c). Although recognizing equality love pretheoretically in this passage, he nonetheless argues, as shown above, that not equality but desire for what is lacking must be the cause of love. Nowhere in the *Lysis* does Socrates state a need-based motivation for equality friendship. However, in the *Protagoras*, Socrates proposes an equality friendship:

> Protagoras, don't think that I have any other desire in conversing with you than to examine things that puzzle me whenever I think about them. I find an important point in Homer, "When two go together, one sees before the other" (*Iliad* 10.224). Somehow *all together* we human beings solve our puzzles better in every thought, word, and deed. And if you do see something or get an idea by yourself, right away you go searching until you find somebody to whom you can demonstrate it and who can confirm it. And I in this circumstance am glad to converse with you rather than anyone else, because I regard you as the best at investigating in general any matters that a sensible man may be expected to examine, and human excellence in particular.
>
> 348c5–e1

Socrates' proposal as lover here is needy: he needs to understand human excellence. Socrates is proposing that Protagoras become his equal partner in an investigation, on the grounds that two can solve puzzles better than one, one seeing before the other and then validating the insight by demonstrating it to the other. Therefore, while Socrates is selective in choosing Protagoras as his investigative teammate for being "best at investigating," he is not proposing to become Protagoras's student in order to acquire Protagoras's character or knowledge. Thus this need-based partnership conforms to the selectivity criterion for equality friendship stated above.

When the mutual need that grounds the partnership is on the level of back scratching, moneymaking, or game playing, the resulting equality friendship is too superficial to be what human beings call true friendship. The relationship between best friends ought to survive the cessation of mutual itching, poverty, or interest in games. But there are more profound problem-solving partnerships involving moral character and conduct, such as involve best friends or marriages, where the partners in friendship or marriage may advise and consult on projects and test and respond in conversation. Such a partnership might well be the case, for example, with the relationship between Crito and Socrates as portrayed by Plato. It is not obvious that anything essential to equality friendship has been left out of such moral partnerships. Yet such partnerships are motivated after all by need, indeed by the most enduring and profound need that human beings experience, namely, for expertise at human well-being. Socrates' reduction of friendship to need is therefore compatible with the human experience of equality love.

Destiny

The *Lysis* gives us an explicit doctrine and a complementary implicit conclusion about both needy and giving love. According to this account, all needy love, that is, all desire, is directed to and only to the intrinsically good. For human beings this good is nothing but expertise at human well-being. A characteristic activity of this wisdom, the activity constituting the happiness of the wise, is to requite the needy love of others with giving love, a care that rules over and indeed owns the lives of the needy as it perfects them. Philosophers have needy love for this wisdom.

According to the *Apology*, it is the philosopher's destiny, as a human being and not a god, never to have this desire satisfied (23a), nor therefore to have divine wisdom and giving love. But there is a giving love appropriate to the philosopher, too, as a religious duty (23b, 37e) and as a consequence of merely Socratic wisdom. The philosopher is surrounded by non-philosophers, who are bad human beings, because they have the delusion that they possess expertise at human well-being. The philosopher's duty is to convert bad human beings to neither-good-nor-bad, which is a lesser state of ignorance in which one is at least aware of not having expertise at human well-being (the *Lysis* 218a–b echoes the *Apology* here). A distinguishing feature of Socratic dialogues is that they portray a Socrates trying in conversation to change the souls of those around him from bad to neither-good-nor-bad by converting them to philosophy. In the course of the *Lysis* Socrates tries to convert the boys, Lysis and Menexenus, in this very way. This Socratic activity is precisely his religious duty of beneficence to others and at the same time his "greatest conceivable happiness" (*Apology* 41c3–4). Yet insofar as Socrates accomplishes his Herculean labor of converting the bad to neither-good-nor-bad, his prospects for friendship are not over. For the neither-good-nor-bad continue to have needs, and to meet such needs Socrates will propose, as he did in the *Protagoras*, problem-solving partnerships between friends of equal standing who seek to investigate together the nature of human excellence.

The next chapter shows Socrates again converting a soul from bad to neither-good-nor-bad, demonstrating in the process the nature of the luck that brings good things to human life.

notes

1 Xenophon records these charges in *Memorabilia* 1.2.49–52.
2 The quotation is from *Clitophon* 408a–b, whose author is either Plato or a student of Plato and who accurately summarizes Socrates' conclusions as Plato presents them at *Euthydemus* 278e–282c. According to Xenophon (*Memorabilia* 1.2.49–50) Socrates at trial was accused of arguing for the lawfulness and beneficence of the wiser imprisoning the more ignorant.
3 On Greek romantic practices, see K. J. Dover, *Greek Popular Morality in the Time of Plato and Aristotle*. Indianapolis: Hackett, 1994.
4 It is significant that there are far more than the two possibilities Socrates mentions. There are in fact 256, as Janet McShane demonstrated to me, if we include reflexive, non-symmetrical, and non-transitive relations. On my reading, Socrates mentions only the two because he wants to emphasize to the audience, as Plato emphasizes to the reader, disjunct a_2.

further reading

Terry Penner and C. J. Rowe, *Plato's Lysis*. Cambridge: Cambridge University Press, 2005. The book gives a commentary and examines philosophical issues in the dialogue as a whole.
George Rudebusch, "True Love is Requited: The Argument of *Lysis* 221d–222a," *Ancient Philosophy* 24 (2004) 1–14. The article gives a detailed defense of a portion of Socrates' argument.

the *euthydemus*

luck

The Divine Sign

In the *Euthydemus*, Socrates, who is now at least 62, relates to his friend Crito a conversation he had the previous day with two sophists before a large crowd. Socrates tells how a god guided him to the conversation in which, oddly enough, he proved that providential luck and wisdom are the same thing: "It was according to some god that I chanced to be sitting alone there" (272e1–2), where the conversation would soon take place, in the dressing room of the Lyceum. Socrates continues: "I had intended to get up, but as I was getting up, the usual sign came to me, the divine sign. And so I sat down again" (272e2–4). A short while later two sophists entered with a crowd of students and began to stroll along the covered walk around the inner courtyard. Socrates remained sitting, doing nothing, in obedience to the uncanny divine sign. "The two had gone around the walk no more than two or three times when young Clinias entered" (273a4–5). Many males, sexually attracted, followed Clinias into the dressing room. When Clinias saw Socrates he went straight to him and sat on his right side, as if seeking some kind of protection. But he had more to worry about than romantic pursuers. The two sophists saw Clinias sitting next to Socrates and surrounded them: "The two came up, and one sat down beside the boy, the other by me on my left" (273b6–7).

The Lyceum was a gymnasium named after a nearby temple to Apollo *Lyceum*, that is, Apollo-*of-the-wolf*. Although the origin of the epithet *of the wolf* is obscure, Athenians knew Apollo as a god of music, medicine, and general rational expertise. At the *Lyceum*, they might have sought his protection, as a kind of Good Shepherd, from many kinds of wolfish dangers. Socrates in that case acted just as we would expect an agent of Apollo to act, namely, with the goal of protecting Clinias from ruin. He declared his intent to the two sophists: "As it happens, I – like all these lovers of his – have a heart's desire for him to become as good as a man can be . . . He is young, and for that reason I fear for him . . . that someone might destroy and ruin him" (275a8–b4).

At Socrates' request, the two sophists agreed to display how they are able to take a man who finds it dubious that "human excellence can be a matter of instruction" (274e1–3) and "convert him to the love of wisdom and to the cultivation of excellence" (275a1–2), using the young man Clinias as an example (275b–c). In fact the two sophists verbally assaulted Clinias (275d–277c) in an exchange that Socrates described as a martial art (277d). Socrates told the boy that the display was a joke, nothing more than the verbal equivalent of "tripping a person trying to walk or pulling a stool away from one trying to sit down" (278b7–8). After Socrates came to the boy's defense, the two sophists turned their attack upon him (283c–d), and the battle continued to the end of their conversation with him, a battle in which the two sophists managed to wound Socrates' reputation before powerful men in the city (305a).

As I understand it, Socrates feels that the god directed him with the divine sign to remain in the Lyceum to protect vulnerable Clinias from the sophists, who threaten to ruin him by leading him to *misology*, the condition where one comes to despise the very possibility of learning through reasoned speech. (On the catastrophe of misology, see chapter 16.)

Conversion to Wisdom

In this chapter I examine a small part of that conversation, when Socrates repeated his request that the two sophists "convert the young man to the cultivation of wisdom and excellence" (278d1–2) and improvised an example of what he had in mind. As he described it the next day to Crito, Socrates began by securing Clinias's agreement to a couple of "no-brainer" (278e5) statements: *Everyone wants to do well in life.* And *One does well by having lots of good things* (278e3–279a4). "And what are these good things?" Socrates asked (279a5). With Socrates, young Clinias began a predictably conventional list of things that "anyone would say" (279a7) cause us to do well and be happy, including wealth, health, good looks, and good birth. When they were nearly done drawing up their list, Socrates suggested another item, as he later relates to Crito:

> "Very well," I went on. "And where in the troupe shall we station wisdom? Among the goods, or where?"
> "Among the goods."
> "Be sure we are not leaving out any of the goods worth mentioning."
> "I do not think we are leaving any out," Clinias said.
>
> 279c1–4

Socrates then remembered one more item:

I remembered and said, "By Zeus, we almost left out the greatest of the goods!"

"What is that?" he said.

"Luckiness, Clinias: a thing which all, even the worst fools, call the greatest of goods."

"You are right," he said.

279c5–8

At this point Socrates made a wild claim about the identity of luckiness, "the greatest of goods."

I reconsidered and said, "You and I have almost made ourselves laughing-stocks in front of our foreigners!"

"Why is this?" he said.

"Because, after putting luckiness in our former list, we have just been discussing the same thing again."

"What's this?"

"Surely it is ridiculous, when a thing has already been before us, to set it forth *again* and list the same thing twice."

"On what grounds," he said, "do you say this?"

"Wisdom," I replied, "is surely luckiness: even a child might see that."

279c9–d7

As Socrates relates this conversation after the fact to Crito, he remarks, "Clinias was incredulous at this – he is still so young and simple" (279d7–8). The remark charms me, because *everyone*, regardless of age and educational level, will be just as incredulous as Clinias upon first hearing that luckiness is nothing but wisdom. I understand the charming remark as an expression of Socrates' modest assessment of his own expertise in explaining this point: his expertise is "nothing to speak of," as he says in the *Apology* (23a7). Socrates' argument demonstrating the identity of luckiness and wisdom needs no special expertise to understand; it is the sort of thing even a teenager is able to see.

In English as in Greek *good luck* has at least two meanings: in a broader sense of *successful outcomes in general* or in a narrower sense of *only those successful outcomes not rationally predictable*. It is important not to confuse these two meanings in following Socrates' argument. The luckiness under discussion is the one Socrates identified as "the greatest of goods" in the passage quoted above (279c5–8). Certainly it is a greater good to cause successful outcomes *in general* than to cause *only* unpredictable successes. So the luckiness at issue is that power – whatever it may be – that causes successful outcomes in general.

In J. K. Rowling's novel *Harry Potter and the Half-Blood Prince*, there is a magic potion called *Felix Felicis*. This potion illustrates the sort of power that Socrates and Clinias agreed is the greatest good. "It's liquid

luck – it makes you lucky! . . . *All your endeavors tend to succeed* . . .
at least until the effects wear off."[1] When the character Ron Weasley
believes himself to have drunk this potion, he enjoys amazing good luck
in a tournament. Ron in fact had not drunk the liquid luck. Instead,
it turns out that the mere belief that he had drunk it gave him self-
confidence that caused his good fortune on the field. Socrates and
Clinias were discussing luckiness as that power, *whatever it is*, that
makes you lucky so that *all your endeavors tend to succeed*. According
to Socrates' argument, such luckiness is neither a magic potion nor
self-confidence but a cognitive power.

Socrates began his argument by showing how wisdom is *correlated*
with lucky results.

> Then I, seeing his incredulity, said, "Can you be unaware, Clinias, that
> at good performances in flute music, the flute players are luckiest?"
> He agreed.
> "And isn't it the case," I said, "that at reading and writing the literate are
> luckiest?"
> "Certainly."
> "Well now, for the risks of a sea-voyage, do you consider any pilots to be
> luckier, all things considered, than the wise ones?"
> "Of course not."
>
> 279d8–e6

Many readers object to Clinias for agreeing so readily in these cases.
The objection is that bad luck – in the form, say, of appendicitis or a
meteor strike – might incapacitate a flute player, reader, or pilot, no matter how skillful or wise, just as performance begins. Surely in such cases
a non-expert might have luckier results and better performance than the
expert.

This objection confuses good performance *at flute playing* with good
performance *in intestinal health* or *in meteorology*. In the passage
above, Socrates is careful to specify that the expert flute player will perform well "in flute music." We ought to interpret Socrates' correlation
between wisdom and lucky results accordingly: lucky results *in some
area* correlate with wisdom *in the same area*. When we are careful to
specify the same area, we find the correlation. At good performances in
intestinal health or *meteor shower safety*, the relevant experts will be
luckiest. I suppose that, if what you are looking for is a good performance
simultaneously in all three areas, the person with *triple* expertise in
flute playing, health, and meteor safety will be luckiest. Charity leads
me to assume that Clinias interprets Socrates' question in such a way,
so that he is right to agree with Socrates.

The correlation explains the *preferences* to which Socrates and Clinias
next agreed:

"Suppose you were on a military campaign. With which kind of general would you more gladly share both the risk and the luck – a wise one, or an ignorant?"

"With a wise one."

"Well, supposing you were sick, with which kind of doctor would you more gladly take your chances, with a wise or an ignorant?"

"With a wise one."

"And your reason," I said, "is this, that acting with a wise person you would make luckier results than with an ignorant one?"

He agreed.

279e7–280a5

All *other* things being equal, anyone who wants a lucky result *in some area* will prefer to take chances with the expert rather than the non-expert *in that area*. We have the preference because we see the correlation.

What explains the correlation between wisdom and lucky results? Socrates inferred that there is a *causal connection*: "Wisdom everywhere *makes* men lucky" (280a6). He gave the following reason for his inference: "Surely wisdom could never err, but necessarily is right in making and hitting upon (literally 'lucking upon') results; otherwise she could no longer be wisdom" (280a7–8). It is the nature of expertise in some matter to calculate the odds correctly and always place the best bet in that matter. This nature explains why wisdom correlates with the luckiest results: its nature *causes* the correlation.

The statement that *wisdom can never err but necessarily is right in its results* is similar to the statement in Socrates' Love Doctrine that "if you are wise . . . you will be useful and good" (*Lysis* 210d1–3, see chapter 8). Socrates expects us to recognize wisdom's inerrancy in right results on the basis of examples such as he has just considered: flute music, reading and writing, sea voyages, military campaigns, and disease. As human beings, of course, our overriding concern is none of these but *human well-being*, which is where we really desire that *all our endeavors tend to succeed*, that is, *luck* in the broad sense.

Socrates at this point ends his narration to Crito of the argument demonstrating the identity of wisdom and luckiness: "We came to an agreement concluding – I don't know just how – that the truth in sum was this: *When wisdom is present, he with whom it is present lacks not a bit of luckiness*" (280b1–3). According to this conclusion, wisdom never travels anywhere without bringing along the whole of luckiness: wisdom never travels alone, as it were. The conclusion leaves open, however, whether luckiness might sometimes travel without wisdom. The conclusion is *weaker*, as logicians say, than the statement Socrates derived with Protagoras, that the powers bravery and wisdom are inseparable, that is, *neither* wisdom nor bravery appears anywhere without the other.

Socrates showed Clinias that wisdom causes lucky results and that wisdom never appears anywhere without luckiness because Clinias "was incredulous" (279d7) when Socrates stated that wisdom and luckiness *are the very same thing*. Clinias was "still so young and simple" (279d7–8) that he did not know we should enter wisdom and luckiness as one item, not two, on a list, an identity that "even a child might see" (279d7).

What, then, is Socrates' argument proving the identity? We might interpret it to be simply the following:

1 When wisdom is present in us, luckiness is present, too.
2 Wisdom is the cause of luck.
3 Therefore wisdom *is* luckiness.

But this is not a good argument. Even if wisdom and luckiness inseparably appeared together, so that whoever was lucky was wise, it would not be safe to conclude that wisdom and luckiness are the same thing. Socrates shows that this sort of reasoning is unsafe in the *Euthyphro*, where he explains that although *something passively being carried* invariably appears together with *something actively carrying*, it does not follow that the passive and active things are the same; indeed they differ as effect and cause (10a). Socrates uses the difference between effect and cause to show that *to be loved by the gods* and *to be reverent* are different, even if they are always found together (10d–11b). Since arguments from co-presence to identity are bad arguments, and since Socrates knows they are bad arguments, charity ought to prevent us from attributing this argument to Socrates.

The words Socrates uses to describe his conclusion with Clinias, "We came to an agreement . . . I don't know just how" (280b1), tell us that Socrates in retelling the conversation has left out part of it, probably something unremarkable. In this way Socrates leaves Crito and us with a puzzle: given Premises 1 and 2 above, what unremarkable premise do we need to add in order to establish the conclusion, that *wisdom is luckiness*, so that even a child might see its truth?

Unremarkable Premise

As it happens, there is an easy solution to the puzzle. In square brackets below, I have added a premise that might easily go without saying:

1 Wisdom is the cause of luck.
2 [*Luckiness* is the cause of luck.]
3 Therefore wisdom *is* luckiness.

If one recognizes that there is such a thing as luckiness, as Clinias does, then such a statement about luckiness – that it is the cause of luck – is the sort of thing even a child such as he ought to know.

In chapter 4 Socrates used a similar unstated premise, that *bravery is the cause of confidence of brave people*, in refuting Protagoras. Such arguments from cause to identity are valid, as my example in chapter 4 of crime scene investigation showed. And so Socrates is right to say that, once you have entered *wisdom* on a list, there is no need to add *luckiness* to the list; it is silly to list the same thing twice (279d1–5).

There is a final question: my statement of Socrates' argument does not use as a premise the statement that *when wisdom is present in us, luckiness is present, too*. Why not? My answer is that this statement is not a premise at all but a further conclusion. Once we know the identity of, say, Superman and Clark Kent, we might conclude that *when Clark Kent is present, Superman is present, too*. Likewise, given the identity of wisdom and luckiness, we might further conclude, as Socrates says, that "when wisdom is present, he with whom it is present lacks not a bit of luckiness" (280b1–3). Unlike inferences from co-presence to identity, such inferences from identity to co-presence are obviously valid.

note

1 J. K. Rowling, *Harry Potter and the Half-Blood Prince* (New York: Scholastic, 2005) p. 187.

further reading

Terence Irwin, *Plato's Ethics*. Oxford: Oxford University Press, 1995. Chapter 4 interprets Socrates' conversation with Clinias in the *Euthydemus*.

the *meno*

desire

S ocrates in the *Meno* is age 67, only three years from the end of life. He reports to the foreigner Meno a general Athenian self-awareness of ignorance:

> Here [at Athens] there is a drought, as it were, of wisdom . . . If you put your question [namely, *Can human excellence be taught?*] to anyone here, they will all laugh and say, "My dear visitor, I guess you think I am blessedly happy – to know whether human excellence can be taught or how it is acquired. The fact is that, far from knowing whether it can be taught, I do not even know what human excellence itself *is*."
> And I am just the same, Meno. I share the poverty of the city in this respect, and I fault myself for not knowing a thing about human excellence.
>
> 70c3–71b3

If Socrates' report is true, I take it that his missionary work among the Athenians (see chapter 2) bore fruit, and he deserves credit for bringing his city to see the truth of divine word about human ignorance. On the other hand, Anytus's hostile reaction to Socrates later in this dialogue (94e3–95a1, quoted in chapter 2), casts doubt upon Socrates' assessment of his city's self-awareness.

Bad Desire

Meno is surprised to hear Socrates profess ignorance of human excellence (71b–c). He thinks it is easy to say what it is (71e). After a couple false starts, Meno defines human excellence as a combination of desire and ability: "Desiring the praiseworthy, to be able to make it happen" (77b6–7).

It seems to me that Meno's combination captures the thought of many people today about morality. Conventionally, we tend to think that morally excellent people must have the will or desire, broadly speaking, to do good things. But our conventional thinking rightly expects more from such people than mere good intentions, since for example careless people can be well meaning yet might be guilty of negligence of the worst sort. Thus we also require some degree of thoughtful competence from excellent people.

After hearing Meno's definition, Socrates uncovers an assumption behind it, that *there are people who desire bad things.*

> MENO: It seems to me, Socrates, that human excellence is, as the poet says, "to rejoice in and to be capable of praiseworthy things," and this is what I myself say excellence is, *desiring the praiseworthy, to be able to secure it.*
>
> SOCRATES: [Do you say this] on the assumption that some people desire bad things, while there are others who desire good things? My good man, doesn't it seem to you that *everyone* desires good things?
>
> MENO: Not to me.
>
> SOCRATES: So [it seems to you that] there are some who desire bad things?
>
> MENO: Yes.
>
> 77b2–c3

Everyone agrees that some, perhaps most, human desire is for good things. But it is conventional wisdom in ancient Greece, just as now, that some people sometimes desire bad things. Although Meno's assumption is a matter of conventional wisdom, then and now, Socrates appears surprised by it. He asks Meno whether he thinks that desire for bad things can arise in cases of both ignorance and knowledge.

> SOCRATES: Do you say [that people desire bad things] thinking that the bad things are good, or that, indeed knowing they are bad, they nonetheless desire them?
>
> MENO: There seem to me to be both cases.
>
> SOCRATES: Does it truly seem to you, Meno, that someone who knows that bad things are bad nonetheless desires them?
>
> MENO: Certainly.
>
> 77c3–7

Socrates clarifies what is at issue between them with a further point: any desire is a desire *to get* something.

> SOCRATES: What is it you call desire? [Isn't it desire] *to get*?
>
> MENO: What else? – It's *to get*.
>
> 77c7–9

Meno's answer, "What else?" tells us he thinks this further point is obviously true. It is possible that Meno has stupidly forgotten that many desires are *to do*, not *to get*. But rather than accuse Meno of stupidity, charity should lead us to interpret this further point in a way that makes it obviously true. The further point is obviously true, if we assume that a desire *to do* something is also a desire *to get* something. For example, a desire to do harm to another might be a desire to get vengeance. In general, it is safe to assume that any desire *to do* will be a desire *to get the satisfaction of doing*. The assumption is safe because desire by nature is correlated with an object, satisfaction. (Hairsplitters might note that in this respect *desire* differs from, say, *intention*. I can *intend* to do something without intending to get the satisfaction of doing it.)

One might ask whether it is possible *to do* a bad thing and *get* a good thing. For example, might *doing wrong to another* be *getting a good thing for oneself*, such as vengeance? This is a good question and relevant to the evaluation of Socrates' argument. If it is possible to *do* bad things so that one *gets* good things, then there might be people who desire to *do* bad things, knowing they are bad and knowing they will *get* good things. Elsewhere, Socrates shows it is not possible to do bad and get good (chapter 12) and therefore rules out the possibility of knowingly desiring to do bad things. But the present argument will not rule out the possibility of such people.

Socrates' clarification establishes that when he and Meno talk about people desiring bad things, they mean people who desire *to get* bad things. Thus Socrates can ask Meno again, in this more precise way, whether people can desire to get bad things in cases of both ignorance and knowledge. To this more precise question, Meno reiterates that both cases are possible:

> There are some who desire to get bad things thinking that bad things are beneficial, and others as well, who desire to get bad things knowing that bad things cause harm.
>
> 77d3–4

Socrates proceeds to argue that both cases – ignorance and knowledge – are impossible.

Ignorant Desire

Socrates begins with the first case, that *there are people who desire to get bad things, thinking that bad things are beneficial.* Meno and Socrates – and certainly we too! – agree that there are people who, to use Meno's word, "secure" (77b5) bad things for themselves, that is, people who *choose and get* bad things. Meno's explanation of those bad choices is that such people *desire* bad things. In the case of ignorant choice, Meno will reject his own explanation when Socrates gives him a better explanation.

But scholars have had trouble understanding the reasoning that rules out Meno's first case. Here is the passage:

SOCRATES: Does it seem to you that those who think bad things are beneficial know that they are bad?
MENO: Such people seem to me not at all aware of this (77d4–7).
SOCRATES: Therefore isn't it obvious that these people do not desire bad things (77d7–e1) – but rather those things that they suppose to be good, although these things are bad (77e1–2), and so the people who are ignorant of these things and suppose them to be good, obviously desire good things (77e2–4).
MENO: Maybe so (77e4).

What has caused scholars trouble are two places in Socrates' second speech where he appears to contradict himself. First, he appears both to affirm and deny that people can desire bad things that they think are good. On the one hand Socrates says they "do *not* desire bad things" (77d7–e1); but in the very next sentence he says they *do* desire "those things that they suppose to be good, although these things are bad" (77e1–2). Second, after stating that ignorant people desire "those things that they suppose to be good" (77e1–2), that is, *apparent* goods, Socrates immediately concludes that such people "obviously desire good things" (77e2–4), that is *real* goods.

I avoid the trouble by interpreting Socrates' argument as a *reductio ad absurdum*. Meno assumes that *there are people who desire to get bad things*, and that the first case of such desire to get bad things occurs when *they think that bad things are beneficial*. Socrates' argument shows that Meno's assumption in the first case leads to a contradiction. The contradiction is therefore not incoherent babble but part of a skillful argument. I shall explain the argument and then show how *reductio ad absurdum* gives a faithful reading of the passage.

Meno and Socrates agree that ignorant people sometimes choose and get bad things. Meno's explanation of such choices is that *such people desire to get bad things*. Socrates has a better explanation: ignorant people choose and get bad things because *they desire to get good things and ignorantly suppose bad things are good*. The better explanation of human choice does not need to postulate desire of any kind for anything bad. A desire to get good things and an ignorant mistake suffice.

To get Meno to see the better explanation, Socrates points out the ignorance of those people who, as Meno claims, desire to get bad things thinking them good.

SOCRATES: Does it seem to you that such people, thinking the bad things are beneficial, know that the bad things are bad?

MENO: Such people seem to me not at all aware of this.

                                                              77d4–7

Since such people are unaware that they are going after bad things and ignorantly suppose they are going to get good things, there must be a reason why they would choose those seeming goods. The reason is obvious, as Socrates says. People who choose bad things "are ignorant of these things and suppose them to be good" (77e2–3). In general, in order to explain why people act as they do, we need to refer to both their thoughts and desires. In cases where the thought is an ignorant mistake of bad for good, only *desire to get something good* (77e3) explains the act of choosing something bad.

When Meno sees this better explanation, he rejects his own explanation of bad choices done by mistake.

SOCRATES: Therefore isn't it obvious that these people do not desire bad
           things? . . .
MENO: Maybe so.

                                                              77d7–e4

Meno is agreeing here that, in explaining the action of such people, *the desire to get bad things* plays no role.

My interpretation faithfully follows the inferences of the text. Socrates marks the two inferences he draws with the words *therefore* and *and so*, which I have underlined at steps 3 and 4 below:

1 *Meno's first case*: There are people who desire bad things "thinking the bad things to be beneficial" (77d3).
2 *Agreed*: Such people, who think bad things are beneficial, are ignorant that the things are bad (77d4–7).
3 "*Therefore* these people [who Meno assumes desire bad things], being ignorant that the things are bad, obviously do *not* desire bad things but rather things *believed* good, which happen to *be* bad" (77d7–e1).

With step 3, Socrates succeeds in reducing Meno's thesis to absurdity by leading it to contradiction: the people who Meno assumes desire bad things do *not* desire bad things. Although the things they desire happen to be bad, to say they desire bad things fails to explain their choice, since they believe these things to be good.

After deriving the contradiction at step 3, Socrates *discharges* (as logicians say) the assumption that led to contradiction and reaches his conclusion.

4   "*And so* [since premise 1 led to the contradiction at 3], people who are ignorant that the things they choose are bad, and who suppose them to be beneficial and good, obviously desire good things" (77e2–4).

Since Meno's first case leads to a contradiction, it is impossible and false. Socrates has successfully ruled out that people desire bad things in the first case of ignorance, proving at the same time that ignorant choice of bad things is the result of desire for good things.

Knowledgeable Desire

It remains for Socrates to show that the second case is also impossible, the case of people who desire to get bad things "*knowing* that bad things cause harm" (77d4). Socrates shows that this case is impossible in two steps. First, *people who knowingly desire to get things that will harm them must knowingly desire to be miserable.*

SOCRATES: Well, about those people who desire the bad things – as you say – and who understand that the bad things harm the person who gets them, do they know that they will be harmed by them?
MENO: They must.
SOCRATES: And don't these people believe that those who are harmed suffer insofar as they are harmed?
MENO: This too they must believe.
SOCRATES: And don't [these people believe] that those who suffer are miserable [insofar as they suffer]?
MENO: *I* certainly think so.

77e5–78a4

To judge from the nature of human understanding, Meno is right to agree to these statements. If I understand that *bad things harm the person who gets them*, certainly I must understand that the bad things would harm *me*, if I got them. Likewise it would not be accurate to describe me as understanding that *the bad things will harm me*, unless as part of that understanding I am aware that *I will suffer insofar as I am harmed* and *I will be miserable insofar as I suffer.*

One might object here by pointing out that the enthusiasm of desire might lead me to forget what I understand, so that I no longer am aware of these connections between harm, suffering, and misery. Socrates and Meno can grant this point, but such forgetting means I no longer *knowingly* desire, and *ignorant* desire was already explained in the first case, above. (See chapter 5 for further, related objections and replies.)

The second step of Socrates' argument is that *no one knowingly desires to be miserable.*

SOCRATES: Is there anyone who wants to suffer and be miserable?
MENO: No one seems that way to me, Socrates.

78a4–5

Given these two steps, Socrates' conclusion ought to compel our assent as well as Meno's.

SOCRATES: Then no one wants bad things, Meno, since no one wishes
[to suffer and be miserable]. For what else is it to suffer than to
desire and get bad things?
MENO: I guess you're right, Socrates. No one wants bad things.

78a6–b2

But there is an objection to Socrates' second step. It seems that some people want to suffer and be miserable. In the tragedy *Medea*, Euripides uses the myth of Jason and Medea to give an extreme example of such a case: a mother who chooses to kill her own children, knowing that it will make her miserable. Euripides first staged this play in 431 BCE, only a couple of years after the dramatic date of Socrates' public conversation with Protagoras, where Socrates argued that people must go after what they calculate to be their best interest. There is no way for us to know whether the dramatic date corresponds to a historical event. But the structure of Medea's soliloquy either is a pointed reply to a Socratic conversation or is a remarkable coincidence.

A princess of the Asian city of Colchis, Medea falls in love with Jason, who comes from Greece on a quest. She betrays her family and city to enable him to steal a sacred ram's fleece, so that he might return to Corinth and take back his throne from the usurper Pelias. When Pelias denies Jason the throne, Medea again saves Jason from failure. She tricks Pelias and kills him. Despite Medea's devotion, Jason eventually divorces her in order to advance his public life by marrying a younger woman of his own race. Medea forms a passionate desire for revenge, with a plan that includes the murder, before she leaves the country, of the two children she bore him.

I like the example of Euripides' Medea, because she articulates so well the passionate deliberation that leads to her choice of a horribly bad thing. While I trust my readers do not entertain passion as bloody-minded as hers, I also surmise that the experience of wrongdoing and wounded pride and the consequent desire to strike back is common to us all. As I see it, Medea's extreme choice illustrates this class of dark human desires. In her deliberation she feels no conflict about her desire to *do* harm to the unfaithful Jason. (As I said above, Socrates does not in this dialogue rule out the possibility of desire to *do* bad things to others.) But led by her sentiments of love for her children and her calculations of her own future pain, she is at one point in her deliberation unwilling to harm Jason in a such a way that she *gets* more harm herself, indeed "twice as much bad."

> My heart is undone when I see the bright eyes of my babes. I am not able to do it – farewell to my earlier wishes! I will bring them – *my* children – away from this land. Why ought I wound their father doing bad to *these*, when the result will be that I will myself get twice as much bad? No, surely I will not do it. Farewell to my wishes!
>
> lines 1042–8

Another part of Medea's soul immediately scorns such sentiments. This other part, her "angry heart," demands revenge and will do anything rather than be mocked.

> And yet what possesses me? Do I wish to leave my enemies unpunished while I am a laughingstock? I must face this deed. To permit soft words of sentiment is badness in me.
>
> 1049–52

In reply Medea speaks for her sentiments and calculates future pleasures she will lose.

> Ah! Ah! Do not, O angry heart, do not do this thing! Let the children go, you wretch – spare the babes! For, living, they will cheer you when we are together away from here.
>
> 1056–9

Her angry heart is unmoved and responds to the sentimental persuasions with three insane arguments. First, the mere possibility of her children being mocked is intolerable, but such a possibility is a consequence of their continued life. Second, her children as mortals cannot escape death, and so it is most fitting that the one who caused their entrance into life should cause their exit. Third, an angry heart, once set on a course of action, will inevitably have its way. The conclusion of all three arguments is the same: she must kill her children.

> Nay, by the avenging furies from down in hell, I shall never let it be possible for my children to be where my enemies can insult them. In any case it is a necessity that they die, and since they must, I who brought forth shall kill. In any case these things are settled and there is no avoiding it.[1]
>
> 1060–5

the *meno*

Medea accepts the desire of her angry heart, which overrules her sentimental desires. She accepts the angry desire, knowing the bad things in it that will make her miserable.

> I shall take a most wretched path and shall send these two on a path still more wretched . . . I know well what sort of bad things I face, but an angry heart – cause of the worst things for mortals – is stronger than my wishes.
>
> 1068–80

Medea's angry heart causes her to accept the desire to kill her children, knowing that to do so will bring her misery. But despite the case of Medea, Meno is right to agree to Socrates' premise that *no one knowingly desires to be miserable.* Misery is not the object of Medea's murderous desire. Her desire, as stated above, is to get revenge and to avoid being a laughingstock. Although she *accepts* it, she does not *desire* misery for herself. She accepts it because, in anger, she sees revenge as *necessary at all costs* and ridicule *to be avoided at all costs.* In her insane calculation, she assesses life without revenge and life open to ridicule as even worse and even more miserable than life without children and life with the guilt of filicide. Seeking to minimize the bad things she will suffer, Medea evidently desires the good in the same way as any profiteer cutting losses. Medea is not an exception to Socrates' premise; she is an illustration of its truth.

Medea's angry desire illustrates Socrates' premise that no one desires to get bad things. But one case does not prove his premise. There are many other cases to examine. Psychologists treat desire for bad things such as pain and death as a disorder, and they look to explain such cases by reference to trauma suffered by the person with the disorder, trauma causing feelings such as fear, anxiety, grief, unworthiness, inadequacy, or failure. Such feelings, in turn, explain the desire to get bad things. In some cases, the bad things are desired to escape from other bad things; in other cases the bad things are desired as deserved punishment, and still other cases are possible. The general hypothesis of such psychological explanations is that the bad object somehow appears good to the person with the disorder. If this explanatory strategy is correct, Socrates is right to assume that no one knowingly desires to be miserable and right to conclude that no one desires bad things. By refuting Meno's assumption, the argument leads to the conclusion that human excellence, understood as the *getting* of good things, is a matter of know-how alone.

SOCRATES: Weren't you saying just now [at 77b2–c3, quoted above] that excellence is both to want and to be able to get good things?

MENO: I was, yes.

SOCRATES:	And since we proved that to want [to get good things] is something everybody does, isn't it true that no one is better than anyone else in this respect?
MENO:	Evidently so.
SOCRATES:	Obviously, then, if one man is better than another, he would be better insofar as he is able to get good things.
MENO:	No doubt.

78b3–c1

Socrates' argument raises a number of questions. Do excellent people desire to get goods only for themselves? What about other people? How might Socrates question someone who believes that excellent people, while *getting* goods for themselves and their loved ones, *give* bad things to their enemies? I present Socrates' answers to these questions in the next two chapters.

note

1 These arguments are so insane that some scholars would cut these lines from the text of the play as spurious. I am not confident that I have interpreted the three arguments correctly, but I can report that in the grip of anger, like this Medea, I have been swayed by insane arguments.

further reading

Terry Penner, "Desire and Power in Socrates: The Argument of *Gorgias* 466a–468e that Orators and Tyrants have No Power in the City," *Apeiron* 24 (1991) 147–202. The article examines the relation between desire and power in Socratic philosophy.

book 1 of the *republic*

benevolence

S ocrates' conversation in the *Lysis* raises the question whether people acting with expertise are bound to act for the well-being of anyone else. His conversation in the *Meno* raises the question whether anyone might desire to get good things by giving bad things to others. His conversation with Thrasymachus in the *Republic* answers these questions. Socrates' argument shows that freely acting expertise invariably acts for the good of others. This is a remarkable answer. It is still more remarkable that Socrates does not simply state this answer, but elicits it from someone who asserts the very opposite.

The Excellence of Exploiting Others

Thrasymachus believes that excellent people always act to get goods for themselves, the more the better. He proposes the thesis that righteousness is "the advantage of the stronger" (338c1–2). Thrasymachus explains what he means: those who are politically stronger in any form of government – tyranny, oligarchy, or democracy – enact laws aimed at their own advantage, so that obedience to the laws of a ruler is righteous – and such obedience is advantageous to the politically strong (338e).

Socrates gets Thrasymachus to admit that such rulers are sometimes mistaken in the laws they enact: they enact a law believing it to be to their advantage, but in fact it harms rather than benefits them (339c). Socrates and Thrasymachus agree that such legislative mistakes can and do occur wherever legislators are active, whether in matters of state security, economy, environment, education, or transportation. Such legislative mistakes harm and sometimes destroy the intended beneficiaries. Moreover, the existence of such mistakes threatens to destroy Thrasymachus's thesis that righteousness is to the advantage of the stronger. For obedience to mistaken laws is righteous, as Thrasymachus has stated, and obedience to such laws is disadvantageous to the politically strong. Thus righteousness, on Thrasymachus's account, is no more properly defined as what is advantageous than as what is disadvantageous to the stronger (339e).

In order to save his definition of righteousness from Socrates' cross-examination, Thrasymachus restricts his claim to the ruler strictly speaking, that is, the *ruler as ruler*:

> Do you call one who is mistaken about the sick a physician in reference to his mistake or one who goes wrong in a calculation a calculator when he goes wrong and in reference to this error? I accept that we speak in such terms – that the physician erred, and the calculator or the grammarian erred. But I also take it that each of these, insofar as he is that which we say him to be, never errs. And so, speaking precisely – since you are such a stickler for precision! – no craftworker ever errs. For it is when his knowledge leaves him that he who goes wrong goes wrong – at which time he is not an expert. And so no craftworker, wise man, or ruler makes a mistake when he is a ruler, though everybody would say that the physician erred and the ruler erred.
>
> 340d2–e6

This restriction lets Thrasymachus re-establish his claim that strong, that is, excellent, people, are the opposite of benevolent. "The ruler, insofar as he is a ruler, never makes errors and unerringly decrees what is best for himself" (340e8–341a2). Socrates proceeds to examine this revised thesis about the ruler in the strict sense, arguing as follows.

The Ruler-as-Ruler Argument

"Strictly speaking" (341c4–5) and "correctly speaking" (341c9), the expert is so called "because of his expertise" (341d3). Moreover, "expertise does not consider its own good but the good of its object" (342c4–6). It follows inescapably that the expert, speaking precisely and correctly – that is, the expert as expert – does not seek his own good but the good of the object of his expertise. For example, the medical expert, strictly and correctly speaking, does not seek his own good but that of the body; likewise the horse expert the good of horses (342c). There is, moreover, a connection between ruling and expertise: "Expertise rules over and is stronger than that at which it is the expertise" (342c8–9). And Thrasymachus's ruler as ruler is by hypothesis inerrant (340e1) and hence expert. It follows that "no one at all, in any ruling position, insofar as he is ruling, considers or commands his own advantage but rather that of the object ruled" (342e6–8).[1] Socrates' conclusion applies to expertise at human well-being. But Thrasymachus raises an objection.

book 1 of the *republic*

An Objection

Socrates has ignored, in his discussion of expertise, that in most actual cases expertise is in service to other goals of the human being who possesses the expertise. Thus, for example, most actual doctors typically refuse to heal others freely, but require some form of payment. Thrasymachus uses such cases to raise an objection to Socrates' argument. The objection is that Socrates is ignoring the plain facts about the real world.

> Shepherds and cowherds consider the good of the sheep and the cattle and fatten and tend them for the sake of . . . the good of their masters and themselves; and likewise the rulers in our cities – those who are actually ruling – . . . consider their subjects as sources of their own profit.
>
> 343b1–c1

Thrasymachus cannot deny Socrates' conclusion that the ruler as ruler cares for the good of the ruler's subjects, but Thrasymachus denies that this conclusion applies to the rulers in our cities. These facts about the real world make Socrates' conclusion seem irrelevant. Accordingly, Socrates turns the inquiry to the actual rulers in our cities.

The Rulers-in-Our-Cities Argument

Thrasymachus's objection refers to two types of different real-world rulers: *private*, such as shepherds and cowherds, and *political*, such as those in our cities. The objection recognizes that there is a specific expertise and benefit associated with each such ruler. Since "shepherds and cowherds consider the good of the sheep and the cattle and fatten and tend them" (343b1–3), they have and make use of shepherding and cow-herding expertise in order to produce good for their objects. In the case of cattle and sheep, they produce this good by giving them nurture in order to cause them to grow. "Likewise" (343b4) the rulers in our cities consider and care for the good of the citizens. In using knowledge to benefit the ones they rule, these *rulers in our cities* are similar to *rulers as rulers*. As the objection puts it, the difference is that rulers in our cities, unlike rulers as rulers, enslave the expertise to serve their own good. For example, shepherds herd sheep and cowherds cattle in order to earn a living themselves; political rulers in our cities rule their subjects in order to make a profit.

Socrates' reply to this objection will be to distinguish expertise at shepherding, cow-herding, and ruling in cities from expertise at money-making. Given this distinction, it will be easy for Socrates to show that, even in actual cities, the benefit from the ruling goes not to the rulers but to their subjects.

Here is the reply, step by step. First Socrates gets Thrasymachus to agree that one expertise differs from another by having a different power and providing a different benefit (346a). Socrates illustrates with the examples of medical expertise, which provides health; the expertise of the ship's captain, which provides safety in sailing; and expertise at moneymaking, which produces profit (346a–b). Thrasymachus is right to agree to this identity condition.

Then Socrates points out that the distinctions about each expertise's proper power and benefit apply to actual experts in our cities, who put one expertise in the service of another. For instance, even if sailing happened to produce health in a ship's captain, the captain's expertise is nonetheless distinct from medical expertise (346b). Likewise, even if medical experts in our cities make money from healing, we ought to distinguish their moneymaking from their medical expertise (346b). Such cases do not cast doubt upon the identity condition, and Thrasymachus is right to agree that, in the real world, a person might practice more than one expertise, and might indeed use one expertise in service to another.

Socrates applies this distinction to people in our cities who use the various branches of expertise to produce a common benefit. "Experts who make money from their various kinds of expertise gain this benefit by using, in addition to their specific branches of expertise, the money-making expertise" (346c9–11). For example, in the case of doctors in the real world, "while their medical expertise produces health, their wage-earning expertise produces a wage" (346d3). In the case of builders in the real world, "while their house-building expertise produces a house, their wage-earning expertise accompanying it produces a wage (346d4–5). In general, "the benefit each expertise produces benefits the object of that expertise" (346d5–6).

Thrasymachus had objected that Socrates did not know how the real world worked, because, he said, rulers in our cities rule for their own good. The reply is that the expertise of such rulers in our cities works to benefit its objects, the same as the expertise of rulers as rulers. The shepherding and cow-herding expertise of real-world shepherds and cowherds produces good for the sheep and cattle, and likewise the political expertise of rulers in our cities, insofar as it is used, produces good for the citizens.

Socrates has shown that expertise at political rule, even in the real world in our cities, works to produce good for the citizens, not the ruler. Socrates has answered the question I raised about the *Lysis*: people acting with expertise are bound to act for the well-being of others. He has answered the question I raised about the *Meno*: people acting with expertise do not desire to get good things by giving bad things to others.

But Thrasymachus's point about real-world rulers remains true: in the real world, rulers put their political expertise into the service of their own personal ends, just as "shepherds and cowherds consider the good of the sheep for the sake of their own good" (343b1–4). So far, Socrates has not shown that Thrasymachus's heroes live miserably or slavishly. He needs further arguments to show their misery (chapter 12) and lack of freedom (chapter 13).

note

1 As an aside, we know that according to Socrates God possesses expertise at human well-being (chapter 2). Such expertise, like all others, would consider not its own good or advantage but rather the advantage of those humans whom it rules. Thus Socrates' argument establishes as a matter of natural theology that God's good will is not due to the mere coincidence that the wise ruler of the universe happens to have a benevolent nature – a good heart, as it were, known to us if at all only by supernatural revelation. Rather, divine benevolence is essential to divine rule and its wisdom.

further reading

Simon Blackburn, *Plato's Republic*. London: Atlantic, 2006. Chapter 2 discusses Thrasymachus.

happiness

After conversation with Socrates, Thrasymachus recognizes that expertise at political rule, even in the real world, even wielded by the most profiteering ruler, produces good for its objects, the citizens, not for the expert, the ruler. Profiteering rulers are those who use their subjects as tools for the sake of their own personal profit. As Socrates has shown in chapter 11, such rulers rule not because they enjoy ruling but in order to make money. Thrasymachus admits this under examination, but it seems an unimportant point to him in contrast to the advantages such rule brings.

Saying openly what many people privately believe, Thrasymachus praises *unrighteousness* as a condition of strength, freedom, and mastery, a condition leading people to take political power when they can and make it serve their own profit and interest at the expense of those they rule. In contrast, he disparages *righteousness* as a condition of personal weakness in servitude to the advantage of the stronger. It is obvious, from his point of view, that unrighteousness produces more profit and advantage in a human life (344c).

Thrasymachus breaks with convention in praising unrighteousness as excellence in a human being. Given his statement that unrighteousness produces strength, freedom, mastery, and a better human life than righteousness, he is reasonable to call it "a human excellence" (348c5–8), making people "intelligent and good" (348d3–4). Righteousness, in contrast, if not exactly a defect in a human being (348c11–12), is an "inborn simplemindedness" (348c12), having no part of excellence or wisdom (348e3).

Socrates admits that there is no superficial contradiction in Thrasymachus's position and warns that an argument in defense of righteousness will not be "easy" (348e5–6). Yet Socrates proceeds to refute first the statement that unrighteousness as Thrasymachus conceives it is something wise and good, and second the statement that such people have a better or more profitable life than the righteous. The conclusion is wild: the righteous, *merely by being righteous*, have a more profitable life than the unrighteous. Indeed the righteous are happy while the unrighteous are wretched. I take up the two arguments in turn.

The Righteous Are Wise and Good

The first argument does the hard work. By showing that righteousness is human wisdom and goodness, Socrates will find it easy to show in the second argument that the righteous are happy. As usual, Socrates draws his premises from the statements of the one he examines. The essential feature of Thrasymachus's unrighteous man is that, in such a man's evaluation, "he ought to have more than *everyone* else" (349c6) and attempts to do so. For Thrasymachus, this selfish evaluation is a sign of a wisdom deeper than conventional righteous thinking, a wisdom that is good because it leads the unrighteous man to a more profitable life.

Socrates is able to refute the claim that unrighteousness is wise and good, because it shares its essential feature – *trying to have ever more* – with ignorance, not expertise. Socrates' refutation works out the details of this insight. The hard work of this argument is to find statements of expert and inexpert behavior that are both general enough to include the *having-ever-more* feature of the unrighteous and essential to why experts are wise and good at what they do.

In order to understand Socrates' argument, it helps to notice that unrighteousness and righteousness, like expertise and ignorance, are in a way *opposites*. In particular, the argument assumes that each unrighteous person, insofar as unrighteous, is *like* every other unrighteous person and *unlike* every righteous person. In the same way, each expert at some skill, insofar as expert, is like every other expert at that skill and unlike every person ignorant of that skill.

There is a distinction (drawn in chapters 2 and 4) between *cautious* and *foolish* ignorance. Some people who are ignorant of a skill are aware of their ignorance: they are humble and cautious in performing or advising about the skill. Other ignorant people are *foolishly ignorant*; they are ignorant even of their ignorance. They see no need to seek out expertise and are willing to act and advise incautiously.

I draw this distinction here again, because, as Socrates will show, the relation between the righteous and unrighteous is like the relation between the expert and the foolishly ignorant. Just as the expert and the foolishly ignorant feel no need to seek each other out for advice, so also the righteous and the unrighteous. There is not the same parallel in the case of the cautiously ignorant, who seek to be guided by experts. Though Socrates and Thrasymachus do not explicitly single out the *foolishly ignorant* in the conversation, the parallel is stronger if we take it to be between the unrighteous (as Thrasymachus conceives them) and the expert, on the one hand, and between the righteous and the foolishly ignorant, on the other.

There is still more to the parallel. First, it is expertise (at, say, medicine) that makes a person wise (about medicine) and good (at producing health), while ignorance of medicine makes a person foolish and bad. In a parallel manner, it is righteousness and unrighteousness that make a person either wise and good or foolish and bad at human life. (Socrates and Thrasymachus disagree not about this parallel but about which of the two – righteousness or unrighteousness – makes one wise and good.) Second, expertise is like unrighteousness (as Thrasymachus conceives it) in that both aim to be productive. Just as unrighteousness aims to produce *profit in human life,* so also each expertise aims to produce something or other. For example, musical expertise produces *harmony* in, say, tuning a lyre; medical expertise produces *health* in, say, prescribing a patient's diet.

Might the parallel be only superficial? One might object that there is a deep difference between expertise and happiness. Expertise is a knowledge of truth. We humans might get closer and closer to the truth, but our knowledge will never, as it were, *go beyond truth* without becoming error. In this way truth limits how far human knowledge can go. But – one might think – there is no limit to how happy a human being can be. That is, one might always have more and ever more happiness. If there is some limit to knowledge that does not apply to happiness, the parallel will fail.

The objection assumes that *there is more and ever more happiness to be gained.* Thrasymachus thinks this idea is part of wisdom; Socrates thinks it is part of foolishness. At issue is ideal human life: must it always fall short of something still better, as Thrasymachus thinks, or is it something perfectly complete? We ought not to prejudge this issue but follow the argument to its conclusion.

Although Socrates and Thrasymachus disagree whether it is righteousness or unrighteousness that is like wisdom, they agree to use the *duck test* to settle the issue: *If a bird looks like a duck, swims like a duck, and quacks like a duck, then it probably is a duck.* As Socrates and Thrasymachus put it: whichever of the two is *like* expertise (in relevant ways) will be the sort of thing that expertise *is,* namely, wise and good at human life (349d).

Socrates does the hard work of the argument with two premises about experts and non-experts and two parallel premises about the righteous and unrighteous. The first premise states how experts "attempt to have more." *Experts attempt to have more than their opposites, the ignorant, but not more than each other* (349e–350a). In terms of musical expertise, for example, Socrates is claiming that the expert, tightening the strings in "tuning the lyre" (349e10–11), attempts to produce – that is, to *have* by virtue of the expertise – *more* harmony than one ignorant of tuning, but not more than the other expert tuners. Again, the medical expert, "in prescribing food or drink" (350a1), attempts to produce more *health* than the non-physician, but not more than the other medical experts. I take it that medical experts do take themselves to produce more health than the foolishly ignorant, but not more than each other, insofar as the correct treatments are known. Although it is true that experts sometimes compete with each other, one can outdo another only at points *unknown* to the other, that is, only at points where the other so-called expert is *ignorant*.

The second premise states how the foolishly ignorant attempt to have more: *Non-experts who are foolishly ignorant attempt to have more than their opposites, the experts, and more than each other* (350a). Such people are the same in relation both to each other and to their opposites. In my experience, most people are willing, like Thrasymachus, to grant Socrates this premise about the foolishly ignorant without further scrutiny. I suppose they are willing because they have memories, as I do, of overdoing actions from ignorance, such as over-tightening a wire or screw until it breaks.

Although Socrates and Thrasymachus do not seek an explanation why the feature, *always trying to have more*, is a consequence of ignorance, such an explanation is possible. Expert action is aimed toward some goal. As Socrates said earlier to Thrasymachus, "The reason why we have discovered medical expertise is that the human body is defective and not self-sufficient; and so we procured expertise for the purpose of producing advantageous results" (341e4–7). I take it that those who are foolishly ignorant of some skill desire the same remedy as experts. The difference is that there is something that the ignorant do not know about the goal, either the proper means to it or the parts of it. For example, suppose one's desire is a tuned lyre, a goal achieved by tightening each string. Experts, knowing precisely how far to tighten the string, are satisfied as soon as they produce the correct tension. They have no desire to have any more tension. But people who are ignorant of the correct tension do not know when they have achieved perfect tune and their desire is satisfied at no definite point. If they are *foolishly* ignorant, they take themselves to know how to produce more satisfaction. And since strings can be tightened indefinitely more and more, there is no limit to how much more they might try to have. It is in this way that the foolishly ignorant try to have ever more, whether in comparison to experts or each other.

The explanation I have given shows why it is no accident that Socrates' two statements are true: the ignorant attempt to have more than everyone else, while experts attempt to have more only than non-experts. Since the activity of expertise as well as foolish ignorance is a consequence of defects in human experience and the desire for remedy, the featured way in which experts attempt to have more is a consequence of their expertise, and the featured way in which the foolishly ignorant attempt to have more is a consequence of their foolish ignorance.

Given the two premises about how experts and non-experts attempt to have more, Socrates elicits two more parallel premises: *the unrighteous are like non-experts* and *the righteous are like experts*. The unrighteous man is like the ignorant because, as Thrasymachus defined him, it is the unrighteous man's evaluation that he ought to have more profit in human life than everyone else, and he "will strive" to do so (349c8).

The second parallel premise is that the righteous are like experts. Is this premise true? Do *the righteous attempt to have more profit in human life than the unrighteous, but not more than the righteous* (349c)? If this is a question about *intentional goals*, then Socrates' argument fails. Consider Socrates' example of the sorts of calculations that a righteous person makes. In his deliberation in the *Crito* about whether or not to escape from prison, Socrates says to Crito, "The only thing to consider is . . . whether we'd be acting righteously" (48c7–8). Socrates says he excludes from his deliberation "considerations of loss of money and reputation" for his friends and lost opportunities "to nurture his children" (48c2–3). To judge from what Socrates includes in his deliberations, I would say that his intentional goal is nothing but right action. In general (see chapter 13) the goal of the righteous is nothing more than to do the right action. They do not make it their goal to *have more than unrighteous people* or to *have as much as other righteous people.* This is why, if *attempt* means *intentional goal*, Socrates' premise is false.

On the other hand, if *attempt* means *natural result*, then Socrates' premise need not be false. Here is an example of people meaning *natural result* when they say *attempt*: when I consult with people about projects I have in mind, they tend to advise me that I am *attempting to do the impossible*. When they say this, they are not claiming that my intended goal is to do the impossible. They are talking about the natural result of my action. Consider, in this way, Socrates' question:

> Would the righteous man's evaluation be that he would have more [profit in human life] than the unrighteous man and would he suppose it right for him to have more? . . . I'm asking whether he would . . . think it right to have more and would desire to have more than an unrighteous man.
>
> 349b8–c2

As I interpret him, he is asking:

> Would the righteous man's evaluation be that *it is the natural result of righteous action that* he would have more profit in human life than *the natural result of the actions of* the unrighteous man, and would the righteous man suppose it is right *that righteous actions would have this natural result for himself?* I'm asking whether the righteous man would

think it right that *a natural result of his righteous action is that* he have more profit in human life and would desire this *as a natural result of his righteous actions.*

What are the correct answers to these questions? I imagine that different camps of people will give different answers. One camp, as I imagine it, answers no. Its members agree with Thrasymachus that righteousness often does require the sacrifice of personal happiness. To use a biblical image, this camp might say that righteous life is like a straight but tiny path that requires us to go through a narrow gate – it can seem to be impossibly narrow! – in contrast to the wide on-ramp leading to the superhighway of unrighteous life. For example, an unrighteous lie, theft, or bit of cheating seems often to produce more advantage, that is, more good things for my personal happiness, than the righteous alternatives – which is why people call such actions *temptations*, after all. According to this camp, such choices test our moral character, because the narrow path is morally correct, while the broad road is tempting precisely because it provides a much more enjoyable life. People who make that narrow path their characteristic choice are, in a way, righteous. But since their enjoyment is inferior, they are not in this life *happy* but rather *long suffering*. If Socrates is asking a question about *the long-suffering righteous*, then the answer is no – his premise is false, and his argument fails.

But *the happy righteous* will answer yes. This second camp disagrees with Thrasymachus's evaluation. Like Jesus, they would not describe the broad road as better in any sense: it leads to nothing but "destruction" (Matt. 7:13). Jesus suggests that considerations of righteousness are unsurpassable grounds for one's personal profit in his rhetorical question, "What shall it profit a man, if he shall gain the whole world and lose his soul?" (Matt. 16:26). Socrates in the *Crito* is another famous example from this second camp: when he says "living well is the same thing as living righteously" (48b8), he is saying that righteous living is every bit of well-being, so that the one who lives so does not lose even a speck of happiness. This camp regards righteousness not as requiring a long-suffering nature but as that which causes human happiness. This camp will answer yes to Socrates' question about the natural result of righteous living.

If we interpret *attempt* as *natural result*, and if we interpret *the righteous* as the *happy righteous*, Socrates' premise is true. This is how I shall use the words *attempt* and *righteous* in this premise and throughout the argument. When the argument began, Thrasymachus took the evaluations and attempts of these people – the happy righteous – to be evidence of their folly at human life. But now Socrates assembles the agreed premises:

"Concerning every expertise and lack of expertise, consider whether it seems to you that whoever is expert is willing to *have more* than any other expert in action and speech, or *have the same* in the same action as one similar in expertise to himself."

"Why, perhaps it must be the latter," he said, "in such cases."

"But what about the non-expert? Won't he attempt to have more than another non-expert in the same way he attempts to have more than an expert?"

"Perhaps."

"And the expert is wise."

"I'll say."

"And the wise is good."

"I'll say."

"Then he who is wise and good, while *not* wishing to have more than another like him, *will* wish to have more than the opposite person who is unlike him."

"So it seems," he said.

"While the bad and foolish wishes to have more than *both* the one like him *and* the one opposite him."

"It appears so."

"Then again, Thrasymachus," I said, "our unrighteous man attempts to have more than *both* the one like him *and* the one unlike him – isn't this what you were saying?"

"Indeed I was," he said.

"And the righteous man, while *not* attempting to have more than the one like him, *will* attempt to have more than the one unlike him."

"Yes."

"Then the righteous man is like the wise and good," I said, "while the unrighteous is like the bad and foolish."

"Maybe."

"But we agreed that whichever is *like* [expertise in these ways] will be *the sort of thing that* [expertise] *is*."

"We did agree."

"Then the righteous man is now revealed to us as wise and good [at human life] and the unrighteous as foolish and bad."

350a6–c11

As I said, the basic idea of this argument is simple: the characteristic feature of the unrighteous – *to have ever more* – is a feature shared with ignorance, not expertise at human life. While the basic idea is simple, the details are intricate and indeed hard work for most readers to follow. It is hard work to produce a statement of expert and inexpert behavior that is both general enough to include the *having-ever-more* feature of the unrighteous and essential to why experts are wise and good at what they do.

The argument in the text is open to a number of objections. These objections in the past have led interpreters to judge the argument not merely a failure, but an obvious failure. I have considered what I think are the best objections and disarmed them. In order to disarm the objections, I went beyond the text in distinguishing foolish from cautious ignorance, happy from long-suffering righteousness, and natural results from intentional goals. I also went beyond the text in taking pains to show that the different ways in which experts and the foolishly inexpert attempt to have more are *consequences of*, not *mere coincidences with*, their expertise. Because of the extra work I needed to do to interpret this argument, it is easy for me to believe Socrates when he says, "Thrasymachus agreed to all these things not in the easy manner I relate here, but with difficulty, dragged along" (350c12–d1). The conclusion of the argument is remarkable and worth all of the effort; it is no surprise that it requires a difficult argument. Socrates has not yet proved that the righteous are happier than the unrighteous, only that the righteous are wise at human life and good at producing more human profit in life, while the unrighteous are foolish and bad at these same things. But the hard work is done.

The Righteous Are Happy

Although the Greek word *eudaimonia* might carry other meanings, Socrates and Thrasymachus use it to mean *our overriding goal as human beings*: call this goal, whatever it is, *excellent human life* (344e). The English word *happiness* can have the same sense, and the argument's conclusion applies to happiness in this sense only. Such happiness is what matters to readers who, like Socrates and Thrasymachus, are interested in the existential question how best to live.

Given that the righteous are wise and good at producing human profit in life, while the unrighteous are foolish and bad, Socrates easily shows that the righteous have better human lives than the unrighteous. He uses an analogy between the eye and the psyche or *soul*, as I call it. Socrates in speaking of the soul makes the same assumption that psychologists today do. The argument makes no controversial assumptions about ghostly substances or a human afterlife. Like the psychologist, he considers the soul to be a natural part of the human organism, as the ear or the eye is. Indeed, the argument works by drawing an analogy between eye and soul, which is easy to view in table 12.1. Under the heading *Soul*, it is at row 2 of the table that Socrates makes use of his previous conclusion that righteousness is goodness at human life, while unrighteousness is badness.

There is a problem at row 3. The problem of external factors seems to falsify the statements at row 3 for both eyes and souls. Eyes insofar as sighted have the *power* to see well, but they do not *actually* see well

Table 12.1   The eye/soul analogy

	Eye	Soul
1	It is by means of the eyes that we see (352e5–6).	It is by means of the soul that we take care of things, rule, deliberate, and live as human beings (353d3–10).
2	The eyes have an excellence, sight, and a defect, blindness, associated with seeing (353b6–7).	The soul has an excellence, righteousness, and a defect, unrighteousness, associated with human life (353e7–8).
3	Thus eyes insofar as sighted see well, while eyes insofar as blind see poorly (353b14–c5).	Thus souls insofar as righteous live well, while souls insofar as unrighteous live poorly (353e10–11).
4	[Thus with sighted eyes we do well as spectators; with blind eyes poorly.]	Thus with a righteous soul we live well as human beings; with an unrighteous soul poorly (353e10–11).
5	[If we have eyes that see well, we are successful as spectators; with eyes that see poorly we are failures as spectators.]	If we have a soul that lives well, we are successful as human beings, that is, happy; with a soul that lives poorly we are failures as human beings, that is, miserable (354a1–3).
6	[Thus the sighted are successful and the blind failures as spectators.]	Thus the righteous are happy and the unrighteous miserable as human beings (354a4–5).

unless external factors permit. When light is absent, eyes with perfect power of sight actually see no better than blind eyes. In the *Nicomachean Ethics* Aristotle stated the problem of external factors for souls. In addition to human excellence, he said, "happiness requires external goods . . . for it is impossible, or not easy, to do the things that matter when you lack resources. Many things are done with *tools*, as it were: with friends and wealth and political power" (1099a31–b2). Aristotle's point is that just as my power of sight is not enough, by itself, for me actually to see well, so too my power, however excellent, to be a friend, lover, husband, or father is not enough, by itself, for me to act as a friend, lover, husband, or father. Aristotle is certainly right that, no matter my personal ability, for me *to act well* as a member of any community is vulnerable to the lack of the appropriate community. The objection, then, is that the power of righteousness alone is no guarantee that I shall have the external resources appropriate to my talent.

Aristotle's objection fails. Righteousness, unlike vision, does not need such external goods. Each moment of human life gives us an opportunity to act righteously, whether we are among friends or in solitude, slave or

book 1 of the *republic*

free, rich or poor, healthy or ill, and whether external factors cause us fear or confidence, pain or pleasure. I suppose that Socrates, in reply to Aristotle's objection about external factors, would say about righteousness what he said in the *Laches* about bravery:

> I want to inquire . . . not only about those who are brave in war, but also those who are brave facing danger at sea, and those who face illness or poverty, or who are brave in community and political affairs, and not only those who are brave facing pain or fear, but also those who battle against desire or pleasure, both in enduring and in avoiding – for, I suppose, there are those who are brave in these sorts of things.
>
> 191c8–e2

There is a reason why righteousness is able to operate no matter what the circumstances. Unlike sight, which we can activate only when we possess eyes and are in light, we can activate righteousness, if we possess it, whenever our souls are in a position "to take care, rule, deliberate and live as human beings" (353d3–10, row 1 of table 12.1).

Elsewhere, Socrates draws a further consequence. Not only is righteousness the sort of thing we can activate regardless of external factors, we can also activate it, if we have it, regardless of our own inner identity. That is, a boy, an old man, and a woman can possess the very same human excellence as a manly man. Socrates draws this further conclusion – much to the surprise of the conventional-minded Meno – from the same premise about when we can activate righteousness, namely whenever we are "managing something that belongs to us" (73b1). Socrates points out that to manage with righteousness does not depend on the *what* but the *how*, not on the object managed but the manner of managing.

MENO: Socrates, it doesn't seem to me that human excellence is the same in the case of boys, old men, women, and men.

SOCRATES: What? Weren't you saying that the excellence of a man is to manage his city well, and for a woman, her household?

MENO: I was.

SOCRATES: Well, is it possible to manage one's city or household or anything else and to do it well without managing sound-mindedly and righteously?

MENO: Surely not.

SOCRATES: And to manage sound-mindedly and righteously is to manage by means of soundness of mind and righteousness?

MENO: Necessarily.

SOCRATES: Then both the woman and the man require the very same two things, if they are going to be good: righteousness and soundness of mind.

MENO: So it seems.

Meno 73a4–b5

happiness | 157

I take it, then, that Aristotle's objection to row 3 is right about vision: eyes insofar as sighted have the *power* to see well, but they do not *actually* see well unless external factors permit. But his objection has little application to righteousness, since a soul can activate righteousness whenever it has sufficient consciousness to manage anything. In an extreme case, a soul that is on a desert island, in solitary confinement, or in a body paralyzed by disease can manage, if nothing else, *itself*.

Such a soul *lives righteously* – that is, *lives excellently as a human being* – and so in some sense *lives well*. Yet does living well in that sense constitute *happiness*? Aristotle rejects Socrates' claim (at row 5 in the analogy) that merely to have a soul that lives well – that is, *excellently* in the sense of *righteously* – is sufficient for complete happiness:

> Human excellence by itself appears to be incomplete. For it seems possible for someone who possesses excellence to . . . suffer the worst luck. No one would call a man happy who was living thus, unless one were defending a thesis at all costs.
>
> 1095b31–1096a2

Human experience is that the worst luck – that is, such things as loss, pain, or untimely death – can happen to the righteous as well as the unrighteous, and that such luck diminishes or destroys the happiness of any human being. The only ones denying the truth of this experience, as it seems to Aristotle, are people who will say anything rather than admit they are wrong, people who will "defend a thesis at all costs."

Unable to accept Socrates' analogy at row 5 – that living *well* (in the sense of *righteously*) is living *happily* – many modern interpreters try to find a tame interpretation of Socrates' words. For example, one might interpret Socrates' words to mean that *righteousness will give us the happiest life possible in our circumstances* – although circumstances that include sufficient loss, pain, and death might mean the life is not happy but only somewhat less miserable than the alternatives – and that *whatever happens to a good man will be better than what would happen to a bad man in the same circumstances*. Most people find such a Socrates more plausible than the Socrates who says the words we actually find in the text.

Unlike these modern interpreters, ancient philosophers took Socrates at face value in his conclusion. Like Aristotle, some found his claim unbelievable. But others, persuaded either by his arguments or the example of his life, agreed. Indeed there were enough others in agreement to be classified as schools, the Cynics and Stoics. The Cynics and Stoics repeatedly give an athlete analogy in defense of the claim that the righteous are happy even in the worst circumstances.[1]

book 1 of the *republic*

In order to illustrate Socrates' argument, then, imagine athletes at the big game, and imagine someone who is ignorant of athletic sport watching them play. The non-athlete observes that the players are straining themselves to the very limits of their powers, and to the non-athlete this mental and physical strain look like suffering terrible misfortune. "No one would call a man happy who was living thus, unless he were maintaining a thesis at all costs," the non-athlete might say.

Such non-athletes presume that it is a universal human experience to prefer easy comfort to utmost exertion. This presumption is wrong. Athletes in sport value excellent performance and notice their sweating and fatigue only as factors to reckon with in their performance, not as misfortune. They are averse not to the strain of active performance but to the inactivity of sitting on a bench on the sidelines. The righteous are like such athletes, except that they value not athletic activity but the specific human activity that is righteousness.

There are objections to the athlete analogy. One objection is that athletes typically value other things besides athletic activity, such as victory, fame, and money. Although athletes might love the athletic activity itself, they also often perform as a means to other ends. No matter how excellent, such athletes might fail to gain these other ends, and in that case the more they love them, the more miserable they are. If the righteous are like such athletes, they might value in addition to righteous activity such things as wealth, health, community, family, and their lives. Yet no matter how excellent their righteous activity, they might fail to gain such other ends. In that case, the more they love them, the more miserable they are. Looked at this way, the athlete analogy shows the falsity of Socrates' conclusion: misfortune can destroy the happiness of the righteous just as it can destroy an athlete's happiness.

As I see it, the objection is right about people who value anything besides righteous activity. Righteous living, no matter how excellent, cannot prevent the loss of other things such people value: wealth, health, community, family, and life itself. Such deprivation will bring them misery. Even before misfortune deprives them, a bit of reflection on their vulnerability will bring them anxiety. If Socrates intends to reassure those of us who have a mind for other things besides righteousness, then his argument is a failure.

But this objection is harmless if we take Socrates in this argument to mean those who are *single-mindedly* righteous, that is, those who value nothing besides righteous activity. These are certainly those whom Socrates means in the *Apology*, where he requires single-mindedness not only of the righteous but of any man "of even a slight bit of value" – any such man ought not "calculate the risk of living or dying when he acts, but rather consider *this only*: whether he acts righteously or unrighteously" (28b7–9).

There is no mystery why poverty, illness, solitude, and even death do not bother the single-minded fanatic. Fanatics simply do not care. Likewise there is no mystery why such events do not bother the single-mindedly righteous. If righteous activity is their only concern, then what Aristotle, in the quote above, calls "suffering the worst luck" will not mar their happiness.

I attribute single-mindedness to the righteous people of Socrates' argument, like the single-mindedness of fanatics. Such single-mindedness saves Socrates from Aristotle's objection, but it raises a new worry. The single-mindedness of a fanatic is a deplorable unsoundness of mind. The new worry is that single-mindedness in a righteous person is likewise deplorable.

For example, Socrates' single-minded focus upon righteousness makes him seem deplorably like a fanatic in the *Crito*. Crito deplores Socrates' intention to submit to his death sentence.

> You do not seem right to me, Socrates, in what you intend to do, abandoning your life when you have the power to save it . . . and also abandoning your children. You have the power to finish their up-bringing and education, yet you would go away and desert them . . . Either one ought not to have children at all, or one ought to see their up-bringing and education through to the end.
>
> 45c5–d5

If Socrates felt conflict in his soul at these terrible consequences of his decision, most people would find it easier to admire his commitment to his principles. But there is no sign of distress or inner conflict in Socrates' reply to Crito's passionate speech or in the remainder of the dialogue. This complacency is a consequence of Socrates' single-mindedness. It looks like deplorable fanaticism, and we ought to be worried.

As I see it, the worry about Socrates' single-mindedness has two parts. There is worry that Socrates is neglecting his duties to his friends and loved ones. And there is worry that Socrates is somehow monstrous not to suffer in his own soul at the suffering of loved ones.

The nature of righteousness eliminates the first part of the worry. Expertise at righteousness will ensure that the single-mindedly righteous person fulfils all duties in the best possible way. We can ask no more of a human being. On the other hand, non-experts who are aware of their lack of expertise, like Socrates, ought always to be willing to re-examine the reasoning that leads to their actions. This is precisely what Socrates does in reply to Crito, saying that they "must consider whether or not to follow" Crito's advice (46b3–4). The remainder of his dialogue with Crito is just such a re-examination. Indeed the first priority for non-experts, a priority trumping all other alleged duties, is the duty to seek to understand how to live right (chapter 2). Such a priority distinguishes Socrates from the deplorable fanatic. It is deplorable to abandon your duties; it is not deplorable, when ignorant, to seek understanding of how best to fulfill your duties.

The nature of love eliminates the second part of the worry. As Socrates recognizes, there are two kinds of love (chapter 8). There is the needy love, for example, of a Romeo for Juliet. And there is the giving love of a Mother Teresa (let us idealize her for the sake of example). A Romeo must suffer horribly if he loses his Juliet. But Teresa, idealized, need not suffer as she gives to the needy around her. How does she do it? If her goal were to save more and ever more lives or souls, such a goal, ever unmet, would cause her enormous suffering. Such a goal might become overwhelming and incapacitating. An ideal Teresa would not have such a goal. Instead, at each moment she is satisfied to be serving her god precisely *in this act*, which is to alleviate the suffering of *this* person at *this* moment. The human object of her love is in no sense treated as a means. On the contrary, that human being's welfare is her single-minded focus. This way of caring for others does not seem evil to me, even though it is an action Teresa can perform with undiminished happiness.

Socrates is no Teresa. Teresa, as I idealize her, believes she benefits others by alleviating their bodily suffering with nursing and by alleviating their emotional suffering with a message of divine compassion. Socrates believes he benefits others by bringing them to desire wisdom as their first priority. Teresa, even when idealized, is also unlike Socrates in that her religious faith leaves her little patience for continual rational re-examination of the grounds of her life. In this respect, Teresa may have more difficulty than Socrates in eliminating the worry that her single-mindedness is deplorable fanaticism. Yet the two are alike in their single-minded focus on what they take to be righteous care or benevolence for others. Socrates shares with Teresa not only untroubled happiness but also admirable benevolence.

Let me summarize my discussion of Socrates' analogy at row 5. Socrates reasons that to have a soul that lives well is to be happy. Aristotle objects that merely living with an excellent soul is no guarantee against suffering the worst luck, that is, horrible circumstances that can destroy happiness. In considering this objection, I have recognized that righteous living will not guarantee happiness for people who value things other than righteousness itself, such as life, health, wealth, and prestige. But righteous living will be happiness for people who in their actions have a mind only for what is right to do. There is a worry about such single-minded people. They are deplorable when they neglect their duties, when they are unconcerned with the well-being of the human beings in their lives, or when they are unwilling to consider their own presuppositions. On my interpretation, Socratic righteousness is single-minded without being deplorable in any of these ways, and so Aristotle's objection to row 5 fails.

In the same passage where he refers to suffering "the worst luck," Aristotle raises a second objection, which applies to Socrates' conclusion at row 6 that the righteous are happy.

> Human excellence by itself appears to be incomplete. For it seems possible for someone who possesses excellence to be asleep, or inactive throughout life . . . No one would call a man happy who was living thus, unless he were maintaining a thesis at all costs.
>
> 1095b31–1096a2

Sleep might deprive a soul of consciousness. So might a coma or dementia. So will death. Deprived of consciousness or life itself, a soul cannot manage anything, no matter how righteous it is.

Certainly Aristotle is right that sleep, death, and other such factors *shorten* the activity of any human life. But no one would deny that a soul might live happily, just as it might live righteously, *so long as it actively lives*, whether that time be short or long.

But I think there is more to Aristotle's objection. To most people, a short happy life seems inferior to a long happy life. Best of all, in their judgment, would be *more and ever more* happy life. Even if we come to accept Socrates' remarkable conclusion that every conscious moment of a righteous life is happy, most people are unable to deny that the over-all value of such a life is diminished and harmed by being shortened. If two years of happiness is good, twenty would have been better, and ever more ever better. Socrates may have shown that the righteous are happy so long as they live, but a short or indeed any finite life nonetheless appears to be harmed by death.

Developed in this way, Aristotle's objection is self-defeating. The goal of ever more life would frustrate us all, since none of us can have it. Foreseeing the frustration, no reflective person could avoid anxiety even now. Yet length of life need not affect our happiness. The single-minded goal of *acting righteously at this moment*, not the goal of ever more life, makes human happiness invulnerable even to death. If Socrates is talking about the single-minded righteous, he is right to claim in the *Apology* that "nothing bad can happen to a good man, neither while living nor after death" (41d1–2).

note

1   See Epictetus *Discourses* 3.20, 3.22, 4.4; also Seneca, *On Providence* 2.

book 1 of the *republic*

further reading

Julia Annas, *The Morality of Happiness*. Oxford: Oxford University Press, 1993. The book examines the relationship of happiness to righteousness in the context of ancient Greek philosophy after Socrates.

George Rudebusch, *Socrates, Pleasure, and Value*. Oxford: Oxford University Press, 1999. Chapter 8 discusses this same argument of Socrates, following the text in more detail and considering alternate interpretations.

freedom

One reason why Thrasymachus praises *unrighteousness* is that, when successful, it leads people to take political power when they can and make it serve their own profit and interest at the expense of those they rule. Such power and mastery, he thinks, is human freedom. In contrast, he disparages *righteousness* as a condition of servitude to those in political power. Socrates refutes Thrasymachus by showing the servitude of such rulers and the freedom of the righteous.

Subordinated Actions

Thrasymachus is right to point out that many rulers in the real world do not rule in order to benefit those they rule but to profit themselves in ruling, say by making money. Such rulers subordinate their expertise at ruling to another expertise, moneymaking. Socrates argues that there is a necessary consequence: such rulers "do not willingly agree to rule" (346e7–9, a restatement of 345e6).

There is an objection to Socrates' consequence. The objection is that Socrates is ignoring an important distinction. Many workers have made great sacrifices, such as leaving their homelands and even risking their lives, in order to have the chance to work for pay. There is a difference between the wills of such workers and the wills of slave laborers. When I work for pay, I myself make the choice to work. When I am a slave, I do not have such a choice; my master makes that decision. Even if the master decided to pay me for my work as a slave, the difference remains: the slave does not get the same choice as the worker. Thus the worker enjoys a kind of freedom that the slave lacks.

The objection is right to say that the distinction between working for pay and slavery is significant. But it is wrong to suppose that it is the only significant distinction relevant to freedom and willing action. There is an equally important distinction, a distinction between actions that are means to other ends and actions that themselves are ends.

Hell, purgatory, and heaven are accurate images of the difference. As Dante describes it, hell is slavish suffering without hope of freedom

(*Inferno* 3). Those in purgatory suffer as slavishly, but *with* hope of escape (*Purgatorio* 3). This is why those in purgatory are of two minds: they want to be in purgatory – as a means to heaven – but they do not ultimately want to be there – because heaven, not purgatory, is their goal. Whereas in purgatory all actions are means to other ends, in heaven every action we take itself is the end (*Paradiso* 31). Since in heaven each action itself precisely *is* the goal and is not done for the sake of some *other* goal, those in heaven are single-minded.

Socrates distinguishes between rulers who do and do not "willingly agree to rule" (346e8–9). If the rulers who *willingly* agree to rule are those for whom the act of ruling is itself the goal, while those who *unwillingly* agree to rule are those for whom the act of ruling is a mere means, then Socrates here in the *Republic* is drawing an important distinction, a distinction between, as it were, heaven and purgatory.

Aristotle, who knew Plato's *Republic*, draws the same distinction in the opening chapter of his *Nicomachean Ethics*: "Some activities *are* their own goals, while other activities aim at goals apart from themselves" (1094a4–5). Karl Marx, who knew Aristotle's work, drew the same distinction between *alienated labor* and its implied contrast, *labor in the workers' paradise*.

> What constitutes the alienation of labor? Firstly, the fact that labor is external to the worker . . . that he, therefore, does not confirm himself in his work, but denies himself, feels miserable and not happy, does not develop free mental and physical energy, but mortifies his flesh and ruins his mind . . . His labor is, therefore, not voluntary but forced, it is forced labor . . . a mere means to satisfy needs outside itself. Its alien character is clearly demonstrated by the fact that as soon as no physical or other compulsion exists, it is shunned like the plague. External labor, labor in which man alienates himself, is a labor of self-sacrifice, of mortification.[1]

It misses the point, therefore, to object that Socrates ignores the distinction between the purgatory of working for pay and the hell of slavery. Thrasymachus holds up the actual rulers in our cities as models of heavenly life. About such rulers, Socrates says, "We must provide a payment to those intending to accept office, either money, prestige, or a penalty if they do not rule" (347a1–6). Socrates' point in calling such rule *unwilling* is that such rulers live in purgatory, not heaven.

Dramatic Images

At this very point in the philosophical conversation, the drama of *Republic* 1 gives us a beautiful contrast between the free and unfree human being.

Glaucon, who is part of the audience, breaks into the conversation precisely here to ask a question. He says that he understands how money and prestige are payments, but he does not understand the third type of "payment" for such rulers – the penalty (347a9). Socrates, before explaining what the penalty is, verifies something he and Glaucon already know: "You know, don't you, that to act from love of prestige or money is said to be and indeed *is* disgraceful?" Glaucon answers, "*I* at any rate know that!" (347b1–4).

Now Glaucon is not just any member of the audience; he is the one who bought and paid for Thrasymachus to teach them all what righteousness is. Before Thrasymachus would consent to teach them, Thrasymachus had required payment for teaching his companions what righteousness is, saying, "Pay money for it!" (337d8). And so Glaucon hired him on behalf of Socrates' companions: "Speak for the sake of money, Thrasymachus!" (337d10–11). Moreover, as Socrates relates, it was clear to the group that Thrasymachus also wanted prestige: "Thrasymachus clearly desired to speak in order to be celebrated" (338a6–7). I take it, then, that when Glaucon says, "*I* at any rate know it is disgraceful to act for love of prestige or money," he is contrasting himself with Thrasymachus. Unlike Glaucon, unlike the rest of the audience, and unlike Socrates, Thrasymachus in this dialogue is working for pay. The others choose this act of shared conversation as itself an end: it is what they love to do. For them, the conversation is a freely chosen end. And Socrates, ruling the conversation with his ingenious albeit inexpert questions, is the most free of all. Thus at the very point of the philosophical conversation where Socrates, with his contrast of willing and unwilling rulers, in effect distinguishes heavenly life from life in purgatory, Plato gives us, in Thrasymachus, a dramatic image of life in purgatory and, in Socrates, an image of heavenly life.

There are other points in the drama where the dialogue reminds us that Thrasymachus is a wage slave. For example, just after his lengthy speech in praise of unrighteousness, on the grounds that it is "stronger, freer, and more masterly than righteousness," Thrasymachus "had in mind to leave" – but was not free to do so: "His audience did not allow it, but compelled him to remain and provide an account of his words" (344c5–d5). Having been hired, Thrasymachus is unfree and weaker than his employer.

Later, Socrates asks Glaucon whether he is persuaded by Thrasymachus's thesis that the unrighteous have more profitable lives than the righteous. When Glaucon says no, Socrates negotiates with him, not Thrasymachus, on the proper form the ensuing conversation will need to take. He gives Glaucon a choice: either a speech opposed to Thrasymachus, which would leave the party in a state of lack, "needing someone else to serve as judge," or "forming agreements with each other

book 1 of the *republic*

at each step of the inquiry" (348b3), so that the conversation is sufficient of itself, empowering the party to be "both judges and advocates" (348b4). Glaucon's choice of the second course of action (348b7) is an image of how to choose free self-sufficiency in life.

Socrates does not need Thrasymachus's permission on the proper course to follow to produce an agreement. As soon as he has the decision from Thrasymachus's wage payer, Glaucon, Socrates simply gives Thrasymachus the command: "Go back to the beginning, Thrasymachus, and answer our questions" (348b8–9). Thus Thrasymachus, working for pay, is an image of the unfree, weak, and slavish in comparison to his free, strong masters. Indeed Thrasymachus recognizes and complains about his servile status, that he is not free to speak according to the method he pleases. His employers "do not allow him to speak" as he wills (350e6). Socrates' treatment of the employee Thrasymachus is especially striking when compared to his many delicate negotiations in the *Protagoras* (316c2–4, 317d1–3, 328e3–329c2, 334c8–336b3, 347b8–348c4, 351e8–9). In all those passages Socrates treats Protagoras with the respect appropriate to another free man, that is, a man who cannot be compelled but must be persuaded to speak and undergo cross-examination.

For Thrasymachus the conversation is good only as a means to other ends. Like the tyrants he praises, he is not doing what he wants, except, like those in purgatory, in his act of choosing servitude. For Socrates and Glaucon, in contrast, the conversation itself is the goal, chosen and enjoyed for its own sake. They live not in purgatory but in heaven.

Nietzsche's Objection

In the *Apology*, Socrates confirms that his conversations are heavenly. Imagining the possibility of afterlife, he says:

> The greatest pleasure would be to pass my time in examining and investigating the people there, as I do those here, to find out who among them is wise and who thinks he is when he is not . . . To converse and associate with them and examine them would be immeasurable happiness.
>
> 41b5–c4

It seems that Socrates is living a heavenly life, right before our eyes, in his dialogues.

Or is he? The *Apology* also suggests another point of view. If we accept what Socrates says, no human being knows how to live, and any life other than philosophy – the search for life's instruction manual, as it were – is guilty of negligence and forbidden as "not worth living"

(38a5–6, see chapter 2). Socrates might seem to condemn us to purgatory: we cannot begin ever to really live as human beings until we understand the manual. But it is worse than that. We never shall possess such know-how. In purgatory there is hope of eventual heavenly life, but if Socrates is correct, our human condition, far from being heavenly, is not even purgatory but rather a hopeless hell. Call this *Nietzsche's objection* to Socrates.

In *Twilight of the Idols*, "The Problem of Socrates," Nietzsche notices that Socrates makes *rationality* – to be more precise, philosophical conversation – mandatory for human beings. "It was not a matter of free choice for either Socrates or his 'invalids' to be rational – it was *de rigueur*, it was their only means" (§10). Nietzsche complains that Socrates is teaching us to enslave ourselves to self-improving work. For Nietzsche, the consequence of any such "improving morality" (§11 – Christianity is another star example for Nietzsche of an improving morality) is that *this life is not heaven*. Nietzsche believes that human life ought to be joyous and free, not debased in servitude. On the grounds that Socrates debases life – indeed teaches us to hate it and to seek death as a cure (see chapter 16) – Nietzsche condemns Socrates and every other "improving moralist" as part of the problem in human life, not part of the solution.

To reply to Nietzsche's objection, Socrates needs explanation. How can Socrates call an eternal life of cross-examination "immeasurable happiness" (41c4)? If we see Socratic philosophy as nothing more than self-interested calculation how best to live, we cannot explain its heavenly aspect. Socratic life would promise to be purgative of ignorance – but with no cure ever to come, in fact it would be hopeless hell. It would be as if philistines enrolled in college and took on the toil of study only because they needed to graduate in order to succeed in life, and then found out that they can never graduate, but must toil fruitlessly forever.

In replying to Nietzsche, then, we do better to refer to the immediate pleasure Socrates takes in his activity than to his rational calculations of self-interest. Certainly ignorance compels him to philosophize as the only life worth living, but – lucky for him – he happens to enjoy the life of cross-examination. His love of the activity makes it itself an end: heavenly fun, not hellish toil.

Socrates' love for his activity gives a better reply to Nietzsche's objection than his calculation of rational self-interest, but it is still incomplete. Nietzsche might well continue to object that to love such a life is perversely masochistic, a Socratic self-humiliation. Masochism, no matter how feverishly enjoyed, is not healthy and thus cannot be heavenly. For those concerned to live a healthy human life, Socrates as a contagion of a masochistic disease is still part of the problem, not part of the solution.

But Socrates has a reply to Nietzsche's continued objection. His reply is that the proper function for human beings is *the examining life*, that is, the life of philosophical cross-examination about the nature of human excellence (chapter 2). As our proper function, philosophy is not a debased, unworthy pursuit that we might masochistically happen to enjoy. As our proper function, the activity is not perverse but healthy in the deepest sense: it is the activity that gives meaning to our lives.

Timeless Life

It is remarkable that, while all the other dialogues that I have considered in this book have more or less definite dramatic dates, the dramatic setting of the first book of the *Republic* is different. It is impossible to assign it any date without "jarring anachronisms" (to quote Debra Nails, p. 324 – see the further reading list for chapter 3). Why is it impossible to assign a dramatic date to book 1 of the *Republic*? Perhaps Plato was careless in writing this dialogue, but it is also possible, and more charitable, to conjecture that he planned it so for a literary effect of timeless life.

As Aristotle notices in the *Nicomachean Ethics*, the experience of the pleasure of free play is timeless in that *it happens at no speed at all*, neither quickly nor slowly: "While it is possible to *get* pleased quickly, as one can get angry quickly, it is not possible to *be* pleased quickly" (1173a34–b1). Likewise Socrates in the *Republic* might *converse* quickly or slowly, but his *joy* in conversation happens at no speed at all, neither quickly nor slowly. This timelessness is an effect of action and goal being one and the same; for movement can only occur between two distinct points. The timeless quality of this dialogue reflects the timelessness of the Socratic life of freedom, a life that happens neither quickly nor slowly, because it is a union of act and goal.

note

1 From Karl Marx, *The Economic and Philosophic Manuscripts*. This is a 1974 translation by Gregor Benton, in *The Communist Manifesto*, by Karl Marx and Frederick Engels, ed. Philip Gasper (Chicago: Haymarket, 2005), p. 149.

further reading

George Rudebusch, "Pleasure," in Georgios Anagnostopoulos, ed., *A Companion to Aristotle*. Oxford: Blackwell, 2009. This chapter examines the relationship between freedom and pleasure in the context of Aristotle's philosophy.

the *euthyphro*

reverence

For religious readers, the question of religious excellence is of ultimate human importance. For secular readers, there is no point to the question. Secular readers usually see the point of a concern how to live a *righteous* life – that is, an upright or excellent life, but religious excellence – that is, *reverence* – is the specific concern how to live excellently *in the presence of the divine*, and secular readers usually sense no such presence and have no commitments to the supernatural.

The *Euthyphro* shows us, at age 70, a religious Socrates. For example, as an aside he says: "What the gods give to us is evident: we possess no good that they did not give" (14e11–15a2). Throughout Socrates' life he senses a divine presence guiding him with an uncanny sign, which Socrates follows as a matter of course (see chapter 9). The *Euthyphro* tells us that Socrates' extraordinary religious experiences were known to many in Athens. Euthyphro attributes Socrates' personal experience of divinity to be the reason why Meletus indicted Socrates for religious heresy (3b). Yet Socrates' train of questions about reverence in the *Euthyphro* lead to the conclusion that reverence does not require religious experience or supernatural commitments. It turns out that the human power to be reverent is nothing different from the goal of secular philosophy, namely, expertise at human well-being. Secular excellence is not an alternative to religious excellence but the very same thing.

To be clear, as chapter 7 shows, the dialogue itself reaches no conclusions about reverence. Every answer that Euthyphro proposes fails. Yet the dialogue challenges the existential reader to wonder what reverence is, and whether there is a successful way to answer Socrates' questions. In this chapter, I propose an answer – namely, that reverence is nothing but righteousness – and argue that no other answer is possible for a reverent person. Unlike the existential reader, the academic reader will simply want to know: What did Socrates believe about reverence? I answer the academic question at the end of this chapter.

Five Relations

Euthyphro has ideas about what reverence is. Most significantly, he tries to define it in terms of what is pleasing to the gods. When those ideas fail, Euthyphro is at a loss. Then Socrates takes the lead and asks Euthyphro to define reverence in relation to righteousness (11e–12d). It is this lead that I follow.

There are five possible relations between reverence and righteousness, that is, between religious and secular excellence. The first is that *nothing righteous is reverent, and nothing reverent is righteous*. The thought behind this answer might be that secular righteousness, like paying taxes to the state or apologizing to a neighbor I have wronged, and sacred duties, like tithing to a church or repenting to God from sin, have nothing to do with each other. The Euler diagram representing this answer contains two non-overlapping circles (see figure 14.1).

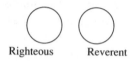

Righteous   Reverent

Figure 14.1   Nothing righteous is reverent, and nothing reverent is righteous

The second answer is that *some but not all righteous items are reverent, and some but not all reverent items are righteous*. The thought behind this answer might be that there are clear examples of purely secular duties, perhaps such as paying taxes. And there are also some purely religious duties, such as tithing. But in addition this answer recognizes that some duties are commanded by both secular and sacred authorities, such as, perhaps, the duty not to rob temples. Because of such cases, the diagram for this answer contains overlapping circles (see figure 14.2).

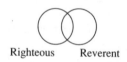

Righteous   Reverent

Figure 14.2   Some but not all righteous items are reverent, and some but not all reverent items are righteous

The third answer is that *everything righteous is reverent, but some reverent items are not righteous*. The thought behind this answer might be that to live righteously among human beings is a divine command. The Bible's Ten Commandments seem to imply this answer. Since all ten are divine commands, our obedience to all ten is a matter of

the *euthyphro*

reverence. Some of these commandments tell us how to revere the divine *directly*: to worship Yahweh above all and without images, to make proper use of his name, and to observe the Sabbath. (As Roman Catholics and Lutherans count, these are the first *three* commandments, while according to Jewish, Orthodox, and most Protestant religions these are the first *four* commandments.) The remaining six (or seven) commandments tell us how to revere God *by righteous human life* – that is, to honor our parents and not to murder, commit adultery, steal, bear false witness, or covet. Taken together, therefore, the Ten Commandments seem to make righteousness a part of reverence, as shown in figure 14.3.

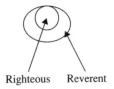

Righteous   Reverent

Figure 14.3   Everything righteous is reverent, but some reverent items are not righteous

The fourth answer is that *everything reverent is righteous, and everything righteous is reverent.* The thought behind this answer might be that God commands us to do good to other human beings and gives us no further commands. On this view, every secular duty is commanded by God, but there are no exclusively sacred duties, so that the diagram for this answer is the same circle for both the righteous and the reverent (see figure 14.4).

Righteous = Reverent

Figure 14.4   Everything reverent is righteous, and everything righteous is reverent

The fifth answer is that *everything reverent is righteous, but some righteous items are not reverent.* The thought that might lead to this answer is that righteousness is not restricted to living *among human beings* – righteousness concerns *everything* one ought to do as a human being. This is how I think of righteousness and how I first introduced it in this book (chapter 2). In that case how a human being ought to behave towards the gods, that is, reverence, will be a mere part of what is righteous, while behavior towards other human beings is the other part. The diagram for this answer makes the reverent a part of the righteous (see figure 14.5).

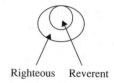

Righteous   Reverent

Figure 14.5 Everything reverent is righteous, but some righteous items are not reverent

Socrates asks Euthyphro about the relation between reverence and righteousness in two steps. First he asks: "See whether it seems necessary to you that everything that is reverent is righteous." "It does," says Euthyphro (11e4–5). Evidently Euthyphro thinks of righteousness the same way I do, that is, as encompassing everything we ought to do as human beings.

By agreeing, Euthyphro has rejected the first three answers and must endorse the fourth or fifth answer: either the very same things are both reverent and righteous, or some things are righteous but not reverent. (Although the dialogue never explicitly considers the first three answers, I find reasons to rule them out below.)

The first step leaves open whether Euthyphro gives the fourth or fifth answer. As a second step, Socrates asks Euthyphro to choose between the fourth and fifth answers: "Then is everything that is righteous also reverent? Or is everything reverent righteous, but not everything righteous reverent – rather, some of it is reverent and some is not" (11e7–12a2). Socrates gives examples that suggest the fifth answer (see chapter 7). Euthyphro agrees with the suggestion, saying it "seems right" (12d4).

Service to the Gods

Having selected the fifth answer, Euthyphro gives the following account of reverence: "This is the part of the righteous that is reverent and holy, Socrates: the part that is service in relation to the gods, and the remaining part of the righteous is service in relation to human beings" (12e5–8). Euthyphro's account is promising, and Socrates says that it "seems well said" (12e9). Socrates asks Euthyphro for more precision, pointing out that many kinds of service, such as of doctors to patients or of therapists to clients, aim to improve the object served. The examples Socrates gives are the services animal trainers provide to animals, such as to horses, dogs, and oxen (13a–b).

Euthyphro and Socrates agree that the reverent human does not aim by reverence to improve the gods in the way that a therapist or trainer improves a client or pet (13a–d). Most people are willing to agree. In my experience, even atheists tend to give a hypothetical agreement ("if there were a god . . ."). But there is a skeptical objection. I sometimes hear people say that part of the purpose of human worship is in some way to sustain or validate God's existence, somewhat as human speech can sustain or validate the existence of a language. Given the diversity of conceptions of the gods, the human intellect appears to be unable to discover evidence to eliminate the metaphysical option that there are gods who need improvement from human beings. Such diversity seems to require skepticism about the nature of God.

A successful reply appeals to the skeptic's reverence. Given indecisive evidence for two options – imperfect or perfect gods – we would be mean-spirited and less reverent to assume the gods are imperfect, while we would be generous and more reverent to assume they are perfect. In the same way, if from the evidence before me I can consistently draw either a cynical or a generous conclusion about your actions, charity requires me to interpret you in the best possible way. I admit that a purely academic skeptic, that is, a skeptic freed from overriding human concerns, will be unmoved by appeals to reverence. But we human beings have an overriding concern to succeed in human life, and this existential concern requires us to be as reverent as possible in the presence of the divine, just as we ought to be as charitable as possible in the presence of our human associates. I interpret Euthyphro and Socrates to have practical human concerns in their dialogue, and accordingly I approve their answer. Moreover, governed myself by practical human concerns, I concur with their answer: if there are gods, reverence cannot be a service aiming to improve them as if they were in need of benefit.

Accordingly, Euthyphro makes his account more precise: the service we give to the gods is not like service that benefits or improves the gods (13c), but like "service that slaves give to masters" (13d5–6). Socrates says, "I understand: it would be a *subordinate* service to the gods," and Euthyphro replies "Very much so" (13d7). What Euthyphro has in mind seems in agreement with Biblical commands to serve God (Deut. 10:12), to be in slave-servitude to God (Rom. 6:22), or to be slaves to God (1 Peter 2:16). A more attractive image for modern readers is Jesus' theme in the Sermon on the Mount to act as *children* of God, but the point that we are to *be obedient to God* seems the same with both the slave and the child images.

There is an objection that *Euthyphro is forgetful* in giving the slavery account of reverence. As interpreters, we might propose the following reasoning: *When a god acts successfully, then the god is benefited. Thus when my obedience contributes to a god's successful action, I am benefiting the god. Thus my slave service to the gods tends to benefit or improve them. But Euthyphro has just agreed that our service* cannot *benefit or improve the gods. So Euthyphro must have forgotten his agreement!* This reasoning, although it is consistent with the text, interprets Euthyphro as stupid. As it happens, there is an alternative interpretation that fits the text just as well, but is more charitable to Euthyphro.

The forgetful-Euthyphro objection assumes that whenever a god acts successfully, it was in a prior state in which it could be improved. Such an assumption not only implies that Euthyphro is stupid; it also proves that any obedience to any god shows that the commanding god is imperfect. Indeed, the reasoning shows it is impossible for a perfect god to act. It would be surprising to be able so easily to show the incoherence of the very idea of a perfect, active being.

There is a way in which a master or parent may act without being in need of improvement or benefit. Sometimes people act from need, but they may also act freely. For example, someone might as well race a chariot *for fun* as from a need to earn money or a prize. Again, a doctor might heal *as a free gift* as well as for pay. Alas, it seems to be our doom as human beings to act for most or all of our lives from necessity rather than freely. But we ought not to imagine the gods to be so desperate, even if they command us as masters or parents do. (Chapter 13 draws the distinction between needy and free action.)

Thus there is also a way in which a slave or child might obey a freely acting commander without benefiting or improving the commander. Sometimes commanders may seek obedient action from slaves and children because they themselves seek some benefit or improvement from the servant. But a command to obey does not require the commander to be in a prior state of need. Many people train and command horses and dogs for fun or as a free gift. Parents and masters may do the same. Imagine a father who races chariots for fun. He might be perfectly able to hold the reins himself yet ask his son to take them. I suppose that such a father's motive with this request is *to give something good to his son*, that is, to give his son pleasure or training. Likewise a doctor might command a slave to diagnose or prescribe to the doctor's patient, not because the doctor needs help but in order *to give something good to the slave*, such as training.

We need not assume that Euthyphro contradicts himself by suggesting that our relationship to the gods is one of slave service. Euthyphro agrees with Socrates' statement that the reverent human does not aim by reverence to improve the gods as a therapist or trainer improves a client or pet (13a–d, reaffirmed at 15a). And Euthyphro does not find it surprising or disagreeable when Socrates says that what the gods give is obvious to everyone, that every good thing we have is a gift from the gods (15a1–2). Therefore when Euthyphro specifies that the kind of service the reverent give to the gods is like the service of slaves to masters, we should interpret Euthyphro to be turning the trainer/animal relationship around, in effect saying that our reverence makes us like animals in relation to benevolent divine trainers or commanders who act freely, not from need. With such an interpretation, I dismiss the forgetful-Euthyphro objection as unnecessary and uncharitable.

Socrates has a further question for Euthyphro. It takes skill to serve in obedience, for example, to hold the reins of a chariot or to diagnose a patient. The skill of holding reins aims to control the steeds; diagnosing aims to identify illness. Even bestial obedience requires rudimentary skill at such things as recognizing commands, heeling, or fetching. Accordingly, Socrates' further question is to the point: "What does service to the gods aim to achieve? . . . What is that single all-good goal that the gods are achieving, using us as servants?" (13e6–11).

Euthyphro gives two answers. His answers are true but vacuous. The first answer is that the gods achieve "many fine things" (13e12). Every reverent person will agree. But, as Socrates points out: "So do generals . . . and farmers" (14a1–5) and indeed every expert! Socrates is right to be dissatisfied with Euthyphro's answer and to repeat his question: as generals achieve many fine things under the heading of *victory in war*, and farmers achieve many fine things under the heading *food from the land*, under what heading are the many fine things that the gods achieve with us as their subordinates? Euthyphro's second answer is that the many fine things reverence achieves in word and deed are under the heading *gratifying to the gods* (14b). Socrates is right to be dissatisfied with this answer, too. One problem with this answer is that it is as vacuous as the first. If the gods are generals, then I gratify them by work under the heading *victory in their war*. If the gods are farmers, then I gratify them under the heading *growing their food*. The same could be said for any expertise, and so this answer tells me nothing substantial about what reverence is. Euthyphro's answers, being vacuous, are failures.

Other answers to Socrates' question are that reverence aims *to love, glorify, revere,* or *obey God.* But these answers, while true, are all as vacuous as Euthyphro's. If God is a general, I love, glorify, revere, and obey him by knowing how to help him achieve *victory in his war*; if God is a farmer, by knowing how to help him *grow his food.* If I do not know what it is that God commands me to do, then telling me to love, glorify, obey, or revere God is not helpful.

Jesus' Answer

Jesus gives an example of a helpful answer to Socrates' question in his account of the Last Judgment.

When the Son of Man comes in his glory, and all the angels with him, he will sit on his glorious throne. All the nations will be gathered before him; and he will separate them from one another, as the shepherd separates the sheep from the goats; and he will put the sheep on his right, and the goats on the left.

The king will say to those on his right, "Come, you who are blessed of my father, inherit the kingdom prepared for you from the foundation of the world. For I was hungry, and you gave me something to eat; I was thirsty, and you gave me something to drink; I was a stranger, and you invited me in; naked, and you clothed me; I was sick, and you visited me; I was in prison, and you came to me."

The righteous will answer him, "Lord, when did we see you hungry, and feed you, or thirsty, and give you something to drink? And when did we see you a stranger, and invite you in, or naked, and clothe you? When did we see you sick, or in prison, and come to you?"

The king will answer and say to them, "Truly I say to you, to the extent that you did it to one of these brothers of mine, even the least of them, you did it to me."

Then he will also say to those on his left, "Depart from me, accursed ones, into the eternal fire which has been prepared for the devil and his angels; for I was hungry, and you gave me nothing to eat; I was thirsty, and you gave me nothing to drink; I was a stranger, and you did not invite me in; naked, and you did not clothe me; sick, and in prison, and you did not visit me."

They also will answer, "Lord, when did we see you hungry, or thirsty, or a stranger, or naked, or sick, or in prison, and did not take care of you?"

He will answer them, "Truly I say to you, to the extent that you did not do it to one of the least of these, you did not do it to me."

These will go away into eternal punishment, but the righteous into eternal life.

Matt. 25:31–46

Jesus' account of the Last Judgment gives us explicit necessary and sufficient conditions for heavenly reward and therefore for reverence: one loves God if and only if one loves human neighbors, where *to love human neighbors* means *to give food and drink to the hungry and thirsty, to welcome strangers, to clothe the naked, to visit the sick and imprisoned.* I take it that the feeding, welcoming, clothing, and visiting in turn mean, to put it under a single heading, *to give good things to our neighbors as human beings.*

Jesus' account of reverence, identifying the divine self with my human neighbors, is wild. Even studious Christians tend to tame these wild words. Unlike my lower-case translation, the *New American Standard* translation capitalizes as follows: "To the extent that you did it to one of these brothers of Mine, even the least of them, you did it to Me." The translators capitalize in this way as a reverent expression of their

Christian reverence to Jesus. This capitalization tames Jesus' words, because it distinguishes Jesus from his human brothers, as if you can honor one without honoring the other. But Jesus in this very passage unequivocally identifies treatment of human neighbors as *the one and only way* to be reverent. A capitalizing translator who does not tame Jesus' account of reverence would write: "To the extent that you did it to one of These Brothers of Mine, even the Least of Them, you did it to Me." Of the capitalizing translations I have seen, not one capitalizes in accordance with Jesus' wild parable.

There is nothing wild in the religious thought that God commands us to act righteously to our human associates. What is wild is to say *that is all* that God requires. On Jesus' account of the Last Judgment, reverence to God is nothing more than righteousness to human beings. Thus Jesus endorses the fourth relation, identifying the righteous and the reverent.

Is Jesus' answer correct? We can prove him wrong by distinguishing service to God, in at least some actions, from service to human beings. The Ten Commandments, Euthyphro, and capitalizing translators of scripture all appear to draw such a distinction. For example, the Ten Commandments appear to give us specific god-related commandments: to worship Yahweh above all and without images, to make proper use of his name, and to observe the Sabbath.

There are two ways to accept these commandments. The first way sees us as somehow *benefiting God* when we worship and speak of him and observe the Sabbath. Perhaps God really is in need of a good reputation among human beings. But, as I argued above, it is irreverent to think of him in such need! So I take it that this way of thinking about the god-related Commandments would be unacceptable to us insofar as we desire to be reverent human beings. The second way sees God as *benefiting us* with his commands, as a trainer might benefit an animal or a master a slave (again, as I argued above). According to this way, the reason why God would command us to worship him above all else is because it would harm us – not God – to worship statues or money or prestige as if they were of ultimate value. Likewise the reason why we should use Yahweh's name properly and remember the Sabbath is because an improper use of the god's name or of his ritual days would put at risk our attitude towards God as supremely valuable in our lives, with damaging consequences for humanity, not God. It is not my point in this paragraph to defend the authority of the Ten Commandments. My point is that reverent people who accept their authority must read them in the second way, not the first.

I use the Ten Commandments only as an illustration. There are scriptural traditions outside of the Bible, with similar commands relating, as it seems, purely to how to treat the divine. As it seems to me, reverent people of any such religious tradition must see all such commandments in the second way, that is, as directed to human, not divine, benefit. The reverent see them this way because the alternative is to see God as in need and imperfect. Thus there can be no acts that directly serve divinity; we serve divinity only by serving humanity.

There is one other attempt to distinguish service to God from service to human beings: perhaps there are some purely righteous acts that are not therefore reverent. One way to make this attempt is to suggest that what is righteous in the eyes of human beings might not be reverent in the eyes of God. For example, suppose that God sometimes requires (or always forbids) capital punishment. Then any nation that always forbids (or sometimes permits) capital punishment will be righteous but not reverent! It seems to me that this way fails. It mistakes a distinction between *the conventional and the true* for *the righteous and the reverent*. Conventional righteousness and reverence is in our eyes; true righteousness and reverence is in divine or expert eyes.

Another way to attempt to distinguish service to God from service to human beings is to suggest that some righteous acts are too trivial to be reverent. For example, one might suggest that *keeping off the grass* is righteous but not reverent. But I judge this way to fail, too. It mistakes a distinction between *trivial and significant* for a distinction between *righteous and reverent*. If keeping off the grass is trivial, it is neither righteous nor reverent; if significant, it is both.

Since I cannot find a distinctively righteous or a distinctively reverent action, it seems to me that Jesus' teaching in the Last Judgment is correct: reverence and righteousness are the very same. We ought to reject every diagram about the relation between reverence and righteousness except the diagram that draws one and the same circle for both powers.

Euthyphro's Failure

Unlike Jesus, Euthyphro failed to define correctly the relation of reverence to righteousness. He failed because he assumed that service to the gods, in at least some aspects, is distinct from our righteous treatment of other human beings. Euthyphro might not have failed had he reflected upon some of his own statements about reverence. For example, in his first attempt to define reverence, Euthyphro says:

> Reverence is doing what I am doing now, prosecuting *him who acts unrighteously*, who commits murder or steals from the temples or does any such thing, whether he be your father, or your mother or anyone else – and not prosecuting him is irreverent. And, Socrates, see what a sure proof I offer you – a proof I have already given to others – that this is established

and correct and that we ought not to let *him who acts irreverently* go unpunished, no matter who he may be.

5d8–e5 (my emphasis)

In this passage Euthyphro talks about *the one acting unrighteously* and *the one acting irreverently* as if they were interchangeable. And he talks about <u>reverence</u> as if it were interchangeable with <u>established and correct</u> action, that is, righteous action. Thus, between the italicized and underlined words, this passage in effect gives us a double equation of reverence and righteousness. Again, in his last attempt to define reverence, Euthyphro calls it the knowledge how to speak and act in prayer and sacrifice, that is, *the knowledge of what to ask from and what to offer to the gods.* Referring to this knowledge, he says that it "is reverence, which preserves individual families and states; and the opposite . . . is irreverent, which overturns and destroys everything" (14b4–7). Surely the business of reverence, to preserve family and state, is one and the same as the business of righteousness. If so, the identity of righteousness and reverence follows: the knowledge how to benefit human society is the very same as knowledge how to live before the gods.

The philosophical interest of the *Euthyphro* is Socrates' line of questions, questions which challenge us to develop a sustainable account of how a human ought to live before the gods. The questioning leads to no conclusion: Euthyphro's definitions of reverence all fail to survive Socrates' examination. I have argued that, although Euthyphro failed, it is possible to give a successful answer to Socrates' question.

Socrates' Answer

In contrast to the philosophical question – *What is reverence?* – is the biographical question, *What did Socrates believe reverence is?* In the *Protagoras*, Socrates plainly tells us: "I myself would say, on my own behalf, that righteousness is a reverent thing and reverence is a righteous thing . . . and I would say that these are surely either the same thing or else righteousness is as similar as can be to reverence" (331b1–5).

Thus Socrates and Jesus agree about the general point that reverence and righteousness are practically the same thing. But the two do not agree about the specifics of righteousness. According to his account of the Last Judgment, Jesus thinks that we give good things to human beings by doing such things as *feeding, welcoming, clothing, and visiting them.* In contrast, Socrates thinks we give good things to human beings with *the act of philosophical conversation* in order to make them aware of their ignorance of human well-being, so that philosophy becomes their first priority. Philosophical investigation is not an alternative to social work but primary social work: it is the primary way to welcome and visit a human being, the primary way to nourish and clothe the soul. Socrates neglects non-philosophical visits and material food as secondary not because he is heartless but because he is ignorant. He does not know when such things are more beneficial to human beings than starvation, nakedness, closed doors, or solitude (as I argue in chapter 2).

further reading

Mark L. McPherran, *The Religion of Socrates*. University Park: Pennsylvania State University Press, 1996. Chapter 2 examines the *Euthyphro*, while chapter 5 discusses Socrates' religious beliefs.

the *euthyphro*

the *crito*

world religion

I have interpreted Plato's account of Socrates' life, from his mastery of the "wisest man", Protagoras, at age 36 to his death sentence at age 70. My interpretation has defended Socrates' wild conclusions:

- No human being knows how to live.
- Bravery, benevolence, righteousness, reverence, the best sort of luck – even the ability to interpret the most divine poetry – are all one and the same thing: expertise at human well-being.
- Such expertise by itself would requite the needy love of any human being, rule the soul without inner conflict, and ensure happiness and freedom.
- Lacking that expertise, we are guilty of the worst sort of negligence if we do not spend our lives trying to discover it – better not to live at all!

These conclusions make Socratic philosophy unique in all history. But there are other more general themes in Socratic philosophy about righteousness and human salvation. These themes, like the specific conclusions above, are opposed to conventional thinking. Socrates shares these themes with the great religions of the Chinese, Indian, and Abrahamic traditions. These shared themes show that Socrates proposed a religion worthy of the world, although distinct from others in its sacrament – not fire, water, bread, or wine, but philosophical cross-examination. My goal in this chapter is to present Socratic philosophy as a world religion, using the *Crito* to identify five Socratic themes. These themes, though opposed to conventional thinking, are shared by world religions.

Five Socratic Themes

1 Excellent human life is not a means but an end

Between Socrates' trial and execution there was a month's imprisonment. In that time, his old and dear friend Crito – the same man Socrates will entrust with his last wishes – comes to him. Crito can easily arrange to get Socrates out of jail and safely into exile. To persuade Socrates, he asks him to consider the loss his friends will suffer of his irreplaceable and beloved companionship, as well as harm to their reputation – since people will think they were too cowardly to save Socrates – and also to consider obligations Socrates has to nurture his young children (44b–45d).

Crito's argument

Crito treats his conversation with Socrates as the only means to a desired goal: saving Socrates' life. He is urgent in his persuasion, because he is bound by the necessity of his circumstances. In contrast, Socrates is an image of freedom, just as he was in the *Republic*. Master of the conversation, yet not coercing Crito, Socrates leads him to "consider the matter in the most measured way" (46c6), that is, by Socratic question and answer, an activity that is Socrates' "heart's desire" (46d4). Socrates does what he ought to do, but his free choice of the activity that he loves doing illustrates the first theme, a man freely doing an action for its own sake. This is how human beings ought to live.

People often think that human life needs a purpose beyond itself, such as service to humanity or God or, more modestly, to its own future security. Perhaps this is true, and our actions give our lives meaning when they aim to serve some other end. As I interpret him, Socrates assumes the opposite in his accounts of happiness and freedom (chapters 12 and 13): each human life and each act of life ought to be an end itself, not a means. Jesus makes a similar point: "The Sabbath was made for man, and not man for the Sabbath" (Mark 2:27), and likewise Confucius says, "The gentleman is not a utensil" (2.12).[1] A person whose acts are themselves ends is not trying to get to an external goal, which explains why it is the mark of a good man for Confucius that "he never takes a short-cut walking" (6.14). In the same way, Krishna teaches the reluctant human warrior Arjuna:

purpose no to a God

> You are indeed entitled to the action, but never to its external goals.
> Never let the external goals of action be your motive.
>
> 2.47

motivation → where should it come from?

2 The proper end of human life is nothing but righteous activity

Socrates elicits from Crito that "to live well and to live righteously are the very same thing" (48b8). "It follows that the question to consider is whether the attempt to escape is righteous or not . . . This is the only thing to consider . . . If we should prove to be acting unrighteously, there is no need to take into account whether any other suffering matters more than acting unrighteously, even if to stay peacefully means death" (48b11–d5). There can be no clearer statement of the second theme.

People often recognize that righteousness can be the means whereby we best attain the goals of everyday life – as if the goals of everyday life, like finding comfort and satisfying physical desires, are the real value of life, while righteousness happens to be a useful tool. The opposite Socratic theme is that the act of seeking comfort in everyday life is valuable only as an opportunity to do righteousness.

Likewise Confucius says, "Gentlemen cherish moral excellence" – no doubt using their property as an opportunity for that end – "while petty men cherish their property" (4.11) – no doubt subordinating moral behavior to that end. He also says, "The gentleman eats without seeking a full belly and lodges without seeking comfort" (1.14). I interpret this statement by comparing the lover of righteousness with the lover of Juliet. In the presence of Juliet, Romeo certainly continues to eat meals and to lodge for shelter. But, like the Confucian gentleman, he does not eat to fill his belly or look for comfort when he lodges. Rather, the meal and the lodge are opportunities to enjoy the presence of his beloved. Confucius is no romantic, but just as Romeo's love converts an ordinary meal into a heavenly encounter with Juliet, so does the gentleman's excellence convert a meal into a heavenly ritual of shared humanity. Both Romeo and the gentleman might use the traditions of courtesy to make the conversion, the romantic celebrating beloved beauty and the righteous celebrating the humanity of the company at the meal. Thus Confucius can predict the behavior of the gentleman:

> If a gentleman abandons *humaneness* [*rén* 仁, discussed in chapter 1], how can he fulfill that name? A gentleman will not, for the space of a meal, depart from humaneness. In haste and flurry, he always adheres to it; in fall and stumble, he always adheres to it."
>
> 4.5

In the same way, Krishna commands the warrior, "Always do what ought to be done *unattached*" (3.19). That is, do *what ought to be done* – that is, righteousness – not for the sake of any external goal but as itself an end. And Jesus says, "No one can serve two masters; for either he will hate the one and love the other, or he will be devoted to one and despise the other. You cannot serve God and wealth" (Matt. 6:24).

3 Righteous actions are holy sacrament

Socrates brings a divine presence into his conversation with Crito. He personifies the Laws of the city of Athens, bringing them into the conversation to speak and ask questions (50a). "Brothers" to the laws governing the afterlife (54c6), the Laws "make covenants" with the citizens of Athens (50c5, 52e2), gave life to Socrates and his ancestors and provided for his upbringing and education (50d), making Socrates and his ancestors their "descendents and servants" (50e3–4). Evidently the Laws are divine beings, who converse with Crito and Socrates in the dialogue. Socrates says he hears their voices in the same paranormal way that religiously ecstatic dancers hear music (54d). The personification of the Laws illustrates the third theme, that Socrates' act of conversation with Crito has the function of linking them to a divine presence. This function makes the conversation a holy sacrament. Socrates' final words of the dialogue emphasize how it links them to the divine presence: ✳"God is leading the way, *right before us*" (54e2).

While it is conventional to draw distinctions between secular righteousness and holy reverence, Socratic argument leads to the same wild conclusion that Jesus preaches in the parable of the Last Judgment (chapter 14): acts promoting human well-being are the proper way to worship God. Jesus' Treasure Parable (chapter 5) is an image of the religious transfiguration of ordinary duty into holy ritual. When a farmer discovers hidden treasure in his fields, land that used to be a place to labor for sustenance becomes a fount of luxury. It is likely that Jesus was inspired by the Hebrew prophet who proclaimed that religious sacrifices apart from righteousness are unacceptable to God, while righteousness by itself – so long as it is "a never-failing stream" – is acceptable (Amos 5:24).

Likewise, a dominant theme in the Qur'an is that only single-minded devotion to righteousness puts us in God's presence.

> He who is truly conscious of God . . .
> Spends his possessions [on others] so that he might grow in purity
> – Not as payment for favors received,
> But only out of a longing for the countenance of his Sustainer,
>   the All-Highest.[2]

And Krishna commands Arjuna to do his battlefield duty "as an act of ritual sacrifice," since any other purpose leaves "this world's actions in bondage" (3.9). Asked about *humaneness* (*rén* 仁), Confucius says it is ✳ "to treat people in the way one handles a great holy sacrament" (12.2).

4 The happiness of the righteous human being is invulnerable

Socrates' single-minded focus upon righteousness makes his life invulnerable to misery. Human beings who value righteousness *and something else to be gained as its external goal*, such as the life of a friend, are insecure in their happiness. Crito is an illustration. The dialogue begins before dawn, when Socrates wakes up in his cell. Crito has already been sitting beside him for a "fairly long time" (43a10), and he explains why. The prospect of Socrates' death has him in a state of "grief and sleeplessness" (43b4). Not so Socrates: Crito is amazed to see "how sweetly" he was sleeping (43b5).

It is conventional to honor righteousness yet to notice that it is often at odds with one's own happiness to such a degree that it is proverbial that "nice guys finish last." In contrast, Socrates explicitly argues that the righteous must be happy and says that the good man cannot be harmed in life or death (chapter 12). Likewise David sings that so long as "Yahweh is my shepherd, I lack nothing" (Psalm 23:1). Krishna tells Arjuna that "staying in the yoke" of single-minded devotion to duty wins the "treasure" of equanimity, come what may:

> Staying in that yoke do your duty,
> O Treasure-winner, letting go of attachment
> and becoming the same in success and failure.
> The attribute of that yoke is equanimity."
>
> 2.48

According to Confucius, the power of the good man is such that he can say, "I have virtue from heaven; no emperor can harm me" (7.23), while to live for the sake of goals external to our actions is a path of misery; the "goal of profit and business" causes "many nights of anguish" (4.12).

5 The righteous are untroubled by death

The *Crito* shows Socrates untroubled by the prospect of death, as the *Phaedo* shows him mindful of one thing only, righteousness, in the act of dying. It is conventional to fear death as an evil. Both the *Crito* and the *Phaedo* (see chapter 16) portray Socrates as untroubled because of his philosophical nature. Likewise world religions take the trouble from death. David sings to his god, "Though I walk through the valley of the shadow of death, I fear no evil, for you are with me" (Psalm 23:4). Confucius says about heaven's way of righteousness, "If at dawn you learn of and tread the way, you can face death at dusk" (4.8). Krishna assures Arjuna that if he establishes his life as righteous duty performed as sacred rite, then just as in the rest of his life "also at the time of death he attains divine bliss" (2.72).

Fairy Tale and Poem

It is conventional to think of righteousness and service to God as like athletic competition, that is, an action done *as a means*, for the sake of some kind of victory. The scriptures of world religions are unconventional to conceive righteousness not as a means but as the end. A fairy tale and poem are my final illustrations. Hans Christian Andersen tells the tale of a little mermaid who had a beautiful voice but trades it away for love. In the end, transfigured into a kind of divine being, she recovers the power to speak, now with an ethereal voice that no earthly music could imitate. With such a voice (to go a bit beyond the fairy tale), this being might now enter into conversation simply *to delight in the power of using her divine voice.* The poet Emily Dickenson, who recognizes that "to be alive and Will" is to be "able as a God," might enter into conversation, as she enters into other human acts, simply *to delight in living and willing.*

Such a mermaid and such a poet are not conversing as a means to something else, but because *each moment of the conversation itself is heavenly perfection,* a way to enjoy godlike power. Likewise Socratic conversation is a godlike power. Socratic conversation is ethereal music; it is being alive and willing, and it is more: righteous communion with others in the presence of the gods.

notes

1 All quotes from Confucius are from the *Analects*, all quotes from Krishna are from the *Bhagavadgita*.
2 Chapter (or *Surah*) 92, verses 17–20. This translation is from *The Message of the Quran*, Muhammad Asad (Chicago: Kazi, 1980).

further reading

Paul Woodruff, *Reverence*. Oxford: Oxford University Press, 2002. The book defends the importance of reverence as a human excellence.

the *crito*

the *phaedo*

last words

Swan Song

The *Phaedo* gives us an account of Socrates' death day. To his already-grieving friends Socrates describes himself as like a dying swan in his religious service, prophetic skill, and joyful spirit.

> *You* probably think that in prophetic skill I am inferior to swans. They, when they perceive that they must die, although having sung their whole life, do then sing mightiest and best, rejoicing that they are about to go away into the presence of the god whose servants they are . . . Because they belong to Apollo, they have prophetic powers; and foreseeing the good things in Hades they on that day above all others sing and are glad. But *I* suppose myself to be in the same service as the swans, dedicated to the same god, to have the prophetic skill from our master no less than swans, and to be released from life no less dispirited.
>
> 84e4–85b7

The legend that swans sing at death must already have been known in Athens in 458 BCE, when Aeschylus has queen Clytemnestra refer to dead Cassandra "as a swan who sang her last, death lament" (*Agamemnon* 1444–5).

Certainly Plato uses the legend to great literary effect in the *Phaedo*. The legend explains a change of character for Socrates. In the *Apology* Socrates professed not to know whether or not the soul survives the death of the body, although he argued that death was something good in either case (40b–41c). Only one month later, on his death day, Socrates gives intricate arguments for the immortality of every living soul, in addition professes without argument an account of the geography of the earth and where the souls of the dead migrate, and – the very last words – commands Crito to make a religious sacrifice to the god of healing. To the skeptical reader who objects that it is inconsistent for Socrates to profess such knowledge, the legend of the swan song gives a mystical answer: the god Apollo gave Socrates such powers on his death day.

Most ancient and modern commentators have denied that swans sing, and sing best, at death. They are in error, confusing the two species found in ancient Greece, the mute swan (*Cygnus olor*), which indeed is as mute at death as in life, with the whooper swan (*Cygnus cygnus*), which can make its most melodious noise at death. The reason is that the whooper has an elongated trachea convoluted within its breastbone. In life the whooper uses the longer trachea to produce a two-tone bugling noise, "the second syllable higher pitched than the first, repeated several times in succession."

> The musicality of this note is a matter of opinion; one authority has compared it to "silver bells," another to the sound of "a clarionet when blown by a novice in music" . . . [But] when [the whooper] dies, the final expiration of air from its collapsing lungs produces a "wailing, flute-like sound given out quite slowly." In modern times this dirge of the dying whooper was first attested by the great ornithologist Peter Pallas in Russia at the beginning of the nineteenth century. It has been more recently observed also in other species of wild swan with similarly convoluted tracheae. The American ornithologist Dr. Daniel Elliott once shot a whistling swan (*Cygnus columbianus*, the American subspecies of the Eurasian Bewick's swan) for the American Museum of Natural History, "and as the bird came sailing down he was amazed to hear a plaintive and musical song, so unlike the call in life, which lasted until the bird reached the water."[1]

Plato may not have known or cared if the legend of the swan song was scientifically accurate. On the other hand, he might have taken pains to be accurate in as many incidental details as possible to enhance the overall credibility of his narration. It would be a mistake to reason that Plato's literary powers required him to invent rather than be accurate in detail.

Hemlock

Those literary powers are at their peak in the *Phaedo's* depiction of Socrates' death by poison. As usual, Socrates acted with ritual propriety. When they saw him drinking the poison, his friends began to cry aloud, one after another. Phaedo narrates how Socrates hushed them:

> "This is one of the main reasons I sent the women away, so that they would not make such offensive noises – for I have heard that one ought to die in reverential silence. Come on: bear up and keep quiet!"
> His words made us ashamed and we held back our tears. But he walked about and, when he said his legs were heavy, lay down on his back, for this had been the advice of the man who administered the poison. This man put his hands on him, let some time pass, and then began to examine his feet

and legs. He pinched his foot hard and asked whether he felt it – Socrates said no – and then his lower legs. Going on upwards he showed us how the numbness and immobility would spread, and touching the place, this man said, "As soon as it reaches his heart, he will be gone."

Now the numbness was in the area of his lower abdomen, and uncovering his face, which had been covered, he said – his last words – "Crito, we owe a cock to Asclepius. Don't forget to pay the debt!"

"It will be paid," said Crito, "But see whether you have anything else to say."

To this question he made no reply. A short time later he moved; the man uncovered him; his eyes were fixed. And when Crito saw it, he closed his mouth and eyes.

117d7–118a14

The literary effect is enhanced by the vivid details of the slowly ascending paralysis that leaves Socrates' mind clear till the very end. Ancient readers tended to accept the account at face value as an answer to the request within the dialogue "to describe every detail as carefully as possible" (58d8–9). Since the seventeenth century, however, medical science and classical scholarship have raised doubts that the details of the text cannot be squared with the medical facts of hemlock poisoning. It was only in 2001 that Enid Bloch dispelled the doubts, identifying the poison as the poison hemlock plant (*Conium maculatum*). While many other members of the same plant family (*Umbelliferae*) are similar in appearance and also poisonous – such as water hemlock and the hemlock known as fool's parsley – they produce death in much more violent ways. Only poison hemlock produces the alkaloids that cause death by slowly ascending paralysis in the manner recorded by Plato.[2]

Though we can have no certainty in this matter, Plato's clinical accuracy about death by hemlock poisoning suggests that he used the same accuracy in his record of Socrates' curious last words. But what is the meaning of those words? What debt was so important to Socrates that an exhortation to pay it was his last speech?

It was ritually proper for ancient Greeks, after healing from disease, to sacrifice a cock to the god Asclepius. Thus Socrates' words, *we owe*, suggest that he and others present at his death had together suffered and then been healed. What disease and what act of healing did Socrates have in mind?

Ultimate Disease

In *Twilight of the Idols*, "The Problem of Socrates," Nietzsche made famous an answer going back to at least 500 CE: Socrates thought that death cures us of the disease of bodily life: "To live – that means to be a long time sick." On this reading, death is seen as a release from the suffering of being imprisoned in a physical body. Socrates never describes embodiment as a disease and regards suicide – unless compelled by a god – as taboo (62b–c), but he does say that any philosopher is eager to die (61b–c). Indeed the entire metaphysical argument of the *Phaedo* is an answer to Cebes' and Simmias's doubts about the goodness of death (62c9–63b5). But Nietzsche is unfaithful to the text, attributing to Socrates these words: "*I* owe a cock to Asclepius," whereas in the text Socrates says to Crito, "*We* owe." Nietzsche must alter the text because, on his interpretation, with death imminent for no one else, only Socrates has a debt to Asclepius.

We get a more faithful interpretation by noticing that in the course of the *Phaedo* Socrates explicitly identifies the worst disease a human being can suffer and worries that he himself suffers from it, while Phaedo, narrating the dialogue, explicitly states that Crito and the rest of those present came to suffer from that disease in the course of the dialogue but were healed by dialogue's end.

According to Socrates, the most dreadful condition is the spiritual illness of *misology*, the distrust and hatred of reasoning.

> "Let us guard against suffering from a certain condition."
> "Of what sort?" I [Phaedo] asked.
> "Let us not become misologists," he said . . . "for no one could suffer from anything worse than this: the hatred of reasoning."[3]
>
> 89c11–d3

The distrust and hatred of reasoning are symptoms of a kind of psychic death, when "reasoning vanishes" from one's soul (89c1–2).

To show Phaedo just how dreadful this kind of psychic death is, Socrates compares it to the death of a beloved friend, referring to the hair-cutting ritual of grief that Phaedo will perform after his beloved Socrates dies:

> "Tomorrow, Phaedo, perhaps you will cut off your beautiful hair."
> "It's likely, Socrates," I said.
> "Not if you do as I say."
> "What's that?" I said.
> "I'll cut my hair *today* and you yours, if reasoning dies for us and we cannot bring it to life again. And I would make a vow, like the Argives, not to let my hair grow until I fight back and defeat the objections of Simmias and Cebes.
>
> 89b4–c4

In comparative terms, Socrates is making a wild claim: the death of reasoning in a soul, not a beloved friend's death, is reason for significant

grief. From such a perspective, a human being can have no greater reason for making a sacrifice to Asclepius than to be healed of misology.

Socrates says that misology is analogous to misanthropy, the condition of disliking and mistrusting all human beings. He speculates that misanthropy develops when a person makes friends uncritically and is repeatedly betrayed by them (89d–e). Likewise misology:

> When people who lack skill at reasoning trust some bit of it to be true, and then a little later the same bit seems false, and this happens over and over – and especially with those who spend their time arguing just to contradict others – you know how it is: they end up thinking that they have become wiser than everyone, and that they alone have discovered that there is nothing healthy or secure in any speech or subject matter . . . The condition is pitiful – assuming that it is possible to discover some true and secure bit of reasoning – since . . . they would be deprived of true understanding of reality.
>
> 90b6–d7

And Socrates worries that he himself suffers from this dreadful illness.

> Let us be on our guard against this, and let us not admit into our souls the notion that there is no health in arguments at all. Let us far rather assume that we ourselves are not yet in healthy condition . . . for I fear that I am not just now *philosophōs* (seeking to know) as regards this particular question, but *philonikōs* (seeking to win a war of words), like uncultured persons.
>
> 90d9–91a3

He is right to worry. As quoted above, only a few minutes earlier he expressed the militant Argive desire to "win" against objections to his reasoning (89c3–4).

Plato uses the structure of the *Phaedo* to draw dramatic attention to misology as a dreadful psychic disease. The first two pages of the *Phaedo* are a conversation between Phaedo and Echecrates (57a–59c), but the remaining sixty pages consist of Phaedo's narration of the story of Socrates' death day (59c–118a) – with a dramatic exception. As Phaedo narrates it, after Socrates' first arguments for the immortality of the soul, Simmias and Cebes raise devastating objections. Phaedo narrates the psychological effect that these objections had upon the people present with Socrates on his last day: "We all felt ill after hearing them speak (as we later told each other). We had been quite convinced by the earlier reasoning [that the soul is immortal]. Now they seemed to have upset and cast into doubt not only the conclusion we had just reached, but also the conclusions we might reach later, whether we were worthless to judge or the subject matter was itself unreliable" (88c1–6). It is at this precise moment – and by page count we are at the very center of the dialogue – that Echecrates breaks into the story, dramatically redoubling the onset of misology:[4]

> By the gods, Phaedo, *I* feel the same way you all did! Hearing this now from you, a thought is coming over me: "What reasoning will we ever trust again? Socrates' reasoning was quite compelling – now it has fallen into disrepute."
>
> 88c8–d3

Such misgivings are symptoms of the onset of misology, as Socrates has described it.

Echecrates at this moment "wants more than anything" to have the soul's immortality established by reasoning (88d6–8): instead of a philosophical desire to know, he desires that Socrates win the argument. He is on the edge of his seat to find out what happens next in the story: "So tell me, by Zeus, how Socrates continued with his reasoning!" (88d8–9).

Phaedo in reply assures Echecrates that Socrates proceeded to heal those present from the dreadful misology. "I have often marveled at Socrates, but never did I admire him more than then. That he had an answer ready was perhaps to be expected; but what astonished me more about him was . . . how well he *healed* us" (88e4–89a5).

I leave aside discussion of the details of that final reasoning whereby Socrates heals himself and his companions. The point I wish to make is that there is no question that Socrates dramatically restores in at least some of his friends their loving trust in reasoning in general as a human activity and their confidence in the particular conclusion that each of us has an immortal soul. Moreover, his friends seem to develop a healthier, more critical attitude towards arguments. Judging from Socrates' account of the cause of misology (90b6–7, quoted above), I take this to be a further sign of good health.

For example, Cebes loves and trusts Socrates' final reasoning. "For my part, Socrates, I have no further objections to state, and I have no doubts about your reasoning" (107a2–3). Cebes does recognize the possibility that, although he cannot think of an objection, others might. "If Simmias here or anyone else has something to say, this is a good time to speak up" (107a3–5). His developing critical attitude is the best way to ward off a relapse of misology in the future.

Likewise Simmias has a healthy reaction, saying, "Nor do I find anything to doubt in the reasoning. However, the vastness of the subject and my recognition of human frailty compel me still to have doubts, for my own part, about what has been said" (107a8–b3).

Socrates, too, has the proper critical attitude along with his trust in reasoning. He endorses Simmias's two points about the subject's magnitude and human frailty and adds another reason for a critical attitude towards the provisionally accepted result: "Not only are you right to make those points, Simmias, but the premises of the reasoning need to be examined more clearly, too, even if you and the others find them trustworthy. And I suppose that, if you go through the premises enough, you will follow the train of reasoning, so far as it is possible for a human being to follow it up. Your inquiry will be over when the reasoning becomes positively clear" (107b4–9). The last sentence does not predict that the reasoning will ever become positively clear. Given that Socrates accepts human frailty in respect to such a large subject and the fallibility of his argument's assumptions, I interpret the last sentence to suggest that human inquiry will never be over in this or any other vast subject.

But it seems that, with respect to misology, Crito at any rate has not been healed, at least not in Socrates' eyes. For when Crito near the end asks Socrates how to bury *him* (instead of asking how to bury *the body* that remains after death), Socrates takes the question to show that Crito does not "trust" (115c6) Socrates' reasoning. Instead of seeing reasoning that compels a provisional rational assent, Socrates says that Crito sees mere "storytelling that reassures one's feelings" (115d5).

Crito's continuing misology makes me want to ask Phaedo about his statement that Socrates "healed" them (89a5). Did Socrates heal others but not Crito from misology? If not Crito, why does Socrates ask Crito and not the others to sacrifice the cock to Asclepius? I conjecture that Phaedo would reply that, although Socrates astonished Phaedo at how well he healed the group, Phaedo never claimed that Socrates had a cure rate of one hundred percent. Socrates' philosophical healing of – if not Crito – at least himself, Simmias, and Cebes is sufficient to incur the obligation of a sacrifice to Asclepius, an obligation that Socrates would want to take care of above all and not forget. And since Crito was in effect the executor of Socrates' wishes, it was ritually proper for Socrates to give to Crito and no one else the request to make a sacrifice in thanks for the group's astonishing recovery, even if Crito himself continues to suffer from misology.

Conclusion

As with the other Socratic dialogues, I take it that Plato's overriding goal in the *Phaedo* is not biography as such but the conversion of the souls of his readers to philosophy as a way of life. But such an overriding goal does not mean that the seeming biography cannot be accurate in detail. Crito's failure to be compelled by Socrates' reasoning is a meticulous detail in Phaedo's account. Such details, like the hemlock poisoning and even the swan song, move me to trust the text as a meticulous portrait, not merely a literary invention.

The call in the *Phaedo* to live a life of inquiry and the thesis that mis-ology is the worst thing that can happen to a human being are both Socratic theses, essential to his divine mission. On the other hand, the argument in the *Phaedo* from the existence of separate Forms to the immortality of the soul has nothing to do with the Socratic dialogues. It is possible that Socrates expanded his philosophical repertoire from ethical concerns and took a metaphysical turn in the last thirty days of life, as the *Phaedo* portrays him. Or it is possible that Plato took Socrates' death day as inspiration for a new, distinctly Platonic, form of dialogue. The choice between these and other possibilities is the topic of my last chapter.

notes

1 W. Geoffrey Arnott, "Swan Songs," *Greece & Rome* 24 (1977) 149–153. Arnott provides references for the testimony he cites. Charles Young told me about this article.
2 Enid Bloch, "Hemlock Poisoning and the Death of Socrates: Did Plato Tell the Truth?" in Thomas C. Brickhouse and Nicholas D. Smith, eds., *The Trial and Execution of Socrates*, Oxford: Oxford University Press, 2001. Also online in the *Journal of the International Plato Society*.
3 Whenever it makes for a natural translation, I translate the Greek noun *logos* in this chapter as "reasoning". But the Greek noun can also mean "speech," and the verb "to speak" as well as "to reason."
4 The only other place where Echecrates breaks into Phaedo's narration is to affirm the existence of Forms such as Tallness separate from and explaining the tallness in us (102a). On separate Forms see the epilogue.

further reading

Sandra Peterson, "An Authentically Socratic Conclusion in Plato's *Phaedo*: Socrates' Debt to Asclepius," in Naomi Reshotko, ed., *Desire, Identity and Existence*. Kelowna: Academic, 2003. The chapter lists 21 different interpretations of Socrates' last words, adding a twenty-second. My interpretation in this chapter is not original; it is the nineteenth option she lists.

epilogue:
socrates or plato?

In terms of philosophical content, all the passages that I have interpreted in this book – drawn from Plato's *Apology, Crito, Euthydemus,
Euthyphro, Ion, Laches, Lysis, Meno, Phaedo, Protagoras,* and
Republic 1 – are primarily concerned with ethics and support the same
position of specific conclusions and general themes about human excellence (chapter 15). Other dialogues share the same primary concern and
contribute to the same position, in particular the *Charmides, Gorgias,*
and *Hippias Major* and *Minor.* It is no surprise that scholars who group
Plato's doctrines by philosophical content tend to place these dialogues
together.[1]

In contrast, the *Phaedo* appears non-Socratic in its content. In the
Phaedo, the character Socrates investigates metaphysics, not ethics,
giving a series of arguments that the human soul is immortal. The final
argument of the *Phaedo* requires a metaphysical account of change in
terms of eternal, unchanging Forms, such as Tallness, distinguishing
"Tallness itself" from "the tallness in us" (102d6–7). In addition to this
change of subject, there are changes in the form of the conversation.
Instead of an inquiry ending in a puzzle, it is a positive demonstration
(106e–107a). Instead of ending with a profession of ignorance and an
exhortation to continue inquiry into the nature of human excellence,
Socrates, after proving the soul is immortal, relates a story of the journey
of the soul at death (107d–108c), asserting unprovable beliefs (108d–e)
about the geography of earth (108e–114d). The dialogue, instead of
reading like an edited transcript of actual oral conversation, reads like
an intricate literary composition.

Aristotle on Socrates

Whereas both the *Phaedo* (among many other such dialogues) and the Socratic dialogues feature a character named Socrates, Aristotle gives us reason to think that the Socratic dialogues give us a *portrait* of the historical Socrates, while the *Phaedo*, among others, gives us a *mouthpiece* for the views of Plato himself.

On the one hand, Aristotle's *Metaphysics* (991b3–4) mentions the *Phaedo* in the course of criticizing Plato for thinking that Forms (such as Tallness itself) are distinct from forms in the world of change (such as the tallness that comes and goes in us). His *On Generation and Corruption* mentions "Socrates in the *Phaedo*" (335b9–17) in the course of criticizing Plato for thinking that such Forms explain change in the world. According to the *Metaphysics* (987a32–b10, 1078b12–1079a4, 1086a37–b11), to distinguish Forms themselves from forms in us (as in the *Phaedo*) is an error Plato, not Socrates, makes, an error attributable to Plato's belief that the world we see is in constant change.

On the other hand, Aristotle also refers to "old man Socrates," distinct from "the Socrates" of dialogues like Plato's *Phaedo*. The distinguishing features Aristotle ascribes to old man Socrates are by and large consistent with the philosophical content present in what I called above the Socratic dialogues. While Aristotle never describes Plato as professing ignorance about how to live well, his work *On Sophistical Refutations* attributes a confession of ignorance to Socrates (183b7–8). The *Metaphysics* attributes to Socrates a concern with ethics and finding definitions of human excellences but, unlike Plato, no concern for nature as a whole (987b1–2, likewise *Posterior Analytics* 642a28–31). The *Nicomachean Ethics* speaks of Socrates but not of Plato denying the possibility that knowledge could be overcome by passion (1145b22–31, 1147b13–17). The same work criticizes Socrates, not Plato, for overstating the place of knowledge in human excellence, for reducing all human excellence to knowledge and ignoring the nonrational part of the soul (1116b3–5, 1144b17–30, likewise *Eudemian Ethics* 1216b3–10). All of these features are marks of the dialogues I have called Socratic, as opposed to the others, such as the metaphysical parts of the *Phaedo*. If Aristotle is reliable, we have a measure of confirmation that the dialogues I have called Socratic are portraying the historical Socrates, while the remaining dialogues give us Plato's, not Socrates', views.

How reliable is Aristotle? Aristotle joined Plato's Academy about thirty-six years after Socrates' death, staying for nearly twenty years. As just shown, he ascribes to Socrates doctrines consistent with the arguments I have interpreted in this book. Yet Aristotle shows no awareness of many of these arguments.

For example, the *Nicomachean Ethics* says, "Bravery seems to be an observable routine – hence Socrates thought it a branch of knowledge" (1116b3–5). Not one of the Socratic dialogues infers that bravery is a branch of knowledge from bravery's *being observable*. On the contrary, in the Socratic dialogues the inference is always from bravery's *being good* to its being a branch of knowledge (see chapters 4 and 6). The *Nicomachean Ethics* also attributes to the historical Socrates the view that "All the human excellences are [numerically distinct] branches of intelligence" (1144b17–18). But in the Socratic dialogues the arguments consistently reduce the excellences to *one* branch of knowledge, the knowledge of human well-being.

It seems likely that in Plato's Academy there was an oral tradition about a man as memorably eccentric as the character in the dialogues I have interpreted, an oral tradition that Aristotle knew. As a rule, oral traditions are like gossip in that they may be superficially accurate but lack the detail and often the accuracy of personal observation. One way to account for the difference between Aristotle's superficial reports and their discrepancies from the dialogues' detailed record of argumentation is that Aristotle's reports derive from an oral tradition distinct from Plato's extensive familiarity with Socrates. If Aristotle is reporting such an oral tradition, his report is independent testimony confirming in rough outline Plato's dialogues as an account of the conclusions of the historical Socrates.

Plato's Contemporaries

We do not know the extent of Aristotle's first-hand knowledge of Plato. The *Physics* refers to unwritten teachings of Plato (209b13–16) as well as to many of Plato's written dialogues (writing as if neither is more valuable than the other as a source indicating Plato's thought). The *Metaphysics* gives us biographical information about Plato (that as a young man Plato associated with Cratylus, 987a32–b1), information not found in any dialogue. However, even if Aristotle had a close acquaintance with Plato, we might doubt his accuracy as a biographer of either Plato or Socrates.

But we do not need to assume first-hand knowledge or scrupulous historical accuracy on the part of Aristotle. He was writing for a contemporary audience, discussing and distinguishing Plato and Socrates in order to criticize their views. If there had been any question at the time whether Aristotle was justified in attributing such wild statements as *there is a Form Tallness apart from the tallness in us* to Plato or *human excellence is nothing but knowledge* to Socrates, we would expect to find Platonic or Socratic defenders questioning Aristotle's attributions.

Although much commentary on Aristotle and many reports of ancient disputes have survived, there is no hint of such a finding. The silence gives us reason to accept Aristotle's distinction of Plato's writings into Socratic as opposed to Platonic dialogues.[2]

Conclusion

As a working hypothesis I accept Aristotle's testimony that the Socrates of the *Phaedo* is a mouthpiece for Plato's own views, despite the fact that I also accept, in the same tentative manner, that the death scene is an accurate historical account (chapter 16). Leaving aside Plato and the Forms, this book has shown that the Socratic dialogues do provide compelling arguments for the sort of wild conclusions Aristotle attributes to the historical Socrates. It remains impossible to know to what extent the many beautiful details of drama and argument are pure literary creation or accurate depiction. The accuracy in detail of death by hemlock in the *Phaedo* gives no certainty but does encourage us to conjecture that Plato is portraying not inventing the details of Socrates' death, even though Plato reports himself as absent from the scene (*Phaedo* 59b). Plato associated with Socrates for at least the last 10 years of Socrates' life and knew older associates of Socrates. Insofar as we are confident to conjecture that the death scene is portrait not invention, we might with a corresponding measure of confidence conjecture that the close psychological and logical details of drama and argument in the Socratic dialogues are more portrait than invention, despite the fact that Plato, born a quarter-century before Socrates' death, set many of these dialogues at times prior to his own birth. Although such conjectures are far from certainty, they are comparable or superior to our grounds for trusting testimonies of the lives and teachings of, say, Confucius, Siddhartha, or Jesus.

In sum, the question is: do any of the dialogues that Plato wrote give us an accurate portrait of Socrates and his philosophy? The correct answer to this question is *no one knows*. The same answer is correct for many questions that arise in ancient history, modern history, and even current events. Police detectives know the unreliability of witnesses; professors know the unreliability of their students or colleagues to understand or accurately restate their arguments and conclusions. But we would lead inferior lives if we made it a general policy to dismiss all such testimony. The best approach must navigate between uncritical trust and complete dismissal, seeking no more certainty in our conclusions than can be expected from the premises, a point Aristotle makes in the *Nicomachean Ethics* (1094b2–4), perhaps learning it from Plato's *Phaedo* (89d–90b). This lack of certainty is not lamentable, since the human value of the Socratic dialogues is not their historical reliability but the power of their arguments to save our lives.

notes

1 For a table comparing the content-based grouping of such scholars, see Debra Nails, *Agora, Academy, and the Conduct of Philosophy* (New York: Springer, 1995), p. 60. Such scholars sometimes add further subdivisions and conjecture that these dialogues were among those written earliest in Plato's career.

The subtle science of stylometrics uses features of a writer's style that, in the best cases, the writer would not be conscious of using. In Greek, these are features analogous to, for example, how frequently the letter "a" appears relative to other letters. Such statistical studies group these same dialogues together for reasons that have nothing to do with philosophical content. On the other hand, such studies fail to separate from this group some dialogues with non-Socratic content, such as Plato's *Phaedo*. At present, stylometrics fails to provide evidence either for distinguishing any definite list as Socratic or for denying such a distinction.

2 In this and the previous section, including all references to Aristotle's work, I follow chapter 1 of Terence Irwin, *Plato's Ethics*. Oxford: Oxford University Press, 1995.

further reading

Debra Nails, *Agora, Academy, and the Conduct of Philosophy*. New York: Springer, 1995. The book examines the relation between the historical Socrates and the character in Plato's dialogues.

index of passages cited

general index

merely one part of human
   excellence, 84
of animals, 83
Brickhouse, Thomas C., 29, 202

Callias, 27, 38
Callicles, xiii, 91
Cassandra, 195
Catholicism, Roman, 175
cause, 56
Cebes, 198–201
Chaerephon, 19, 30, 33, 39–44
charity, 12, 92, 94, 124, 126, 133, 177,
   178
Charmides, 39
Christianity, 21, 28, 65, 168, 180
   Orthodox, 175
Circe, 62
Clinias, 121–7
Clytemnestra, 195
cognition, 72
Colchis, 137
coma, 162
confidence, 51–3
Confucius, xiv, 5, 9, 12, 188–92, 206
Conium maculatum, 197
consciousness, 162
conversation, 166
conversation, Socratic, 166
   see also philosophy, Socratic
Corinth, 137
Corinthians, 17
corpse, 7
crime, 23
Critias, 6, 7, 9, 37, 38, 39
Crito, 60, 78, 114, 115, 121–6, 152,
   160, 187–201
Cynics, 158

Daedalus, 96
Damon, 34
Dante, 164
dared, 82, 84
David, the Psalmist, 191
death, 162, 191
   as cure for life, 197
   psychic, 198
delight, 192

Delium, 35, 36
Delphi, 19, 20, 28–44, 104
deme, 33
dementia, 162
deprivation, 111
Desdemona, 82
desire, 63, 111, 131
   always *to get* something, 132
   brute, 65, 71
   causes love, 110
   cognitive, 72
   for bad, 131
   for heavenly life, 65
   for misery, 137
   ignorant, 133
   knowledgeable, 136
   psychology of, 139
destiny, 116
devotion, religious, xiv, 5
Dickenson, Emily, 9, 192
dikaios, 25
dikaiosunē, 25
dikē, 25
Dionysus, xiii
disability, 25
disease, 197
disjunction, 112
disrespect, 7
divers, 52
Dover, K. J., 117
dreaded, 82, 84
drives, blind, 72
duck, 150
duty, 116

Echecrates, 199–202
Elliott, Daniel, 196
ends, 164, 187
Engels, Frederick, 169
enthusiasm, 136
Epictetus, 162
eudaimonia, 155
Euripides, 137
Euthyphro, 88–98, 126, 173–84
Evenus, 27
excellence
   as expertise, 139
   combines desire and ability, 131

excellence (*cont'd*)
exploits others, 143
has parts, 50, 84
in human life, 155
secular and religious, 173
teachable, 122
existential, 11, 12, 80, 86, 89, 104, 155,
173, 177
see also practical
expertise
and happiness, 150
and knowledge, 52
and ruling, 144
as bravery, 80
attempts to have more than its
opposite, 150
different for sciences and the
humanities, 10
identity conditions of, 8, 146
in all branches of knowledge, 6
in backcountry guiding, 9
in battlefield good and evil, 85
in benefiting human society, 183
in biography, 3
in chariot racing, 4, 5
in corpse bartering, 7
in desert hiking, 9
in fishing, 5
in history, 3
in Homer, 5, 8
in human well-being, xii, xiii, 6, 7,
37, 81, 106
in judging words and actions, 4
in judgments of relative value, 85
in living before gods, 183
in medical risk, 4
in medicine, 10
in moneymaking, 146
in mountain climing, 9
in navigation, 10
in pharmacy, 9
in poetry, 4, 5, 7, 8
in political rule, 148
in prayer and sacrifice, 183
in prophecy, 5
in psychology, 10
in service, 143, 145, 179
in surgery, 9

in what is to be dreaded and dared,
82
in what will be best, 83
in when best to die, 82
in woodcutting, 7
makes one wise and good, 149
of the general, 6
of the rhapsode, 4
of the seer, 82
requites love, 108
skepticism about, 83
see also knowledge, skill, wisdom
extrinsic, 110

fanatics, 160
fearlessness, 84
Felix Felicis, 123
Forms, Plato's, 202
freedom, 164, 167, 178
fun, 178
function, human, 169

Gasper, Philip, 169
geography, 195
Glaucon, 166, 167
and freedom, 167
glorify, 179
goal, 165, 169
god, 175, 192
god(s)
and human beings, 4
at Delphi, 28
genesis of, 4
good will of, 147
mission from, 17
perfection of, 177
saving word of, 21
service to, 176
skepticism about, 177
sun, 62
goods, 122, 156, 159
guilt
four degrees of, 23
freedom from, 24
of unsocratic life, 25

Hades, 195
happiness, 148, 190

and expertise, 150
and external goods, 156
and righteousness, 155
  ever more to be gained, 150
heaven, 164, 192
hedonism, 66
hell, 164
hemlock, 196
Hercules, 21, 26
heroes, 4
Hesiod, 11
hetairos, 42
Hippocrates, 36, 39, 90–92
Hipponicus, 27
Hippothales, 105, 111
Hollywood, 24
Homer, 3–12, 42, 72, 115
homicide, 23
Horatio, 56
humaneness, 190
hunger, 71

identity, 56
ignorance
  always tries to have more, 151
  and confidence, 52
  cautious vs. foolish, 107, 149
  makes one foolish and bad, 150
immortality, 195
impotence, 63
impropriety, 40
incommensurability, 65
intellectualism, 41, 139
intention, 133
intrinsic, 110
involuntary, 23
invulnerability, 162, 190
Ion, 3–12, 17, 20, 90
Ionians, 43
Irwin, Terence, 127, 207

Jason, 137, 138
Jesus, xiv, 64–73, 153, 177–90, 206
joy, 169
Judaism, 175
Juliet, 83–5, 161, 189
justice, 25
  see also righteousness

kalos, 61
Kent, Clark, 127
knowledge
  and expertise, 52
  of best course of action, 63
  of good and bad, 6
  impotent, 63, 107
  rules and saves, 73
  see also expertise
Koran *see* Qur'an
Krishna, xiv, 188–92

labor, alienated, 165
Laches, 21–5, 33–9, 45, 73, 77–98
Lamb, W. R. M., 106
Last Judgment, 179
Laws of Athens, 189
lǐ 禮, 5
life
  examining, 169
  excellent, 187
  heavenly, 70
  loss of, 162
  unexamined, 22
logicians, 125, 135
logos, 202
love, 103, 161
luck
  and wisdom, 121
  two meanings of, 123
luckiness, 123, 126
Lutheranism, 175
luxury, 190
Lyceum, 121
Lysimachus, 33–5, 45, 77
Lysis, 104–17

Marx, Karl, 165, 169
McPherran, Mark L., 184
McShane, Janet, 117
means, 164, 187
Medea, 137–40
Melesias, 77
Meletus, 18, 21, 26–9, 91, 173
Menexenus, 105, 109, 115, 116
Meno, 131
mermaid, 192
mind, soundness of, 51